Praise for *TypeSct*

In *TypeScript Cookbook*, Stefan Baumgartner deftly covers everything from project setup to advanced typing techniques, providing a wealth of practical examples and valuable insights to make you a TypeScript expert ready for any challenge.

—Addy Osmani
Head of Chrome Developer Experience, Google

Typescript Cookbook is an essential resource for developers who want to learn how to use TypeScript effectively. Stefan packs clear and concise recipes for solving real-world problems into a comprehensive playbook that upskills you from novice to expert.

—Simona Cotin
Engineering Manager for Angular, Google

TypeScript Cookbook shows you how to solve all sorts of problems with advanced types. Even better, it teaches you how to use TypeScript's features to write new types for yourself.

—Nathan Shively-Sanders
Software Engineer on the TypeScript team

TypeScript Cookbook is an extremely valuable reference for anyone working with TypeScript. It condenses a ton of valuable information into a format you can dip into and out of easily.

—Matt Pocock
Author of Total TypeScript

TypeScript can sometimes slow developers down, but *TypeScript Cookbook* is the perfect remedy! The comprehensive solutions offered for common TypeScript problems make it an indispensable tool for improving productivity.

—Vanessa Böhner
Lead Front-End Developer, Zavvy

TypeScript Cookbook is a lovely read and a fount of information. I thoroughly enjoyed the succinct questions and answers followed by well-crafted discussions of the nuances behind them. I learned a ton of neat tricks and snazzy new patterns from each of the chapters. It would behoove any TypeScript developer to learn those nuances, tricks, and patterns—in particular from this book. Would highly recommend!

—*Josh Goldberg*
Author of Learning TypeScript

I recognized so many issues that I'd come across in my own TypeScript and found Stefan's advice on them to be clear, precise, and insightful. I feel more confident with TypeScript with this reference by my side.

—*Phil Nash, Developer Advocate, Sonar*

TypeScript Cookbook
Real World Type-Level Programming

Stefan Baumgartner

Beijing · Boston · Farnham · Sebastopol · Tokyo

TypeScript Cookbook

by Stefan Baumgartner

Copyright © 2023 Stefan Baumgartner. All rights reserved.

Published by O'Reilly Media, Inc., 1005 Gravenstein Highway North, Sebastopol, CA 95472.

O'Reilly books may be purchased for educational, business, or sales promotional use. Online editions are also available for most titles (*http://oreilly.com*). For more information, contact our corporate/institutional sales department: 800-998-9938 or *corporate@oreilly.com*.

Acquisitions Editor: Amanda Quinn
Development Editor: Shira Evans
Production Editor: Elizabeth Faerm
Copyeditor: Piper Editorial Consulting, LLC
Proofreader: Shannon Turlington

Indexer: WordCo Indexing Services, Inc.
Interior Designer: David Futato
Cover Designer: Karen Montgomery
Illustrator: Kate Dullea

August 2023: First Edition

Revision History for the First Edition

2023-08-08: First Release

See *http://oreilly.com/catalog/errata.csp?isbn=9781098136659* for release details.

978-1-098-13665-9

[LSI]

Table of Contents

Foreword

I am always excited to witness the evolution of programming languages and the impact they make on software development. TypeScript, a superset of JavaScript, is no exception. In fact, TypeScript has swiftly risen to become one of the most widely used programming languages, carving out a unique space for itself in the world of web development. As this language has garnered significant adoption and praise, it is only fitting that it be given the comprehensive treatment it deserves in *TypeScript Cookbook*.

As an avid TypeScript user, I must say that the precision and robustness it has brought to JavaScript have been both empowering and astonishing. One of the key reasons behind this is its type safety, which has addressed a long-standing criticism of JavaScript. By allowing developers to define strict types for variables, TypeScript has made it easier to catch errors during the compilation process, significantly improving code quality and maintainability.

TypeScript Cookbook is a much-needed guide. The preface rightly establishes Type-Script's skyrocketing popularity. However, this rising interest in TypeScript also brings to light the challenges developers face in adopting it. It is here that this book is set to make a difference.

Drenched in practicality, this book is meticulously designed to address real-world challenges faced by TypeScript users. It is an amalgamation of more than one hundred recipes that deal with a gamut of concepts ranging from basic to advanced. As developers, we often find ourselves fighting the type-checker, and that's where this book will serve as your sword and shield. With in-depth explanations, you will not only learn how to work with TypeScript efficiently but also understand the thought processes behind the concepts.

One of the many laudable aspects of *TypeScript Cookbook* is its approach toward embracing TypeScript's rapid evolution. With TypeScript getting regular releases per year, staying up to date is a Herculean task. This book does a splendid job focusing on the long-lasting aspects of TypeScript and ensures that your learning remains relevant despite the ever-changing landscape.

In addition to a plethora of recipes, the book encourages you to comprehend the intricate connection between JavaScript and TypeScript. Understanding the symbiotic relationship between these two languages is paramount in unlocking TypeScript's true potential. Whether you are struggling with type assertions, generics, or even integrating TypeScript with popular libraries and frameworks such as React, this book covers it all.

This book also excels in serving as both a guide and a reference. As a guide, it seamlessly takes you from novice to expert. As a reference, it serves as a reliable companion throughout your TypeScript journey. The organization of the book is impeccable, ensuring that each chapter can be consumed in isolation, yet forming a cohesive knowledge base when put together.

With TypeScript's popularity showing no signs of slowing down, *TypeScript Cookbook* is poised to be an essential resource for every TypeScript enthusiast. From real-world examples to a treasure trove of solutions, this book is the compass you need to navigate the exciting world of TypeScript.

Whether you are getting your feet wet or looking to dive into the depths of TypeScript, this book is a beacon of knowledge. I extend my heartfelt congratulations to Stefan Baumgartner for crafting this masterpiece and welcome you all to savor the recipes of success in TypeScript.

Let the journey into TypeScript begin.

—Addy Osmani
Engineering Lead
Google Chrome
July 2023

Preface

The only way you can read this sentence is by opening this book, either physically or digitally. This tells me you are interested in TypeScript, one of the most popular programming languages in recent years. According to the 2022 State of JavaScript survey (*https://2022.stateofjs.com*), almost 70% of all participants actively use TypeScript. The 2022 StackOverflow survey (*https://survey.stackoverflow.co/2022*) lists TypeScript as one of the top five most popular languages and the fourth highest in user satisfaction. At the beginning of 2023, TypeScript counts more than 40 million weekly downloads on NPM (*https://oreil.ly/ZHWn8*).

Without a doubt: TypeScript is a phenomenon!

Despite its popularity, TypeScript still gives a lot of developers a hard time. *Fighting the type-checker* is one phrase you hear often; another one is *throwing a couple of any's in there so it shuts up*. Some people feel slowed down, writing just to please the compiler when they know their code *has* to work. However, TypeScript's sole purpose is to make JavaScript developers more productive and efficient. Does the tool ultimately fail to meet its goals, or do we as developers expect something different from the tool than it is designed to deliver?

The answer is somewhere in the middle, and this is where *TypeScript Cookbook* comes in. In this book, you will find more than one hundred recipes that deal with everything from complex project setups to advanced typing techniques. You will learn about the intricacies and inner workings of the type system, as well as the trade-offs and exceptions it has to make to not interfere with its foundation: JavaScript. You also will learn methodologies, design patterns, and development techniques to create better and more robust TypeScript code. In the end, you will understand not only *how* to do something but also *why*.

My goal is to give you a guide that takes you from novice to expert, as well as a quick reference you can use well after you've read the book. With TypeScript's four releases per year, it's impossible to list all the most up-to-date features in a single book. This is why we focus on long-lasting aspects of the programming language, to prepare you for all the changes to come. Welcome to the TypeScript cookbook.

Who This Book Is For

This book is for developers, engineers, and architects who know enough JavaScript to be dangerous and have gotten their feet wet in TypeScript. You understand the fundamental concepts of types and how to apply them, and you understand the immediate benefits of static types. You are at a point where things get interesting: you need a deeper knowledge of the type system, and you need to actively work with TypeScript not only to ensure a robust and scaleable application but also to guarantee collaboration between you and your colleagues.

You want to learn about how something behaves in TypeScript, as well as understand the reasoning behind its behavior. This is what you get in *TypeScript Cookbook*. You will learn project setup, quirks, and behavior of the type system; complex types and their use cases; and working with frameworks and applying type development methodology. This book is designed to take you from novice to apprentice, and eventually to expert. If you need a guide to actively learn more of TypeScript's sophisticated features, but also a reference you can rely on throughout your career, this book will do right by you.

What's in This Book?

A predominant goal of writing *TypeScript Cookbook* was to focus on solutions for everyday problems. TypeScript is a remarkable programming language, and the features of the type system are so powerful that we reach a point where people challenge themselves with advanced TypeScript puzzles (*https://tsch.js.org*). While these brain teasers are entertaining, they often lack real-world context and thus are not part of this book.

I want to make sure that the content presented is something you will encounter in your day-to-day life as a TypeScript developer, with problems that stem from real-world situations and solutions that are holistic. I will teach you techniques and methodologies you can use in multiple scenarios, not just in a single recipe. Throughout the book you will find references to earlier recipes, showing you how a specific techique can be applied in a new context.

The examples are either ripped directly from the source code of real projects or stripped down to essentials to illustrate a concept without requiring too much domain knowledge. While some examples are very specific, you will also see a lot of `Person` objects that have the name "Stefan" (and you will be able to see me age throughout the book).

The book will focus almost exclusively on the features TypeScript adds on top of Java-Script; thus, to understand the example fully, you need to understand a reasonable amount of JavaScript. I don't expect you to be a JavaScript guru but being able to read basic JavaScript code is a must. Since JavaScript and TypeScript have this strong relationship, some chapters in the book discuss JavaScript features and their behavior, but always through the lens of TypeScript.

A cookbook is designed to give you a quick solution to a problem: a recipe. In this book, every recipe ends with a *discussion*, giving you broader context and meaning for the solution. Depending on the style of the author, the focus of O'Reilly's cookbooks lies either on the solution or on the discussion. *TypeScript Cookbook* is unmistakably a *discussion* book. In my almost 20-year career as a person who writes software, I've never encountered situations in which one solution fits all problems. That's why I want to show you in detail how we came to our conclusions, their meaning, and the trade-offs. Ultimately, this book should be a guide for discussions like that. Why make an educated guess when you have proper arguments for your decisions?

Organization of This Book

TypeScript Cookbook takes you through the language from start to finish. We start with project setup, talk about basic types and the inner workings of the type system, and ultimately go into advanced territory like conditional types and helper types. We continue with chapters that explore very specific features, like the duality of classes and support for React, and end with learnings on how to best approach type development.

While there is a thread and buildup, each chapter and each recipe can be consumed on its own. Each lesson has been designed to point out the connection to previous (or next!) recipes in the book, but each chapter is ultimately self-contained. Feel free to consume it from start to finish, or use the "choose your own adventure" approach with its many references. Here is a brief overview of the content.

TypeScript wants to work with all flavors of JavaScript, and there are a lot of different flavors. In Chapter 1, "Project Setup" you will learn about configuration possibilities for different language runtimes, module systems, and target platforms.

Chapter 2, "Basic Types" guides you through the type hierarchy, tells you the difference between any and unknown, teaches you which code contributes to which namespace, and answers the age-old question of whether to choose a type alias or an interface to describe your object types.

One of the longer chapters in the book is Chapter 3, "The Type System". Here you will learn everything about union and intersection types, how to define discriminated union types, how to use the *assert never* and *optional never* techniques, and how to narrow and widen types based on your use case. After this chapter, you will understand why TypeScript has type assertions and no type casts, why enums are generally frowned upon, and how you find the nominal bits in a structural type system.

TypeScript has a generic type system, which we will see in detail in Chapter 4, "Generics". Generics not only make your code more reusable but are also the entrance to the more advanced features of TypeScript. This chapter marks the point where you ascend from TypeScript basics to the more sophisticated areas of the type system, a fitting end to the first part.

Chapter 5, "Conditional Types" explains why the TypeScript type system is also its own metaprogramming language. With the possibility of choosing types based on certain conditions, people invented the most outstanding things, like a full-fledged SQL parser or a dictionary in the type system. We use conditional types as a tool to make a static type system more flexible for dynamic situations.

In Chapter 6, "String Template Literal Types" you see how TypeScript integrates a string parser in the type system. Extracting names from format strings, defining a dynamic event system based on string input, and creating identifiers dynamically: nothing seems impossible!

You get a little taste of *functional programming* in Chapter 7, "Variadic Tuple Types". The *tuple* has a special meaning in TypeScript and helps describe function parameters and object-like arrays, and it creates flexible helper functions.

Even more metaprogramming happens in Chapter 8, "Helper Types". TypeScript has a few built-in helper types that make it easier for you to derive types from other types. In this chapter, you learn not only how to use them but also how to create your own. This chapter also marks the next breakpoint in *TypeScript Cookbook* because at this point you have learned all the basic ingredients of the language and type system, which you then can apply in the next part.

After spending eight chapters understanding all the nitty-gritty of the type system, it's time to integrate your knowledge with type definitions done by others in Chapter 9, "The Standard Library and External Type Definitions". In this chapter you will see situations that work differently than expected, and see how you can bend the built-in type definitions to your will.

In Chapter 10, "TypeScript and React" you will learn how one of the most popular JavaScript frameworks is integrated in TypeScript, features that make the syntax extension *JSX* possible, and how this fits into the overall concept of TypeScript. You will also learn how to write robust types for components and hooks, and how to deal with a type definition file that has been attached to the actual library after the fact.

The next chapter is about classes, a staple of object-oriented programming that was available in TypeScript long before their counterpart existed in JavaScript. This leads to an interesting duality of features discussed in detail in Chapter 11, "Classes".

The book ends with Chapter 12, "Type Development Strategies". Here I focus on giving you the skills to create advanced types on your own, to make the right decisions on how to move your project along, and to deal with libraries that validate types for you. You also will learn about special workarounds and hidden features, and discuss how to name generics or if advanced types are a bit too much. This chapter is particularly fun because after a long journey from novice to apprentice, you will reach expert status.

All examples are available as a TypeScript playground or CodeSandbox project at the book's website (*https://typescript-cookbook.com*). The playgrounds in particular offer an intermediate state, so you can fiddle around on your own and play with the behaviors. I always say that you can't learn a programming language just by reading about it; you need to actively code and get your hands dirty to understand how everything plays together. See this as an invitation to have fun with programming types.

Conventions Used in This Book

Programming Conventions

TypeScript allows for many programming styles and formatting options. To avoid *bike-shedding*, I chose to autoformat all examples using Prettier (*https://prettier.io*). If you are used to a different formatting style—maybe you prefer commas instead of semicolons after each property declaration of your types—you are more than welcome to continue with your preference.

TypeScript Cookbook has a lot of examples and deals with a lot of functions. There are many ways to write functions, and I've chosen to write mostly *function declarations* instead of *function expressions*, except where it was crucial to explain the differences between both notations. On all other occasions, it's mostly a matter of taste rather than for technical reasons.

All examples have been checked against TypeScript 5.0, the most recent release at the time of this book's writing. TypeScript changes constantly and so do the rules. This book ensures that we mostly focus on things that are long-lasting and can be trusted across versions. Where I expect further development or fundamental change, I provide respective warnings and notes.

Typesetting Conventions

The following typographical conventions are used in this book:

Italic

> Indicates new terms, URLs, email addresses, filenames, and file extensions.

`Constant width`

> Used for program listings, as well as within paragraphs to refer to program elements such as variable or function names, databases, data types, environment variables, statements, and keywords.

`Constant width italic`

> Shows text that should be replaced with user-supplied values or by values determined by context.

This element signifies a tip or suggestion.

This element signifies a general note.

This element indicates a warning or caution.

Using Code Examples

Supplemental material (code examples, exercises, etc.) is available for download at *https://typescript-cookbook.com*.

If you have a technical question or a problem using the code examples, please send email to *support@oreilly.com*.

This book is here to help you get your job done. In general, if example code is offered with this book, you may use it in your programs and documentation. You do not need to contact us for permission unless you're reproducing a significant portion of the code. For example, writing a program that uses several chunks of code from this book does not require permission. Selling or distributing examples from O'Reilly books does require permission. Answering a question by citing this book and quoting example code does not require permission. Incorporating a significant amount of example code from this book into your product's documentation does require permission.

We appreciate, but do not require, attribution. An attribution usually includes the title, author, publisher, and ISBN. For example: "*TypeScript Cookbook* by Stefan Baumgartner (O'Reilly). Copyright 2023 Stefan Baumgartner, 978-1-098-13665-9."

If you feel your use of code examples falls outside fair use or the permission given above, feel free to contact us at *permissions@oreilly.com*.

O'Reilly Online Learning

O'REILLY® For more than 40 years, *O'Reilly Media* has provided technology and business training, knowledge, and insight to help companies succeed.

Our unique network of experts and innovators share their knowledge and expertise through books, articles, and our online learning platform. O'Reilly's online learning platform gives you on-demand access to live training courses, in-depth learning paths, interactive coding environments, and a vast collection of text and video from O'Reilly and 200+ other publishers. For more information, visit *https://oreilly.com*.

How to Contact Us

Please address comments and questions concerning this book to the publisher:

O'Reilly Media, Inc.
1005 Gravenstein Highway North
Sebastopol, CA 95472
800-998-9938 (in the United States or Canada)
707-829-0515 (international or local)
707-829-0104 (fax)
support@oreilly.com
https://www.oreilly.com/about/contact.html

We have a web page for this book, where we list errata, examples, and any additional information. You can access this page at *https://oreil.ly/typescript-cookbook*.

For news and information about our books and courses, visit *https://oreilly.com*.

Find us on LinkedIn: *https://linkedin.com/company/oreilly-media*.

Follow us on Twitter: *https://twitter.com/oreillymedia.*

Watch us on YouTube: *https://youtube.com/oreillymedia.*

Acknowledgments

Alexander Rosemann, Sebastian Gierlinger, Dominik Angerer, and Georg Kothmeier are the first people I go to if I have something new cooking. Our regular meetings and interactions not only are entertaining but also provide me with the necessary feedback to evaluate all my choices. They are the first people that heard about the book, and also the first ones that gave feedback.

Interacting with Matt Pocock, Joe Previte, Dan Vanderkam, Nathan Shively-Sanders, and Josh Goldberg on social media brought plenty of new ideas to the table. Their approach to TypeScript might differ from mine, but they ultimately broadened my horizon and made sure that I didn't end up too opinionated.

Phil Nash, Simona Cotin, and Vanessa Böhner have not only been early reviewers of the final manuscript but also long-time companions and friends who are always here to sanity-check my ideas. Addy Osmani has been an inspiration throughout my entire career, and I'm very proud that he agreed to open my new book.

Lena Matscheko, Alexandra Rapeanu, and Mike Kuss did not hesitate to bombard me with technical challenges and questions based on their real-world experiences. Where I lacked a good example, they flooded me with excellent source material to distill.

I would lose track of all of TypeScript's developments if it wasn't for Peter Kröner, who constantly knocks on my door when there's a new TypeScript version coming out. Our podcast episodes together on TypeScript releases are legendary, and also increasingly not about TypeScript.

My tech editors Mark Halpin, Fabian Friedl, and Bernhard Mayr provided the best technical feedback I could wish for. They challenged every assumption, checked on every code sample, and made sure all my reasoning made sense and that I didn't skip a beat. Their love of detail and their ability to discuss on such a high level ensured that this book is not just another collection of hot takes but a guide and reference that stands on a solid foundation.

This book would not exist if not for Amanda Quinn. After writing *TypeScript in 50 Lessons* in 2020, I thought I'd said everything I needed to say about TypeScript. It was Amanda who pursued me to give the idea of a cookbook a go, to see which ideas I would find that wouldn't make the cut for my first book. After three hours I had a complete proposal and table of contents with more than one hundred entries. Amanda was right: I had so much more to say, and I'm eternally grateful for her support and her guidance.

Where Amanda helped in the early phases, Shira Evans made sure that the project made good progress and didn't derail. Her feedback was invaluable, and her pragmatic and hands-on approach made it a joy to work together.

Elizabeth Faerm and Theresa Jones took care of the production. Their eye for detail is outstanding, and they made sure that the production phase is exciting and actually a lot of fun! The final result is a beautiful experience I can't get enough of.

During writing I had great assistance from Porcupine Tree, Beck, Nobuo Uematsu, Camel, The Beta Band, and many others.

The biggest contribution to this book comes from my family. Doris, Clemens, and Aaron are everything I've ever wished for, and without their endless love and support, I wouldn't be able to pursue my ambitions. Thank you for everything.

CHAPTER 1

Project Setup

You want to get started with TypeScript, fantastic! The big question is: how do you start? You can integrate TypeScript into your projects in many ways, and all are slightly different depending on your project's needs. Just as JavaScript runs on many runtimes, there are plenty of ways to configure TypeScript so it meets your target's needs.

This chapter covers all the possibilities of introducing TypeScript to your project, as an extension next to JavaScript that gives you basic autocompletion and error indication, up to full-fledged setups for full-stack applications on Node.js and the browser.

Since JavaScript tooling is a field with endless possibilities—some say that a new JavaScript build chain is released every week, almost as much as new frameworks—this chapter focuses more on what you can do with the TypeScript compiler alone, without any extra tool.

TypeScript offers everything you need for your transpilation needs, except the ability to create minified and optimized bundles for web distribution. Bundlers like ESBuild (*https://esbuild.github.io*) or Webpack (*https://webpack.js.org*) take care of this task. Also, there are setups that include other transpilers like Babel.js (*https://babeljs.io*) that can play nicely with TypeScript.

Bundlers and other transpilers are not within the scope of this chapter. Refer to their documentation for the inclusion of TypeScript and use the knowledge in this chapter to get the right configuration setup.

TypeScript being a project with more than a decade of history, it carries some remains from older times that, for the sake of compatibility, TypeScript can't just get rid of. Therefore, this chapter will spotlight modern JavaScript syntax and recent developments in web standards.

If you still need to target Internet Explorer 8 or Node.js 10, first: I'm sorry, these platforms are really hard to develop for. However, second: you will be able to put together the pieces for older platforms with the knowledge from this chapter and the official TypeScript documentation (*https://typescriptlang.org*).

1.1 Type-Checking JavaScript

Problem

You want to get basic type-checking for JavaScript with the least amount of effort possible.

Solution

Add a single-line comment with @ts-check at the beginning of every JavaScript file you want to type-check. With the right editors, you already get red squiggly lines whenever TypeScript encounters things that don't quite add up.

Discussion

TypeScript has been designed as a superset of JavaScript, and every valid JavaScript is also valid TypeScript. This means TypeScript is also really good at figuring out potential errors in regular JavaScript code.

We can use this if we don't want a full-blown TypeScript setup but want some basic hints and type-checks to ease our development workflow.

A good prerequisite if you only want to type-check JavaScript is a good editor or IDE. An editor that goes really well with TypeScript is Visual Studio Code (*https://code.visu alstudio.com*). Visual Studio Code—or VSCode for short—was the first major project to utilize TypeScript, even before TypeScript's release.

A lot of people recommend VSCode if you want to write JavaScript or TypeScript. But really, every editor is great as long as it features TypeScript support. And nowadays most of them do.

With Visual Studio Code we get one very important thing for type-checking JavaScript: red squiggly lines when something doesn't quite add up, as you can see in Figure 1-1. This is the lowest barrier to entry. TypeScript's type system has different levels of strictness when working with a codebase.

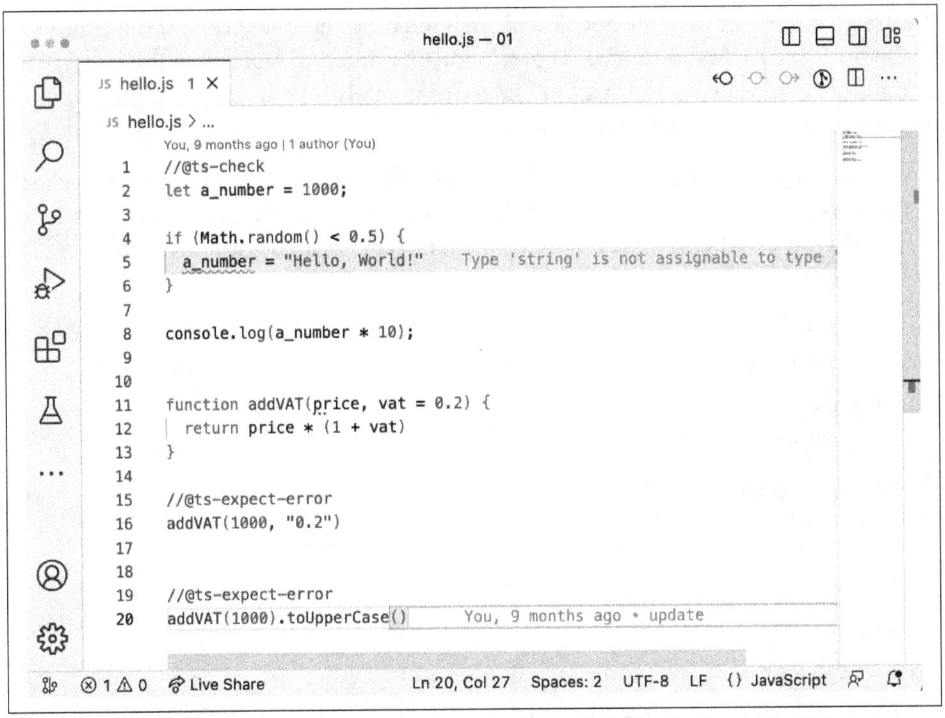

Figure 1-1. Red squiggly lines in code editors: first-level feedback if something in your code doesn't add up

First, the type system will try to *infer* types from JavaScript code through usage. If you have a line like this in your code:

```
let a_number = 1000;
```

TypeScript will correctly infer `number` as the type of `a_number`.

One difficulty with JavaScript is that types are dynamic. Bindings via `let`, `var`, or `const` can change type based on usage.[1] Take a look at the following example:

```
let a_number = 1000;

if (Math.random() < 0.5) {
  a_number = "Hello, World!";
}

console.log(a_number * 10);
```

---

[1] Objects assigned to a `const` binding can still change values and properties, and thus change their types.

We assign a number to a_number and change the binding to a string if the condition in the next line evaluates to true. This wouldn't be much of a problem if we didn't try to multiply a_number on the last line. In approximately 50% of all cases, this example will produce unwanted behavior.

TypeScript can help here. With the addition of a single-line comment with @ts-check at the very top of our JavaScript file, TypeScript activates the next strictness level: type-checking JavaScript files based on the type information available in the JavaScript file.

In our example, TypeScript will figure out that we tried to assign a string to a binding that TypeScript has inferred to be a number. We will get an error in our editor:

```
// @ts-check
let a_number = 1000;

if (Math.random() < 0.5) {
  a_number = "Hello, World!";
// ^-- Type 'string' is not assignable to type 'number'.ts(2322)
}

console.log(a_number * 10);
```

Now we can start to fix our code, and TypeScript will guide us.

Type inference for JavaScript goes a long way. In the following example, TypeScript infers types by looking at operations like multiplication and addition as well as default values:

```
function addVAT(price, vat = 0.2) {
  return price * (1 + vat);
}
```

The function addVat takes two arguments. The second argument is optional, as it has been set to a default value of 0.2. TypeScript will alert you if you try to pass a value that doesn't work:

```
addVAT(1000, "a string");
//            ^-- Argument of type 'string' is not assignable
//                to parameter of type 'number'.ts(2345)
```

Also, since we use multiplication and addition operations within the function body, TypeScript understands that we will return a number from this function:

```
addVAT(1000).toUpperCase();
//            ^-- Property 'toUpperCase' does not
//                exist on type 'number'.ts(2339)
```

In some situations you need more than type inference. In JavaScript files, you can annotate function arguments and bindings through JSDoc type annotations. JSDoc (*https://jsdoc.app*) is a comment convention that allows you to describe your variables and function interfaces in a way that's not only readable for humans but also interpretable by machines. TypeScript will pick up your annotations and use them as types for the type system:

```
/** @type {number} */
let amount;

amount = '12';
//        ^-- Argument of type 'string' is not assignable
//            to parameter of type 'number'.ts(2345)

/**
 * Adds VAT to a price
 *
 * @param {number} price The price without VAT
 * @param {number} vat The VAT [0-1]
 *
 * @returns {number}
 */
function addVAT(price, vat = 0.2) {
  return price * (1 + vat);
}
```

JSDoc also allows you to define new, complex types for objects:

```
/**
 * @typedef {Object} Article
 * @property {number} price
 * @property {number} vat
 * @property {string} string
 * @property {boolean=} sold
 */

/**
 * Now we can use Article as a proper type
 * @param {[Article]} articles
 */
function totalAmount(articles) {
  return articles.reduce((total, article) => {
    return total + addVAT(article);
  }, 0);
}
```

The syntax might feel a bit clunky, though; we will find better ways to annotate objects in Recipe 1.3.

Given that you have a JavaScript codebase that is well documented via JSDoc, adding a single line on top of your files will give you a really good understanding if something goes wrong in your code.

1.2 Installing TypeScript

Problem

Red squigglies in the editor are not enough: you want command-line feedback, status codes, configuration, and options to type-check JavaScript and compile TypeScript.

Solution

Install TypeScript via Node's primary package registry: NPM (*https://npmjs.com*).

Discussion

TypeScript is written in TypeScript, compiled to JavaScript, and uses the Node.js JavaScript runtime (*https://nodejs.org*) as its primary execution environment.[2] Even if you're not writing a Node.js app, the tooling for your JavaScript applications will run on Node. So, make sure you get Node.js from the official website (*https://nodejs.org*) and get familiar with its command-line tools.

For a new project, make sure you initialize your project's folder with a fresh *package.json*. This file contains all the information for Node and its package manager NPM to figure out your project's contents. Generate a new *package.json* file with default contents in your project's folder with the NPM command-line tool:

```
$ npm init -y
```

 Throughout this book, you will see commands that should be executed in your terminal. For convenience, we show these commands as they would appear on BASH or similar shells available for Linux, macOS, or the Windows subsystem for Linux. The leading $ sign is a convention to indicate a command, but it is not meant to be written by you. Note that all commands also work on the regular Windows command-line interface as well as PowerShell.

NPM is Node's package manager. It comes with a CLI, a registry, and other tools that allow you to install dependencies. Once you initialize your *package.json*, install TypeScript from NPM. We install it as a development dependency, meaning that TypeScript won't be included if you intend to publish your project as a library to NPM itself:

```
$ npm install -D typescript
```

---

2 TypeScript also works in other JavaScript runtimes, such as Deno and the browser, but they are not intended as main targets.

You can globally install TypeScript so you have the TypeScript compiler available everywhere, but I strongly suggest installing TypeScript separately per project. Depending on how frequently you visit your projects, you will end up with different TypeScript versions that are in sync with your project's code. Installing (and updating) TypeScript globally might break projects you haven't touched in a while.

 If you install frontend dependencies via NPM, you will need an additional tool to make sure that your code also runs in your browser: a bundler. TypeScript doesn't include a bundler that works with the supported module systems, so you need to set up the proper tooling. Tools like Webpack (*https://webpack.js.org*) are common, and so is ESBuild (*https://esbuild.github.io*). All tools are designed to execute TypeScript as well. Or you can go full native, as described in Recipe 1.8.

Now that TypeScript is installed, initialize a new TypeScript project. Use NPX for that: it allows you to execute a command-line utility that you installed relative to your project.

With:

```
$ npx tsc --init
```

you can run your project's local version of the TypeScript compiler and pass the init flag to create a new *tsconfig.json*.

The *tsconfig.json* is the main configuration file for your TypeScript project. It contains all the configuration needed so that TypeScript understands how to interpret your code, how to make types available for dependencies, and if you need to turn certain features on or off.

Per default, TypeScript sets these options for you:

```
{
  "compilerOptions": {
    "target": "es2016",
    "module": "commonjs",
    "esModuleInterop": true,
    "forceConsistentCasingInFileNames": true,
    "strict": true,
    "skipLibCheck": true
  }
}
```

Let's look at them in detail.

target is es2016, which means that if you run the TypeScript compiler, it will compile your TypeScript files to an ECMAScript 2016 compatible syntax. Depending on your supported browsers or environments, you can set that either to something more recent (ECMAScript versions are named after the year of release) or to something older such as es5 for people who have to support very old Internet Explorer versions. Of course, I hope you don't have to.

module is commonjs. This allows you to write ECMAScript module syntax, but instead of carrying this syntax over to the output, TypeScript will compile it to the CommonJS format. This means that:

```
import { name } from "./my-module";

console.log(name);
//...
```

becomes:

```
const my_module_1 = require("./my-module");
console.log(my_module_1.name);
```

once you compile. CommonJS was the module system for Node.js and has become very common because of Node's popularity. Node.js has since adopted ECMAScript modules as well, something we'll tackle in Recipe 1.9.

esModuleInterop ensures modules that aren't ECMAScript modules are aligned to the standard once imported. forceConsistentCasingInFileNames helps people using case-sensitive file systems cooperate with folks who use case-insensitive file systems. And skipLibCheck assumes that your installed type definition files (more on that later) have no errors. So your compiler won't check them and will become a little faster.

One of the most interesting features is TypeScript's strict mode. If set to true, TypeScript will behave differently in certain areas. It's a way for the TypeScript team to define their view on how the type system should behave.

If TypeScript introduces a breaking change because the view on the type system changes, it will get incorporated in strict mode. This ultimately means that your code might break if you update TypeScript and always run in strict mode.

To give you time to adapt to changes, TypeScript also allows you to turn certain strict mode features on or off, feature by feature.

In addition to the default settings, I strongly recommend two more:

```
{
  "compilerOptions": {
    //...
    "rootDir": "./src",
    "outDir": "./dist"
  }
}
```

This tells TypeScript to pick up source files from a *src* folder and put the compiled files into a *dist* folder. This setup allows you to separate your built files from the ones you author. You will have to create the *src* folder, of course; the *dist* folder will be created after you compile.

Oh, compilation. Once you have your project set up, create an *index.ts* file in src:

```
console.log("Hello World");
```

The *.ts* extension indicates it's a TypeScript file. Now run:

```
$ npx tsc
```

in your command line and see the compiler at work.

1.3 Keeping Types on the Side

Problem

You want to write regular JavaScript with no extra build step but still get some editor support and proper type information for your functions. However, you don't want to define your complex object types with JSDoc as shown in Recipe 1.1.

Solution

Keep type definition files "on the side" and run the TypeScript compiler in the "check JavaScript" mode.

Discussion

Gradual adoption has always been a dedicated goal for TypeScript. With this technique, which I dubbed "types on the side," you can write TypeScript syntax for object types and advanced features like generics and conditional types (see Chapter 5) instead of clunky JSDoc comments, but you still write JavaScript for your actual app.

Somewhere in your project, maybe in a *@types* folder, create a type definition file. Its ending is *.d.ts*, and as opposed to regular *.ts* files, its purpose is to hold declarations but no actual code.

This is where you can write your interfaces, type aliases, and complex types:

```
// @types/person.d.ts

// An interface for objects of this shape
export interface Person {
  name: string;
  age: number;
}
```

```
// An interface that extends the original one
// this is tough to write with JSDoc comments alone.
export interface Student extends Person {
  semester: number;
}
```

Note that you export the interfaces from the declaration files. This is so you can import them in your JavaScript files:

```
// index.js
/** @typedef { import ("../@types/person").Person } Person */
```

The comment on the first line tells TypeScript to import the `Person` type from *@types/person* and make it available under the name `Person`.

Now you can use this identifier to annotate function parameters or objects just like you would with primitive types like `string`:

```
// index.js, continued

/**
 * @param {Person} person
 */
function printPerson(person) {
  console.log(person.name);
}
```

To make sure that you get editor feedback, you still need to set `@ts-check` at the beginning of your JavaScript files as described in Recipe 1.1. Or, you can configure your project to always check JavaScript.

Open *tsconfig.json* and set the `checkJs` flag to `true`. This will pick up all the JavaScript files from your *src* folder and give you constant feedback on type errors in your editor. You also can run `npx tsc` to see if you have errors in your command line.

If you don't want TypeScript to transpile your JavaScript files to older versions of JavaScript, make sure you set `noEmit` to `true`:

```
{
  "compilerOptions": {
    "checkJs": true,
    "noEmit": true,
  }
}
```

With that, TypeScript will look at your source files and will give you all the type information you need, but it won't touch your code.

This technique is also known to scale. Prominent JavaScript libraries like Preact (*https://preactjs.org*) work like this and provide fantastic tooling for their users as well as their contributors.

1.4 Migrating a Project to TypeScript

Problem

You want to get the full benefits of TypeScript for your project, but you need to migrate an entire codebase.

Solution

Rename your modules file by file from *.js* to *.ts*. Use several compiler options and features that help you iron out errors.

Discussion

The benefit of having TypeScript files instead of JavaScript files with types is that your types and implementations are in one file, which gives you better editor support and access to more TypeScript features, and increases compatibility with other tools.

However, just renaming all files from *.js* to *.ts* most likely will result in tons of errors. This is why you should go file by file and gradually increase type safety as you go along.

The biggest problem when migrating is that you're suddenly dealing with a TypeScript project, not with JavaScript. Still, lots of your modules will be JavaScript and, with no type information, they will fail the type-checking step.

Make it easier for yourself and for TypeScript by turning off type-checking for JavaScript, but allow TypeScript modules to load and refer to JavaScript files:

```
{
  "compilerOptions": {
    "checkJs": false,
    "allowJs": true
  }
}
```

Should you run `npx tsc` now, you will see that TypeScript picks up all JavaScript and TypeScript files in your source folder and creates respective JavaScript files in your destination folder. TypeScript will also transpile your code to be compatible with the specified target version.

If you are working with dependencies, you will see that some of them don't come with type information. This will also produce TypeScript errors:

```
import _ from "lodash";
//          ^- Could not find a declaration
//             file for module 'lodash'.
```

Install third-party type definitions to get rid of this error. See Recipe 1.5.

Once you migrate file by file, you might realize that you won't be able to get all typings for one file in one go. There are dependencies, and you will quickly go down the rabbit hole of having too many files to adjust before you can tackle the one that you actually need.

You can always decide just to live with the error. By default, TypeScript sets the compiler option noEmitOnError to false:

```
{
  "compilerOptions": {
    "noEmitOnError": false
  }
}
```

This means that no matter how many errors you have in your project, TypeScript will generate result files, trying not to block you. This might be a setting you want to turn on after you finish migrating.

In strict mode, TypeScript's feature flag noImplicitAny is set to true. This flag will make sure that you don't forget to assign a type to a variable, constant, or function parameter. Even if it's just any:

```
function printPerson(person: any) {
  // This doesn't make sense, but is ok with any
  console.log(person.gobbleydegook);
}

// This also doesn't make sense, but any allows it
printPerson(123);
```

any is the catchall type in TypeScript. Every value is compatible with any, and any allows you to access every property or call every method. any effectively turns off type-checking, giving you some room to breathe during your migration process.

Alternatively, you can annotate your parameters with unknown. This also allows you to pass everything to a function but won't allow you to do anything with it until you know more about the type.

You can also decide to ignore errors by adding a @ts-ignore comment before the line you want to exclude from type-checking. A @ts-nocheck comment at the beginning of your file turns off type-checking entirely for this particular module.

A comment directive that is fantastic for migration is @ts-expect-error. It works like @ts-ignore as it will swallow errors from the type-checking progress but will produce red squiggly lines if no type error is found.

When migrating, this helps you find the spots that you successfully moved to Type-Script. When there are no @ts-expect-error directives left, you're done:

```
function printPerson(person: Person) {
  console.log(person.name);
}

// This error will be swallowed
// @ts-expect-error
printPerson(123);


function printNumber(nr: number) {
  console.log(nr);
}

// v- Unused '@ts-expect-error' directive.ts(2578)
// @ts-expect-error
printNumber(123);
```

The great thing about this technique is that you flip responsibilities. Usually, you have to make sure that you pass in the right values to a function; now you can make sure that the function is able to handle the right input.

All possibilities for getting rid of errors throughout your migration process have one thing in common: they're explicit. You need to explicitly set @ts-expect-error comments, annotate function parameters as any, or ignore files entirely from type-checking. With that, you can always search for those escape hatches during the migration process and make sure that, over time, you got rid of them all.

1.5 Loading Types from Definitely Typed

Problem

You rely on a dependency that hasn't been written in TypeScript and therefore lacks typings.

Solution

From Definitely Typed (*https://oreil.ly/nZ4xZ*), install community-maintained type definitions.

Discussion

Definitely Typed is one of the biggest and most active repositories on GitHub and collects high-quality TypeScript type definitions developed and maintained by the community.

The number of maintained type definitions is close to 10,000, and there is rarely a JavaScript library not available.

All type definitions are linted, checked, and deployed to the Node.js package registry NPM under the @types namespace. NPM has an indicator on each package's information site that shows if Definitely Typed type definitions are available, as you can see in Figure 1-2.

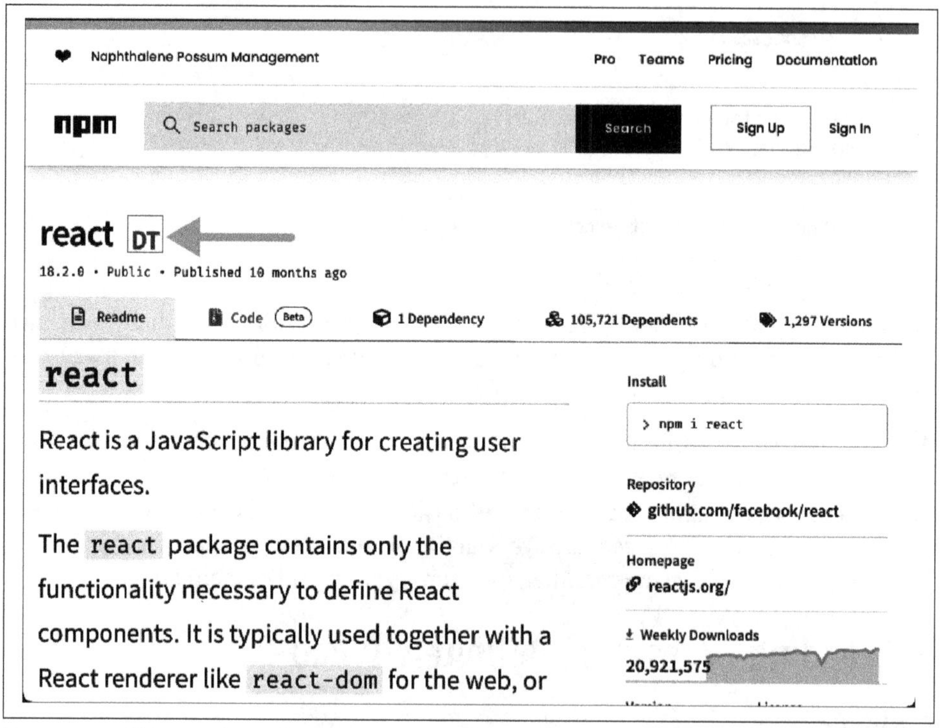

Figure 1-2. The NPM site for React shows a DT logo next to the package name; this indicates available type definitions from Definitely Typed

Clicking on this logo leads you to the actual site for type definitions. If a package has first-party type definitions already available, it shows a small TS logo next to the package name, as shown in Figure 1-3.

npm   🔍 Search packages   Search   Sign Up   Sign In

@types/react **TS** ⬅

18.2.0 · Public · Published 4 days ago

📄 Readme   📄 Code (Beta)   📦 3 Dependencies   ⚓ 15,141 Dependents   🏷 457 Versions

Installation

```
npm install --save @types/react
```

Summary

This package contains type definitions for React
(https://react.dev/).

Details

Install
```
> npm i @types/react
```

Repository
◈ github.com/DefinitelyTyped/D...

Homepage
🔗 github.com/DefinitelyTyped/D...

⬇ Weekly Downloads
23,309,365

Figure 1-3. Type definitions for React from Definitely Typed

To install, for example, typings for the popular JavaScript framework React, you install the @types/react package to your local dependencies:

```
# Installing React
$ npm install --save react

# Installing Type Definitions
$ npm install --save-dev @types/react
```

In this example we install types to development dependencies, since we consume them while developing the application, and the compiled result has no use of the types anyway.

By default, TypeScript will pick up type definitions it can find that are in visible *@types* folders relative to your project's root folder. It will also pick up all type definitions from *node_modules/@types*; note that this is where NPM installs, for example, @types/react.

We do this because the `typeRoots` compiler option in *tsconfig.json* is set to `@types` and `./node_modules/@types`. Should you need to override this setting, make sure to include the original folders if you want to pick up type definitions from Definitely Typed:

```
{
  "compilerOptions": {
    "typeRoots": ["./typings", "./node_modules/@types"]
  }
}
```

Note that just by installing type definitions into *node_modules/@types*, TypeScript will load them during compilation. This means that if some types declare globals, TypeScript will pick them up.

You might want to explicitly state which packages should be allowed to contribute to the global scope by specifying them in the `types` setting in your compiler options:

```
{
  "compilerOptions": {
    "types": ["node", "jest"]
  }
}
```

Note that this setting will only affect the contributions to the global scope. If you load node modules via import statements, TypeScript still will pick up the correct types from *@types*:

```
// If `@types/lodash` is installed, we get proper
// type defintions for this NPM package
import _ from "lodash"

const result = _.flattenDeep([1, [2, [3, [4]], 5]]);
```

We will revisit this setting in Recipe 1.7.

1.6 Setting Up a Full-Stack Project

Problem

You want to write a full-stack application targeting Node.js and the browser, with shared dependencies.

Solution

Create two *tsconfig* files for each frontend and backend, and load shared dependencies as composites.

Discussion

Node.js and the browser both run JavaScript, but they have a very different under-standing of what developers should do with the environment. Node.js is meant for servers, command-line tools, and everything that runs without a UI—*headless*. It has its own set of APIs and standard library. This little script starts an HTTP server:

```
const http = require('http'); ❶

const hostname = '127.0.0.1';
const port = process.env.PORT || 3000; ❷

const server = http.createServer((req, res) => {
  res.statusCode = 200;
  res.setHeader('Content-Type', 'text/plain');
  res.end('Hello World');
});

server.listen(port, hostname, () => {
  console.log(`Server running at http://${hostname}:${port}/`); ❸
});
```

While it's without a doubt JavaScript, some things are unique to Node.js:

❶ "http" is a built-in Node.js module for everything related to HTTP. It is loaded via require, which is an indicator for Node's module system called *CommonJS*. There are other ways to load modules in Node.js as we see in Recipe 1.9, but recently CommonJS has been the most common.

❷ The process object is a global object containing information on environment variables and the current Node.js process in general. This is also unique to Node.js.

❸ The console and its functions are available in almost every JavaScript runtime, but what it does in Node is different from what it does in the browser. In Node, it prints on STDOUT; in the browser, it will print a line to the development tools.

There are of course many more unique APIs for Node.js. But the same goes for Java-Script in the browser:

```
import { msg } from `./msg.js`; ❶

document.querySelector('button')?.addEventListener("click", () => { ❷
  console.log(msg); ❸
});
```

❶ After years without a way to load modules, ECMAScript modules have found their way into JavaScript and the browsers. This line loads an object from another JavaScript module. This runs in the browser natively and is a second module system for Node.js (see Recipe 1.9).

❷ JavaScript in the browser is meant to interact with UI events. The `document` object and the idea of a `querySelector` that points to elements in the *Document Object Model (DOM)* are unique to the browser. So is adding an event listener and listening on "click" events. You don't have this in Node.js.

❸ And again, `console`. It has the same API as in Node.js, but the result is a bit different.

The differences are so big, it's hard to create one TypeScript project that handles both. If you are writing a full-stack application, you need to create two TypeScript configuration files that deal with each part of your stack.

Let's work on the backend first. Let's assume you want to write an Express.js server in Node.js (Express is a popular server framework for Node). First, you create a new NPM project as shown in Recipe 1.1. Then, install Express as a dependency:

```
$ npm install --save express
```

And install type definitions for Node.js and Express from Definitely Typed:

```
$ npm install -D @types/express @types/node
```

Create a new folder called *server*. This is where your Node.js code goes. Instead of creating a new *tsconfig.json* via `tsc`, create a new *tsconfig.json* in your project's *server* folder. Here are the contents:

```
// server/tsconfig.json
{
  "compilerOptions": {
    "target": "ESNext",
    "lib": ["ESNext"],
    "module": "commonjs",
    "rootDir": "./",
    "moduleResolution": "node",
    "types": ["node"],
    "outDir": "../dist/server",
    "esModuleInterop": true,
    "forceConsistentCasingInFileNames": true,
    "strict": true,
    "skipLibCheck": true
  }
}
```

You should already know a lot of this, but a few things stand out:

- The `module` property is set to `commonjs`, the original Node.js module system. All `import` and `export` statements will be transpiled to their CommonJS counterpart.
- The `types` property is set to `["node"]`. This property includes all the libraries you want to have globally available. If `"node"` is in the global scope, you will get type information for `require`, `process`, and other Node.js specifics that are in the global space.

To compile your server-side code, run:

```
$ npx tsc -p server/tsconfig.json
```

Now for the client:

```
// client/tsconfig.json
{
  "compilerOptions": {
    "target": "ESNext",
    "lib": ["DOM", "ESNext"],
    "module": "ESNext",
    "rootDir": "./",
    "moduleResolution": "node",
    "types": [],
    "outDir": "../dist/client",
    "esModuleInterop": true,
    "forceConsistentCasingInFileNames": true,
    "strict": true,
    "skipLibCheck": true
  }
}
```

There are some similarities, but again, a few things stand out:

- You add `DOM` to the `lib` property. This gives you type definitions for everything related to the browser. Where you needed to install Node.js typings via Definitely Typed, TypeScript ships the most recent type definitions for the browser with the compiler.
- The `types` array is empty. This will *remove* `"node"` from our global typings. Since you only can install type definitions per *package.json*, the `"node"` type definitions we installed earlier would be available in the entire code base. For the `client` part, however, you want to get rid of them.

To compile your frontend code, run:

```
$ npx tsc -p client/tsconfig.json
```

Please note that you configured two distinct *tsconfig.json* files. Editors like Visual Studio Code pick up configuration information only for *tsconfig.json* files per folder. You could as well name them *tsconfig.server.json* and *tsconfig.client.json* and have them in your project's root folder (and adjust all directory properties). `tsc` will use the correct configurations and throw errors if it finds any, but the editor will mostly stay silent or work with a default configuration.

Things get a bit hairier if you want to have shared dependencies. One way to achieve shared dependencies is to use project references and composite projects. This means that you extract your shared code in its own folder, but tell TypeScript that this is meant to be a dependency project of another one.

Create a *shared* folder on the same level as *client* and *server*. Create a *tsconfig.json* in *shared* with these contents:

```
// shared/tsconfig.json
{
    "compilerOptions": {
      "composite": true,
      "target": "ESNext",
      "module": "ESNext",
      "rootDir": "../shared/",
      "moduleResolution": "Node",
      "types": [],
      "declaration": true,
      "outDir": "../dist/shared",
      "esModuleInterop": true,
      "forceConsistentCasingInFileNames": true,
      "strict": true,
      "skipLibCheck": true
    },
  }
```

Two things stand out again:

- The flag `composite` is set to `true`. This allows other projects to reference this one.
- The `declaration` flag is also set to `true`. This will generate *d.ts* files from your code so other projects can consume type information.

To include them in your client and server code, add this line to *client/tsconfig.json* and *server/tsconfig.json*:

```
// server/tsconfig.json
// client/tsconfig.json
{
  "compilerOptions": {
    // Same as before
  },
  "references": [
    { "path": "../shared/tsconfig.json" }
  ]
}
```

And you are all set. You can write shared dependencies and include them in your client and server code.

There is a caveat, however. This works great if you share, for example, only models and type information, but the moment you share actual functionality, you will see that the two different module systems (CommonJS in Node, ECMAScript modules in the browser) can't be unified in one compiled file. You either create an ESNext module and can't import it in CommonJS code or create CommonJS code and can't import it in the browser.

There are two things you can do:

- Compile to CommonJS and let a bundler take care of the module resolution work for the browser.
- Compile to ECMAScript modules and write modern Node.js applications based on ECMAScript modules. See Recipe 1.9 for more information.

Since you are starting out new, I strongly recommend the second option.

1.7 Setting Up Tests

Problem

You want to write tests, but the globals for testing frameworks interfere with your production code.

Solution

Create a separate *tsconfig* for development and build, and exclude all test files in the latter one.

Discussion

In the JavaScript and Node.js ecosystem, there are a lot of unit testing frameworks and test runners. They vary in detail, have different opinions, or are tailored for certain needs. Some of them might just be prettier than others.

While test runners like Ava (*https://oreil.ly/R6xFr*) rely on importing modules to get the framework into scope, others provide a set of globals. Take Mocha (*https://mochajs.org*), for example:

```
import assert from "assert";
import { add } from "..";

describe("Adding numbers", () => {
  it("should add two numbers", () => {
```

```
    assert.equal(add(2, 3), 5);
  });
});
```

`assert` comes from the Node.js built-in assertion library, but `describe`, `it`, and many more are globals provided by Mocha. They also only exist when the Mocha CLI is running.

This provides a bit of a challenge for your type setup, as those functions are necessary to write tests but aren't available when you execute your actual application.

The solution is to create two different configuration files: a regular *tsconfig.json* for development that your editor can pick up (remember Recipe 1.6) and a separate *tsconfig.build.json* that you use when you want to compile your application.

The first one includes all the globals you need, including types for Mocha; the latter makes sure no test file is included within your compilation.

Let's go through this step by step. We look at Mocha as an example, but other test runners that provide globals like Jest (*https://jestjs.io*) work just the same way.

First, install Mocha and its types:

```
$ npm install --save-dev mocha @types/mocha @types/node
```

Create a new *tsconfig.base.json*. Since the only differences between development and build are the set of files to be included and the libraries activated, you want to have all the other compiler settings located in one file you can reuse for both. An example file for a Node.js application would look like this:

```
// tsconfig.base.json
{
  "compilerOptions": {
    "target": "esnext",
    "module": "commonjs",
    "esModuleInterop": true,
    "forceConsistentCasingInFileNames": true,
    "strict": true,
    "outDir": "./dist",
    "skipLibCheck": true
  }
}
```

The source files should be located in *src*; test files should be located in an adjacent folder *test*. The setup you create in this recipe will also allow you to create files ending with *.test.ts* anywhere in your project.

Create a new *tsconfig.json* with your base development configuration. This one is used for editor feedback and for running tests with Mocha. You extend the basic settings from *tsconfig.base.json* and inform TypeScript which folders to pick up for compilation:

```
// tsconfig.json
{
  "extends": "./tsconfig.base.json",
  "compilerOptions": {
    "types": ["node", "mocha"],
    "rootDirs": ["test", "src"]
  }
}
```

Note that you add `types` for Node and Mocha. The `types` property defines which globals are available and, in the development setting, you have both.

Additionally, you might find that compiling your tests before executing them is cumbersome. There are shortcuts to help you. For example, `ts-node` runs your local installation of Node.js and does an in-memory TypeScript compilation first:

```
$ npm install --save-dev ts-node
$ npx mocha -r ts-node/register tests/*.ts
```

With the development environment set up, it's time for the build environment. Create a *tsconfig.build.json*. It looks similar to *tsconfig.json*, but you will spot the difference right away:

```
// tsconfig.build.json
{
  "extends": "./tsconfig.base.json",
  "compilerOptions": {
    "types": ["node"],
    "rootDirs": ["src"]
  },
  "exclude": ["**/*.test.ts", "**/test/**"]
}
```

In addition to changing `types` and `rootDirs`, you define which files to exclude from type-checking and compilation. You use wild-card patterns that exclude all files ending with *.test.ts* that are located in test folders. Depending on your taste, you can also add *.spec.ts* or *spec* folders to this array.

Compile your project by referring to the right JSON file:

```
$ npx tsc -p tsconfig.build.json
```

You will see that in the result files (located in `dist`), you won't see any test file. Also, while you still can access `describe` and `it` when editing your source files, you will get an error if you try to compile:

```
$ npx tsc -p tsconfig.build.json

src/index.ts:5:1 - error TS2593: Cannot find name 'describe'.
Do you need to install type definitions for a test runner?
Try `npm i --save-dev @types/jest` or `npm i --save-dev @types/mocha`
and then add 'jest' or 'mocha' to the types field in your tsconfig.
```

```
5 describe("this does not work", () => {})
  ~~~~~~~~
```

```
Found 1 error in src/index.ts:5
```

If you don't like polluting your globals during development mode, you can choose a similar setup as in Recipe 1.6, but it won't allow you to write tests adjacent to your source files.

Finally, you can always opt for a test runner that prefers the module system.

1.8 Typing ECMAScript Modules from URLs

Problem

You want to work without bundlers and use the browser's module-loading capabilities for your app, yet you still want to have all the type information.

Solution

Set `target` and `module` in your *tsconfig*'s compiler options to esnext and point to your modules with a *.js* extension. In addition, install types to dependencies via NPM, and use the `path` property in your *tsconfig* to tell TypeScript where to look for types:

```
// tsconfig.json
{
  "compilerOptions": {
    "target": "esnext",
    "module": "esnext",
    "paths": {
      "https://esm.sh/lodash@4.17.21": [
        "node_modules/@types/lodash/index.d.ts"
      ]
    }
  }
}
```

Discussion

Modern browsers support module loading out of the box. Instead of bundling your app into a smaller set of files, you can use the raw JavaScript files directly.

Content Delivery Networks (CDNs) like esm.sh (*https://esm.sh*), unpkg (*https://unpkg.com*), and others are designed to distribute node modules and JavaScript dependencies as URLs, consumable by native ECMAScript module loading.

With proper caching and state-of-the-art HTTP, ECMAScript modules become a real alternative for apps.

TypeScript does not include a modern bundler, so you would need to install an extra tool anyway. But if you decide to go module first, there are a few things to consider when working with TypeScript.

What you want to achieve is to write `import` and `export` statements in TypeScript but preserve the module-loading syntax and let the browser handle module resolution:

```
// File module.ts
export const obj = {
  name: "Stefan",
};

// File index.ts
import { obj } from "./module";

console.log(obj.name);
```

To achieve this, tell TypeScript to:

1. Compile to an ECMAScript version that understands modules
2. Use the ECMAScript module syntax for module code generation

Update two properties in your *tsconfig.json*:

```
// tsconfig.json
{
  "compilerOptions": {
    "target": "esnext",
    "module": "esnext"
  }
}
```

`module` tells TypeScript how to transform import and export statements. The default converts module loading to CommonJS, as seen in Recipe 1.2. Setting `module` to esnext will use ECMAScript module loading and thus preserve the syntax.

`target` tells TypeScript the ECMAScript version you want to transpile your code to. Once a year, there's a new ECMAScript release with new features. Setting `target` to esnext will always target the latest ECMAScript version.

Depending on your compatibility goals, you might want to set this property to the ECMAScript version compatible with the browsers you want to support. This is usually a version with a year (e.g. `es2015`, `es2016`, `es2017`, etc). ECMAScript modules work with every version from `es2015` on. If you go for an older version, you won't be able to load ECMAScript modules natively in the browser.

Changing these compiler options already does one important thing: it leaves the syntax intact. A problem occurs once you want to run your code.

Usually, import statements in TypeScript point to files without an extension. You write import { obj } from "./module", leaving out *.ts*. Once you compile, this extension is still missing. But the browser needs an extension to actually point to the respective JavaScript file.

The solution: Add a *.js* extension, even though you are pointing to a *.ts* file when you develop. TypeScript is smart enough to pick that up:

```
// index.ts

// This still loads types from 'module.ts', but keeps
// the reference intact once we compile it.
import { obj } from './module.js';

console.log(obj.name);
```

For your project's modules, that's all you need!

It gets a lot more interesting when you want to use dependencies. If you go native, you might want to load modules from a CDN, like esm.sh (*https://esm.sh*):

```
import _ from "https://esm.sh/lodash@4.17.21"
//                  ^- Error 2307

const result = _.flattenDeep([1, [2, [3, [4]], 5]]);

console.log(result);
```

TypeScript will error with the following message: "Cannot find module … or its corresponding type declarations. (2307)"

TypeScript's module resolution works when files are on your disk, not on a server via HTTP. To get the info we need, we have to provide TypeScript with a resolution of our own.

Even though we are loading dependencies from URLs, the type information for these dependencies lives with NPM. For lodash, you can install type information from Definitely Typed:

```
$ npm install -D @types/lodash
```

For dependencies that come with their own types, you can install the dependencies directly:

```
$ npm install -D preact
```

Once the types are installed, use the `path` property in your compiler options to tell TypeScript how to resolve your URL:

```
// tsconfig.json
{
  "compilerOptions": {
    // ...
    "paths": {
      "https://esm.sh/lodash@4.17.21": [
        "node_modules/@types/lodash/index.d.ts"
      ]
    }
  }
}
```

Be sure to point to the right file!

There's also an escape hatch if you don't want to use typings, or if you just can't find typings. Within TypeScript, we can use `any` to intentionally disable type-checking. For modules, we can do something very similar—ignore the TypeScript error:

```
// @ts-ignore
import _ from "https://esm.sh/lodash@4.17.21"
```

`ts-ignore` removes the *next* line from type-checking and can be used everywhere you want to ignore type errors (see Recipe 1.4). This effectively means that you won't get any type information for your dependencies and you might run into errors, but it might be the ultimate solution for unmaintained, old dependencies that you just need but won't find any types for.

1.9 Loading Different Module Types in Node

Problem

You want to use ECMAScript modules in Node.js and the CommonJS interoperability feature for libraries.

Solution

Set TypeScript's module resolution to `"nodeNext"` and name your files *.mts* or *.cts*.

Discussion

With the advent of Node.js, the CommonJS module system has become one of the most popular module systems in the JavaScript ecosystem.

The idea is simple and effective: define exports in one module and require them in another:

```
// person.js
function printPerson(person) {
  console.log(person.name);
}

exports = {
  printPerson,
};

// index.js
const person = require("./person");
person.printPerson({ name: "Stefan", age: 40 });
```

This system has been a huge influence on ECMAScript modules and also has been the default for TypeScript's module resolution and transpiler. If you look at the ECMAScript modules syntax in Example 1-1, you can see that the keywords allow for different transpilations. This means that with the commonjs module setting, your import and export statements are transpiled to require and exports.

Example 1-1. Using the ECMAScript module system

```
// person.ts
type Person = {
  name: string;
  age: number;
};

export function printPerson(person) {
  console.log(person.name);
}

// index.ts
import * as person from "./person";
person.printPerson({ name: "Stefan", age: 40 });
```

With ECMAScript modules stabilizing, Node.js has also started to adopt them. Even though the basics of both module systems seem to be very similar, there are some differences in the details, such as handling default exports or loading ECMAScript modules asynchronously.

As there is no way to treat both module systems the same but with different syntax, the Node.js maintainers decided to give both systems room and assigned different file endings to indicate the preferred module type. Table 1-1 shows the different endings, how they're named in TypeScript, what TypeScript compiles them to, and what they can import. Thanks to the CommonJS interoperability, it's fine to import CommonJS modules from ECMAScript modules, but not the other way around.

Table 1-1. *Module endings and what they import*

Ending	TypeScript	Compiles to	Can import
.js	.ts	CommonJS	.js, .cjs
.cjs	.cts	CommonJS	.js, .cjs
.mjs	.mts	ES Modules	.js, .cjs, .mjs

Library developers who publish on NPM get extra information in their *package.json* file to indicate the main type of a package (`module` or `commonjs`), and to point to a list of main files or fallbacks so module loaders can pick up the right file:

```
// package.json
{
  "name": "dependency",
  "type": "module",
  "exports": {
    ".": {
      // Entry-point for `import "dependency"` in ES Modules
      "import": "./esm/index.js",
      // Entry-point for `require("dependency")` in CommonJS
      "require": "./commonjs/index.cjs",
    },
  },
  // CommonJS Fallback
  "main": "./commonjs/index.cjs"
}
```

In TypeScript, you write mainly ECMAScript module syntax and let the compiler decide which module format to create in the end. Now there are possibly two: CommonJS and ECMAScript modules.

To allow for both, you can set module resolution in your *tsconfig.json* to `NodeNext`:

```
{
  "compilerOptions": {
    "module": "NodeNext"
    // ...
  }
}
```

With that flag, TypeScript will pick up the right modules as described in your dependencies *package.json*, will recognize *.mts* and *.cts* endings, and will follow Table 1-1 for module imports.

For you as a developer, there are differences in importing files. Since CommonJS didn't require endings when importing, TypeScript still supports imports without endings. The example in Example 1-1 still works, if all you use is CommonJS.

Importing with file endings, just like in Recipe 1.8, allows modules to be imported in both ECMAScript modules and CommonJS modules:

```
// index.mts
import * as person from "./person.js"; // works in both
person.printPerson({ name: "Stefan", age: 40});
```

Should CommonJS interoperability not work, you can always fall back on a `require` statement. Add `"node"` as global types to your compiler options:

```
// tsconfig.json
{
  "compilerOptions": {
    "module": "NodeNext",
    "types": ["node"],
  }
}
```

Then, import with this TypeScript-specific syntax:

```
// index.mts
import person = require("./person.cjs");

person.printPerson({ name: "Stefan", age: 40 });
```

In a CommonJS module, this will be just another `require` call; in ECMAScript modules, this will include Node.js helper functions:

```
// compiled index.mts
import { createRequire as _createRequire } from "module";
const __require = _createRequire(import.meta.url);
const person = __require("./person.cjs");
person.printPerson({ name: "Stefan", age: 40 });
```

Note that this will reduce compatibility with non-Node.js environments like the browser, but it might eventually fix interoperability issues.

1.10 Working with Deno and Dependencies

Problem

You want to use TypeScript with Deno, a modern JavaScript runtime for applications outside the browser.

Solution

That's easy; TypeScript is built in.

Discussion

Deno is a modern JavaScript runtime created by the same people who developed Node.js. Deno is similar to Node.js in many ways, but with significant differences:

- Deno adopts web platform standards for their main APIs, meaning that you will find it easier to port code from the browser to the server.

- It allows file system or network access only if you explicitly activate it.

- It doesn't handle dependencies via a centralized registry, but—again adopting browser features—via URLs.

Oh, and it comes with built-in development tooling and TypeScript!

Deno is the tool with the lowest barrier if you want to try TypeScript. No need to download any other tool (the `tsc` compiler is already built in), no need for TypeScript configurations. You write *.ts* files, and Deno handles the rest:

```
// main.ts
function sayHello(name: string) {
  console.log(`Hello ${name}`);
}

sayHello("Stefan");

$ deno run main.ts
```

Deno's TypeScript can do everything `tsc` can do, and it is updated with every Deno update. However, there are some differences when you want to configure it.

First, the default configuration has differences in its default settings as opposed to the default configuration issued by `tsc --init`. Strict mode feature flags are set differently, and it includes support for React (on the server side!).

To make changes to the configuration, you should create a *deno.json* file in your root folder. Deno will automatically pick this up, unless you tell it not to. *deno.json* includes several configurations for the Deno runtime, including TypeScript compiler options:

```
{
  "compilerOptions": {
    // Your TSC compiler options
  },
  "fmt": {
    // Options for the auto-formatter
  },
  "lint": {
    // Options for the linter
  }
}
```

You can see more possibilities on the Deno website (*https://oreil.ly/zGA--*).

The default libraries are different as well. Even though Deno supports web platform standards and has browser-compatible APIs, it needs to make some cuts because there is no graphical user interface. That's why some types—for example, the DOM library—clash with what Deno provides.

Some libraries of interest are:

- *deno.ns*, the default Deno namespace
- *deno.window*, the global object for Deno
- *deno.worker*, the equivalent for Web Workers in the Deno runtime

DOM and subsets are included in Deno, but they are not switched on by default. If your application targets both the browser and Deno, configure Deno to include all browser and Deno libraries:

```
// deno.json
{
  "compilerOptions": {
    "target": "esnext",
    "lib": ["dom", "dom.iterable", "dom.asynciterable", "deno.ns"]
  }
}
```

Aleph.js (*https://alephjs.org*) is an example of a framework that targets both Deno and the browser.

Also different with Deno is how type information for dependencies is distributed. External dependencies in Deno are loaded via URLs from a CDN. Deno itself hosts its standard library at *https://deno.land/std*.

But you can also use CDNs like esm.sh (*https://esm.sh*) or unpkg (*https://unpkg.com*), like in Recipe 1.8. These CDNs distribute types by sending an X-TypeScript-Types header with the HTTP request, showing Deno was to load type declarations. This also goes for dependencies that don't have first-party type declarations but rely on Definitely Typed.

So the moment you install your dependency, Deno will fetch not only the source files but also all the type information.

If you don't load a dependency from a CDN but rather have it locally, you can point to a type declaration file the moment you import the dependency:

```
// @deno-types="./charting.d.ts"
import * as charting from "./charting.js";
```

or include a reference to the typings in the library itself:

```
// charting.js
/// <reference types="./charting.d.ts" />
```

This reference is also called a *triple-slash directive* and is a TypeScript feature, not a Deno feature. There are various triple-slash directives, mostly used for pre-ECMAScript module dependency systems. The documentation (*https://oreil.ly/ EvUWm*) gives a really good overview. If you stick with ECMAScript modules, you most likely won't use triple-slash directives, though.

1.11 Using Predefined Configurations

Problem

You want to use TypeScript for a certain framework or platform but don't know where to start with your configuration.

Solution

Use a predefined configuration from *tsconfig/bases* (*https://oreil.ly/ljsVT*) and extend from there.

Discussion

Just like Definitely Typed hosts community-maintained type definitions for popular libraries, *tsconfig/bases* hosts a set of community-maintained recommendations for TypeScript configurations you can use as a starting point for your own project. This includes frameworks like Ember.js, Svelte, or Next.js as well as JavaScript runtimes like Node.js and Deno.

The configuration files are reduced to a minimum, dealing mostly with recommended libraries, modules, and target settings, and a bunch of strict mode flags that make sense for the respective environment.

For example, this is the recommended configuration for Node.js 18, with a recommended strict mode setting and with ECMAScript modules:

```
{
  "$schema": "https://json.schemastore.org/tsconfig",
  "display": "Node 18 + ESM + Strictest",
  "compilerOptions": {
    "lib": [
      "es2022"
    ],
    "module": "es2022",
    "target": "es2022",
    "strict": true,
```

```
        "esModuleInterop": true,
        "skipLibCheck": true,
        "forceConsistentCasingInFileNames": true,
        "moduleResolution": "node",
        "allowUnusedLabels": false,
        "allowUnreachableCode": false,
        "exactOptionalPropertyTypes": true,
        "noFallthroughCasesInSwitch": true,
        "noImplicitOverride": true,
        "noImplicitReturns": true,
        "noPropertyAccessFromIndexSignature": true,
        "noUncheckedIndexedAccess": true,
        "noUnusedLocals": true,
        "noUnusedParameters": true,
        "importsNotUsedAsValues": "error",
        "checkJs": true
    }
}
```

To use this configuration, install it via NPM:

```
$ npm install --save-dev @tsconfig/node18-strictest-esm
```

and wire it up in your own TypeScript configuration:

```
{
    "extends": "@tsconfig/node18-strictest-esm/tsconfig.json",
    "compilerOptions": {
        // ...
    }
}
```

This will pick up all the settings from the predefined configuration. You can now start setting your own properties, for example, root and out directories.

CHAPTER 2

Basic Types

Now that you are all set up, it's time to write some TypeScript! Starting out should be easy, but you will soon run into situations where you're unsure if you're doing the right thing. Should you use interfaces or type aliases? Should you annotate or let type inference do its magic? What about any and unknown: are they safe to use? Some people on the internet said you should never use them, so why are they part of TypeScript?

All these questions will be answered in this chapter. We will look at the basic types that make TypeScript and learn how an experienced TypeScript developer will use them. You can use this as a foundation for the upcoming chapters, so you get a feel for how the TypeScript compiler gets to its types and how it interprets your annotations.

This is about the interaction between your code, the editor, and the compiler. And it's about going up and down the type hierarchy, as we will see in Recipe 2.3. Whether you're an experienced TypeScript developer or just starting out, you'll find useful information in this chapter.

2.1 Annotating Effectively

Problem

Annotating types is cumbersome and boring.

Solution

Annotate only when you want your types checked.

Discussion

A type annotation is a way to explicitly tell which types to expect. You know, the prominent stuff in other programming languages, where the verbosity of `String Builder stringBuilder = new StringBuilder()` makes sure that you're really, really dealing with a `StringBuilder`. The opposite is type inference, where Type-Script tries to figure out the type for you:

```
// Type inference
let aNumber = 2;
// aNumber: number

// Type annotation
let anotherNumber: number = 3;
// anotherNumber: number
```

Type annotations are also the most obvious and visible syntax difference between TypeScript and JavaScript.

When you start learning TypeScript, you might want to annotate everything to express the types you'd expect. This might feel like the obvious choice, but you can also use annotations sparingly and let TypeScript figure out types for you.

A type annotation is a way for you to express where contracts have to be checked. If you add a type annotation to a variable declaration, you tell the compiler to check if types match during the assignment:

```
type Person = {
  name: string;
  age: number;
};

const me: Person = createPerson();
```

If `createPerson` returns something that isn't compatible with `Person`, TypeScript will throw an error. Do this if you really want to be sure you're dealing with the right type.

Also, from this moment on, `me` is of type `Person`, and TypeScript will treat it as a `Person`. If there are more properties in `me`—for example, a `profession`—TypeScript won't allow you to access them. It's not defined in `Person`.

If you add a type annotation to a function signature's return value, you tell the compiler to check if types match the moment you return that value:

```
function createPerson(): Person {
  return { name: "Stefan", age: 39 };
}
```

If you return something that doesn't match `Person`, TypeScript will throw an error. Do this if you want to be completely sure that you return the correct type. This especially comes in handy if you are working with functions that construct big objects from various sources.

If you add a type annotation to a function signature's parameters, you tell the compiler to check if types match the moment you pass along arguments:

```
function printPerson(person: Person) {
  console.log(person.name, person.age);
}

printPerson(me);
```

In my opinion this is the most important and unavoidable type annotation. Everything else can be inferred:

```
type Person = {
  name: string;
  age: number;
};

// Inferred!
// return type is { name: string, age: number }
function createPerson() {
  return { name: "Stefan", age: 39 };
}

// Inferred!
// me: { name: string, age: number}
const me = createPerson();

// Annotated! You have to check if types are compatible
function printPerson(person: Person) {
  console.log(person.name, person.age);
}

// All works
printPerson(me);
```

You can use inferred object types where you expect an annotation because TypeScript has a *structural type system*. In a structural type system, the compiler will only take into account the members (properties) of a type, not the actual name.

Types are compatible if all members of the type to check against are available in the type of the value. We also say that the *shape* or *structure* of a type has to match:

```
type Person = {
  name: string;
  age: number;
};
```

```
type User = {
  name: string;
  age: number;
  id: number;
};

function printPerson(person: Person) {
  console.log(person.name, person.age);
}

const user: User = {
  name: "Stefan",
  age: 40,
  id: 815,
};

printPerson(user); // works!
```

User has more properties than Person, but all properties that are in Person are also in User, and they have the same type. This is why it's possible to pass User objects to printPerson, even though the types don't have any explicit connection.

However, if you pass a literal, TypeScript will complain that there are excess properties that should not be there:

```
printPerson({
  name: "Stefan",
  age: 40,
  id: 1000,
  // ^- Argument of type '{ name: string; age: number; id: number; }'
  //    is not assignable to parameter of type 'Person'.
  //    Object literal may only specify known properties,
  //    and 'id' does not exist in type 'Person'.(2345)
});
```

This makes sure that you didn't expect properties to be present in this type and then wonder why changing them has no effect.

With a structural type system, you can create interesting patterns with carrier variables with the type inferred, and you can reuse the same variable in different parts of your software, with no similar connection to each other:

```
type Person = {
  name: string;
  age: number;
};

type Studying = {
  semester: number;
};

type Student = {
```

```
  id: string;
  age: number;
  semester: number;
};

function createPerson() {
  return { name: "Stefan", age: 39, semester: 25, id: "XPA" };
}

function printPerson(person: Person) {
  console.log(person.name, person.age);
}

function studyForAnotherSemester(student: Studying) {
  student.semester++;
}

function isLongTimeStudent(student: Student) {
  return student.age - student.semester / 2 > 30 && student.semester > 20;
}

const me = createPerson();

// All work!
printPerson(me);
studyForAnotherSemester(me);
isLongTimeStudent(me);
```

Student, Person, and Studying have some overlap but are unrelated to each other. createPerson returns something that is compatible with all three types. If you have annotated too much, you would need to create a lot more types and a lot more checks than necessary, without any benefit.

So annotate wherever you want to have your types checked, at least for function arguments.

2.2 Working with any and unknown

Problem

There are two top types in TypeScript, any and unknown. Which one should you use?

Solution

Use any if you effectively want to deactivate typing; use unknown when you need to be cautious.

Discussion

Both any and unknown are top types, which means that every value is compatible with any or unknown:

```
const name: any = "Stefan";
const person: any = { name: "Stefan", age: 40 };
const notAvailable: any = undefined;
```

Since any is a type every value is compatible with, you can access any property without restriction:

```
const name: any = "Stefan";
// This is ok for TypeScript, but will crash in JavaScript
console.log(name.profession.experience[0].level);
```

any is also compatible with every subtype, except never. This means you can narrow the set of possible values by assigning a new type:

```
const me: any = "Stefan";
// Good!
const name: string = me;
// Bad, but ok for the type system.
const age: number = me;
```

Being so permissive, any can be a constant source of potential errors and pitfalls since you effectively deactivate type-checking.

While everybody seems to agree that you shouldn't use any in your codebases, there are some situations where any is really useful:

Migration

When you go from JavaScript to TypeScript, chances are that you already have a large codebase with a lot of implicit information on how your data structures and objects work. It might be a chore to get everything spelled out in one go. any can help you migrate to a safer codebase incrementally.

Untyped third-party dependencies

You might have a JavaScript dependency that still refuses to use TypeScript (or something similar). Or even worse: there are no up-to-date types for it. Definitely Typed is a great resource, but it's also maintained by volunteers. It's a formalization of something that exists in JavaScript but is not directly derived from it. There might be errors (even in such popular type definitions like React's), or they just might not be up to date!

This is where any can help you. When you know how the library works, if the documentation is good enough to get you going, and if you use it sparingly, any can be an option instead of fighting types.

JavaScript prototyping

TypeScript works a bit differently from JavaScript and needs to make a lot of trade-offs to ensure that you don't run into edge cases. This also means that if you write certain things that would work in JavaScript, you'd get errors in TypeScript:

```
type Person = {
  name: string;
  age: number;
};

function printPerson(person: Person) {
  for (let key in person) {
    console.log(`${key}: ${person[key]}`);
// Element implicitly has an 'any' --^
// type because expression of type 'string'
// can't be used to index type 'Person'.
// No index signature with a parameter of type 'string'
// was found on type 'Person'.(7053)
  }
}
```

Find out why this is an error in Recipe 9.1. In cases like this, any can help you to switch off type-checking for a moment because you know what you're doing. And since you can go from every type to any, but also back to every other type, you have little, explicit unsafe blocks throughout your code where you are in charge of what's happening:

```
function printPerson(person: any) {
  for (let key in person) {
    console.log(`${key}: ${person[key]}`);
  }
}
```

Once you know this part of your code works, you can start adding the right types, work around TypeScript's restrictions, and type assertions:

```
function printPerson(person: Person) {
  for (let key in person) {
    console.log(`${key}: ${person[key as keyof Person]}`);
  }
}
```

Whenever you use any, make sure you activate the noImplicitAny flag in your *tsconfig.json*; it is activated by default in strict mode. TypeScript needs you to explicitly annotate any when you don't have a type through inference or annotation. This helps find potentially problematic situations later on.

An alternative to any is unknown. It allows for the same values, but the things you can do with it are very different. Where any allows you to do everything, unknown allows you to do nothing. All you can do is pass values around; the moment you want to call a function or make the type more specific, you first need to do type-checks:

```
const me: unknown = "Stefan";
const name: string = me;
//    ^- Type 'unknown' is not assignable to type 'string'.(2322)
const age: number = me;
//    ^- Type 'unknown' is not assignable to type 'number'.(2322)
```

Type-checks and control flow analysis help you do more with unknown:

```
function doSomething(value: unknown) {
  if (typeof value === "string") {
    // value: string
    console.log("It's a string", value.toUpperCase());
  } else if (typeof value === "number") {
    // value: number
    console.log("it's a number", value * 2);
  }
}
```

If your apps work with a lot of different types, unknown is great for making sure that you can carry values throughout your code but don't run into any safety problems because of any's permissiveness.

2.3 Choosing the Right Object Type

Problem

You want to allow for values that are JavaScript objects, but there are three different object types: object, Object, and {}. Which one should you use?

Solution

Use object for compound types like objects, functions, and arrays. Use {} for everything that has a value.

Discussion

TypeScript divides its types into two branches. The first branch, *primitive types*, includes number, boolean, string, symbol, bigint, and some subtypes. The second branch, *compound types*, includes everything that is a subtype of an object and is ultimately composed of other compound types or primitive types. Figure 2-1 provides an overview.

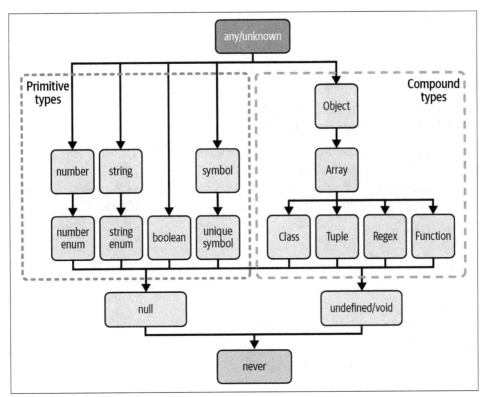

Figure 2-1. The type hierarchy in TypeScript

In some situations you want to target values that are *compound types*, either because you want to modify certain properties or because you just want to be safe that you don't pass any primitive values. For example `Object.create` creates a new object and takes its prototype as the first argument. This can only be a *compound type*; otherwise, your runtime JavaScript code would crash:

```
Object.create(2);
// Uncaught TypeError: Object prototype may only be an Object or null: 2
//     at Function.create (<anonymous>)
```

In TypeScript, three types seem to do the same thing: The empty object type {}, the uppercase O `Object` interface, and the lowercase O `object` type. Which one do you use for compound types?

{} and `Object` allow for roughly the same values, which are everything but `null` or `undefined` (given that `strict` mode or `strictNullChecks` is activated):

```
let obj: {}; // Similar to Object
obj = 32;
obj = "Hello";
obj = true;
```

```
obj = () => { console.log("Hello") };
obj = undefined; // Error
obj = null; // Error
obj = { name: "Stefan", age: 40 };
obj = [];
obj = /.*/;
```

The `Object` interface is compatible with all values that have the `Object` prototype, which is every value from every primitive and compound type.

However, `Object` is a defined interface in TypeScript, and it has some requirements for certain functions. For example, the `toString` method, which is `toString() => string` and part of any non-nullish value, is part of the `Object` prototype. If you assign a value with a different `tostring` method, TypeScript will error:

```
let okObj: {} = {
  toString() {
    return false;
  }
}; // OK

let obj: Object = {
  toString() {
    return false;
  }
// ^- Type 'boolean' is not assignable to type 'string'.ts(2322)
}
```

`Object` can cause some confusion due to this behavior, so in most cases, you're good with `{}`.

TypeScript also has a *lowercase* `object` type. This is more the type you're looking for, as it allows for any compound type but no primitive types:

```
let obj: object;
obj = 32; // Error
obj = "Hello"; // Error
obj = true; // Error
obj = () => { console.log("Hello") };
obj = undefined;  // Error
obj = null; // Error
obj = { name: "Stefan", age: 40 };
obj = [];
obj = /.*/;
```

If you want a type that excludes functions, regexes, arrays, and the like, see Chapter 5, where we create one on our own.

2.4 Working with Tuple Types

Problem

You are using JavaScript arrays to organize your data. The order is important, and so are the types at each position. But TypeScript's type inference makes it really cumbersome to work with.

Solution

Annotate with tuple types.

Discussion

Like objects, JavaScript arrays are a popular way to organize data in a complex object. Instead of writing a typical `Person` object as we did in other recipes, you can store entries element by element:

```
const person = ["Stefan", 40]; // name and age
```

The benefit of using arrays over objects is that array elements don't have property names. When you assign each element to variables using destructuring, it becomes really easy to assign custom names:

```
// objects.js
// Using objects
const person = {
  name: "Stefan",
  age: 40,
};

const { name, age } = person;

console.log(name); // Stefan
console.log(age); // 40

const { anotherName = name, anotherAge = age } = person;

console.log(anotherName); // Stefan
console.log(anotherAge); // 40

// arrays.js
// Using arrays
const person = ["Stefan", 40]; // name and age

const [name, age] = person;

console.log(name); // Stefan
console.log(age); // 40
```

```
const [anotherName, anotherAge] = person;

console.log(anotherName); // Stefan
console.log(anotherAge); // 40
```

For APIs where you need to assign new names constantly, using arrays is very comfortable, as explained in Chapter 10.

When using TypeScript and relying on type inference, however, this pattern can cause some issues. By default, TypeScript infers the array type from an assignment. Arrays are open-ended collections with the same element in each position:

```
const person = ["Stefan", 40];
// person: (string | number)[]
```

So TypeScript thinks that person is an array, where each element can be either a string or a number, and it allows for plenty of elements after the original two. This means when you're destructuring, each element is also of type string or number:

```
const [name, age] = person;
// name: string | number
// age: string | number
```

That makes a comfortable pattern in JavaScript really cumbersome in Typescript. You would need to do control flow checks to narrow the type to the actual one, where it should be clear from the assignment that this is not necessary.

Whenever you think you need to do extra work in JavaScript just to satisfy TypeScript, there's usually a better way. In that case, you can use tuple types to be more specific about how your array should be interpreted.

Tuple types are a sibling of array types that work on a different semantic. While arrays can be potentially endless in size and each element is of the same type (no matter how broad), tuple types have a fixed size, and each element has a distinct type.

All you need to do to get tuple types is to explicitly annotate:

```
const person: [string, number] = ["Stefan", 40];

const [name, age] = person;
// name: string
// age: number
```

Fantastic! Tuple types have a fixed length; this means the length is also encoded in the type. So assignments that go out of bounds are not possible; TypeScript will throw an error:

```
person[1] = 41; // OK!
person[2] = false; // Error
//^- Type 'false' is not assignable to type 'undefined'.(2322)
```

TypeScript also allows you to add labels to tuple types. This is just metainformation for editors and compiler feedback, but it allows you to be clearer about what to expect from each element:

```
type Person = [name: string, age: number];
```

This will help you and your colleagues to understand what to expect, just like with object types.

Tuple types can also be used to annotate function arguments. This function:

```
function hello(name: string, msg: string): void {
    // ...
}
```

can also be written with tuple types:

```
function hello(...args: [name: string, msg: string]): {
    // ...
}
```

And you can be very flexible in defining it:

```
function h(a: string, b: string, c: string): void {
    //...
}
// equal to
function h(a: string, b: string, ...r: [string]): void {
    //...
}
// equal to
function h(a: string, ...r: [string, string]): void {
    //...
}
// equal to
function h(...r: [string, string, string]): void {
    //...
}
```

These are also known as *rest* elements, something that we have in JavaScript that allow you to define functions with an almost limitless argument list; when it is the last element, the *rest* element sucks all excess arguments in. When you need to collect arguments in your code, you can use a tuple before you apply them to your function:

```
const person: [string, number] = ["Stefan", 40];

function hello(...args: [name: string, msg: string]): {
    // ...
}

hello(...person);
```

Tuple types are useful for many scenarios. For more information about tuple types, see Chapters 7 and 10.

2.5 Understanding Interfaces Versus Type Aliases

Problem

TypeScript declares object types in two ways: interfaces and type aliases. Which one should you use?

Solution

Use type aliases for types within your project's boundary, and use interfaces for contracts that are meant to be consumed by others.

Discussion

Both approaches to defining object types have been the subject of many blog articles over the years. And all of them became outdated over time. As of this writing there is little difference between type aliases and interfaces. And everything that *was* different has been gradually aligned.

Syntactically, the difference between interfaces and type aliases is nuanced:

```
type PersonAsType = {
  name: string;
  age: number;
  address: string[];
  greet(): string;
};

interface PersonAsInterface {
  name: string;
  age: number;
  address: string[];
  greet(): string;
}
```

You can use interfaces and type aliases for the same things, in the same scenarios:

- In an implements declaration for classes
- As a type annotation for object literals
- For recursive type structures

However, there is one important difference that can cause side effects you usually don't want to deal with: interfaces allow for declaration merging, but type aliases don't. Declaration merging allows for adding properties to an interface even after it has been declared:

```
interface Person {
  name: string;
}

interface Person {
  age: number;
}

// Person is now { name: string; age: number; }
```

TypeScript often uses this technique in *lib.d.ts* files, making it possible to just add deltas of new JavaScript APIs based on ECMAScript versions. This is a great feature if you want to extend, for example, Window, but it can backfire in other scenarios, for example:

```
// Some data we collect in a web form
interface FormData {
  name: string;
  age: number;
  address: string[];
}

// A function that sends this data to a backend
function send(data: FormData) {
  console.log(data.entries()) // this compiles!
  // but crashes horrendously in runtime
}
```

So, where does the entries() method come from? It's a DOM API! FormData is one of the interfaces provided by browser APIs, and there are a lot of them. They are globally available, and nothing keeps you from extending those interfaces. And you get no notification if you do.

You can of course argue about proper naming, but the problem persists for all interfaces that you make available globally, maybe from some dependency where you aren't even aware they add an interface to the global space.

Changing this interface to a type alias immediately makes you aware of this problem:

```
type FormData = {
//    ^-- Duplicate identifier 'FormData'.(2300)
  name: string;
  age: number;
  address: string[];
};
```

Declaration merging is a fantastic feature if you are creating a library that is consumed by other parts in your project, maybe even other projects written entirely by other teams. It allows you to define an interface that describes your application but allows your users to adapt it to reality. Think of a plug-in system, where loading new modules enhances functionality: declaration merging is a feature that you do not want to miss.

Within your module's boundaries, however, using type aliases prevents you from accidentally reusing or extending already declared types. Use type aliases when you don't expect others to consume them.

Performance

Using type aliases over interfaces has sparked some discussion, as interfaces have been considered much more performant in their evaluation than type aliases, even resulting in a performance recommendation on the official TypeScript wiki (*https://oreil.ly/8Y0hP*). This recommendation should be taken with a grain of salt.

On creation, simple type aliases may perform faster than interfaces because interfaces are never closed and might be merged with other declarations. But interfaces may perform faster in other places because they're known ahead of time to be object types. Ryan Canavaugh from the TypeScript team expects performance differences to be measurable with an extraordinary number of interfaces or type aliases to be declared: around five thousand according to this tweet (*https://oreil.ly/Y_2oS*).

If your TypeScript code base doesn't perform well, it's not because you declared too many type aliases instead of interfaces, or vice versa.

2.6 Defining Function Overloads

Problem

Your function's API is very flexible and allows for arguments of various types, where context is important. This is hard to type in just a single function signature.

Solution

Use function overloads.

Discussion

JavaScript is very flexible when it comes to function arguments. You can pass basically any parameters, of any length. As long as the function body treats the input correctly, you're good. This allows for very ergonomic APIs, but it's also very tough to type.

Think of a conceptual task runner. With a `task` function you define new tasks by name and either pass a callback or pass a list of other tasks to be executed. Or both—a list of tasks that needs to be executed *before* the callback runs:

```
task("default", ["scripts", "styles"]);

task("scripts", ["lint"], () => {
    // ...
});

task("styles", () => {
    // ...
});
```

If you're thinking, "this looks a lot like Gulp six years ago," you're right. Its flexible API where you couldn't do much wrong was also one of the reasons Gulp was so popular.

Typing functions like this can be a nightmare. Optional arguments, different types at the same position—this is tough to do even if you use union types:[1]

```
type CallbackFn = () => void;

function task(
    name: string, param2: string[] | CallbackFn, param3?: CallbackFn
): void {
//...
}
```

This catches all variations from the preceding example, but it's also wrong, as it allows for combinations that don't make any sense:

```
task(
    "what",
    () => {
        console.log("Two callbacks?");
    },
    () => {
        console.log("That's not supported, but the types say yes!");
    }
);
```

Thankfully, TypeScript has a way to solve problems like this: function overloads. Its name hints at similar concepts from other programming languages: the same definition but with different behavior. The biggest difference in TypeScript, as opposed to other programming languages, is that function overloads work only on a type system level and have no effect on the actual implementation.

The idea is that you define every possible scenario as its own function signature. The last function signature is the actual implementation:

---

1 Union types are a way to combine two different types into one (see more in Chapter 3).

```
// Types for the type system
function task(name: string, dependencies: string[]): void;
function task(name: string, callback: CallbackFn): void
function task(name: string, dependencies: string[], callback: CallbackFn): void
// The actual implementation
function task(
  name: string, param2: string[] | CallbackFn, param3?: CallbackFn
): void {
//...
}
```

A couple of things are important to note here.

First, TypeScript only picks up the declarations before the actual implementation as possible types. If the actual implementation signature is also relevant, duplicate it.

Also, the actual implementation function signature can't be anything. TypeScript checks if the overloads can be implemented with the implementation signature.

If you have different return types, it is your responsibility to make sure that inputs and outputs match:

```
function fn(input: number): number
function fn(input: string): string
function fn(input: number | string): number | string {
  if(typeof input === "number") {
    return "this also works";
  } else {
    return 1337;
  }
}

const typeSaysNumberButItsAString = fn(12);
const typeSaysStringButItsANumber = fn("Hello world");
```

The implementation signature usually works with a very broad type, which means you have to do a lot of checks that you would need to do in JavaScript anyway. This is good as it urges you to be extra careful.

If you need overloaded functions as their own type, to use them in annotations and assign multiple implementations, you can always create a type alias:

```
type TaskFn = {
  (name: string, dependencies: string[]): void;
  (name: string, callback: CallbackFn): void;
  (name: string, dependencies: string[], callback: CallbackFn): void;
}
```

As you can see, you only need the type system overloads, not the actual implementation definition.

2.7 Defining this Parameter Types

Problem

You are writing callback functions that make assumptions about this, but you don't know how to define this when writing the function standalone.

Solution

Define a this parameter type at the beginning of a function signature.

Discussion

One source of confusion for aspiring JavaScript developers is the ever-changing nature of the this object pointer:

> Sometimes when writing JavaScript, I want to shout, "This is ridiculous!" But then I never know what *this* refers to.
>
> —Unknown JavaScript developer

The preceding statement is true especially if your background is a class-based object-oriented programming language, where this always refers to an instance of a class. this in JavaScript is entirely different but not necessarily harder to understand. What's more, TypeScript can greatly help get more closure about this in usage.

this lives within the scope of a function, and that points to an object or value bound to that function. In regular objects, this is pretty straightforward:

```
const author = {
  name: "Stefan",
  // function shorthand
  hi() {
    console.log(this.name);
  },
};

author.hi(); // prints 'Stefan'
```

But functions are values in JavaScript, and they can be bound to a different context, effectively changing the value of this:

```
const author = {
  name: "Stefan",
};

function hi() {
  console.log(this.name);
}
```

```
const pet = {
  name: "Finni",
  kind: "Cat",
};

hi.apply(pet); // prints "Finni"
hi.call(author); // prints "Stefan"

const boundHi = hi.bind(author);

boundHi(); // prints "Stefan"
```

It doesn't help that the semantics of this change again if you use arrow functions instead of regular functions:

```
class Person {
  constructor(name) {
    this.name = name;
  }

  hi() {
    console.log(this.name);
  }

  hi_timeout() {
    setTimeout(function() {
      console.log(this.name);
    }, 0);
  }

  hi_timeout_arrow() {
    setTimeout(() => {
      console.log(this.name);
    }, 0);
  }
}

const person = new Person("Stefan")
person.hi(); // prints "Stefan"
person.hi_timeout(); // prints "undefined"
person.hi_timeout_arrow(); // prints "Stefan"
```

With TypeScript, we can get more information on what this is and, more importantly, what it's supposed to be through this parameter types.

Take a look at the following example. We access a button element via DOM APIs and bind an event listener to it. Within the callback function, this is of type HTMLButton Element, which means you can access properties like classList:

```
const button = document.querySelector("button");
button?.addEventListener("click", function() {
```

```
    this.classList.toggle("clicked");
  });
```

The information on this is provided by the addEventListener function. If you extract your function in a refactoring step, you retain the functionality, but Type-Script will error, as it loses context for this:

```
const button = document.querySelector("button");
button.addEventListener("click", handleToggle);

function handleToggle() {
  this.classList.toggle("clicked");
// ^- 'this' implicitly has type 'any'
//    because it does not have a type annotation
}
```

The trick is to tell TypeScript that this is supposed to be a specific type. You can do this by adding a parameter at the very first position in your function signature named this:

```
const button = document.querySelector("button");
button?.addEventListener("click", handleToggle);

function handleToggle(this: HTMLButtonElement) {
  this.classList.toggle("clicked");
}
```

This argument gets removed once compiled. TypeScript now has all the information it needs to make sure this needs to be of type HTMLButtonElement, which also means that you get errors once you use handleToggle in a different context:

```
handleToggle();
// ^- The 'this' context of type 'void' is not
//    assignable to method's 'this' of type 'HTMLButtonElement'.
```

You can make handleToggle even more useful if you define this to be HTMLElement, a supertype of HTMLButtonElement:

```
const button = document.querySelector("button");
button?.addEventListener("click", handleToggle);

const input = document.querySelector("input");
input?.addEventListener("click", handleToggle);

function handleToggle(this: HTMLElement) {
  this.classList.toggle("clicked");
}
```

When working with this parameter types, you might want to use two helper types that can either extract or remove this parameters from your function type:

```
function handleToggle(this: HTMLElement) {
  this.classList.toggle("clicked");
```

```
    }

    type ToggleFn = typeof handleToggle;
    // (this: HTMLElement) => void

    type WithoutThis = OmitThisParameter<ToggleFn>
    // () = > void

    type ToggleFnThis = ThisParameterType<ToggleFn>
    // HTMLElement
```

There are more helper types for this in classes and objects. See more in Recipes 4.8 and 11.8.

2.8 Working with Symbols

Problem

You see the type symbol popping up in some error messages, but you don't know what symbols mean or how you can use them.

Solution

Create symbols for object properties you want to be unique and not iterable. They're great for storing and accessing sensitive information.

Discussion

symbol is a primitive data type in JavaScript and TypeScript, which, among other things, can be used for object properties. Compared to number and string, symbols have some unique features.

Symbols can be created using the Symbol() factory function:

```
    const TITLE = Symbol('title')
```

Symbol has no constructor function. The parameter is an optional description. By calling the factory function, TITLE is assigned the unique value of this freshly created symbol. This symbol is now unique and distinguishable from all other symbols, and it doesn't clash with any other symbols that have the same description:

```
    const ACADEMIC_TITLE = Symbol('title')
    const ARTICLE_TITLE = Symbol('title')

    if(ACADEMIC_TITLE === ARTICLE_TITLE) {
      // This is never true
    }
```

The description helps you to get info on the symbol during development time:

```
console.log(ACADEMIC_TITLE.description) // title
console.log(ACADEMIC_TITLE.toString()) // Symbol(title)
```

Symbols are great if you want to have comparable values that are exclusive and unique. For runtime switches or mode comparisons:

```
// A really bad logging framework
const LEVEL_INFO = Symbol('INFO')
const LEVEL_DEBUG = Symbol('DEBUG')
const LEVEL_WARN = Symbol('WARN')
const LEVEL_ERROR = Symbol('ERROR')

function log(msg, level) {
  switch(level) {
    case LEVEL_WARN:
      console.warn(msg); break
    case LEVEL_ERROR:
      console.error(msg); break;
    case LEVEL_DEBUG:
      console.log(msg);
      debugger; break;
    case LEVEL_INFO:
      console.log(msg);
  }
}
```

Symbols also work as property keys but are not iterable, which is great for serialization:

```
const print = Symbol('print')

const user = {
  name: 'Stefan',
  age: 40,
  [print]: function() {
    console.log(`${this.name} is ${this.age} years old`)
  }
}

JSON.stringify(user) // { name: 'Stefan', age: 40 }
user[print]() // Stefan is 40 years old
```

A global symbols registry allows you to access tokens across your whole application:

```
Symbol.for('print') // creates a global symbol

const user = {
  name: 'Stefan',
  age: 37,
  // uses the global symbol
  [Symbol.for('print')]: function() {
    console.log(`${this.name} is ${this.age} years old`)
  }
}
```

The first call to Symbol.for creates a symbol, and the second call uses the same symbol. If you store the symbol value in a variable and want to know the key, you can use Symbol.keyFor():

```
const usedSymbolKeys = []

function extendObject(obj, symbol, value) {
  //Oh, what symbol is this?
  const key = Symbol.keyFor(symbol)
  //Alright, let's better store this
  if(!usedSymbolKeys.includes(key)) {
    usedSymbolKeys.push(key)
  }
  obj[symbol] = value
}

// now it's time to retreive them all
function printAllValues(obj) {
  usedSymbolKeys.forEach(key => {
    console.log(obj[Symbol.for(key)])
  })
}
```

Nifty!

TypeScript has full support for symbols, and they are prime citizens in the type system. symbol itself is a data type annotation for all possible symbols. See the extend Object function in the preceding code block. To allow for all symbols to extend our object, we can use the symbol type:

```
const sym = Symbol('foo')

function extendObject(obj: any, sym: symbol, value: any) {
  obj[sym] = value
}

extendObject({}, sym, 42) // Works with all symbols
```

There's also the subtype unique symbol. A unique symbol is closely tied to the declaration, allowed only in const declarations, and referencing this exact symbol and nothing else.

You can think of a nominal type in TypeScript for a very nominal value in JavaScript.

To get to the type of unique symbol, you need to use the typeof operator:

```
const PROD: unique symbol = Symbol('Production mode')
const DEV: unique symbol = Symbol('Development mode')

function showWarning(msg: string, mode: typeof DEV | typeof PROD) {
  // ...
}
```

At the time of writing, the only possible nominal type is TypeScript's structural type system.

Symbols stand at the intersection between nominal and opaque types in TypeScript and JavaScript. They are the closest things we get to nominal type-checks at runtime.

2.9 Understanding Value and Type Namespaces

Problem

It's confusing that you can use certain names as type annotations and not others.

Solution

Learn about type and value namespaces, and which names contribute to what.

Discussion

TypeScript is a superset of JavaScript, which means it adds more things to an already existing and defined language. Over time you learn to spot which parts are JavaScript and which parts are TypeScript.

It really helps to see TypeScript as this additional layer of types upon regular Java-Script, a thin layer of metainformation that will be peeled off before your JavaScript code runs in one of the available runtimes. Some people even speak about TypeScript code "erasing to JavaScript" once compiled.

TypeScript being this layer on top of JavaScript also means that different syntax contributes to different layers. While a `function` or `const` creates a name in the Java-Script part, a `type` declaration or an `interface` contributes a name in the TypeScript layer:

```
// Collection is in TypeScript land! --> type
type Collection = Person[]

// printCollection is in JavaScript land! --> value
function printCollection(coll: Collection) {
  console.log(...coll.entries)
}
```

We also say that declarations contribute a name to either the *type namespace* or the *value namespace*. Since the type layer is on top of the value layer, it's possible to consume values in the type layer, but not vice versa. We also have explicit keywords for that:

```
// a value
const person = {
  name: "Stefan",
```

```
};

// a type
type Person = typeof person;
```

`typeof` creates a name available in the type layer from the value layer below.

It gets irritating when there are declaration types that create both types and values. Classes, for instance, can be used in the TypeScript layer as a type as well as in Java-Script as a value:

```
// declaration
class Person {
  name: string;

  constructor(n: string) {
    this.name = n;
  }
}

// used as a value
const person = new Person("Stefan");

// used as a type
type Collection = Person[];

function printPersons(coll: Collection) {
  //...
}
```

And naming conventions can trick you. Usually, we define classes, types, interfaces, enums, and so on with a capital first letter. And even if they may contribute values, they for sure contribute types. Well, until you write uppercase functions for your React app, as the convention dictates.

If you're used to using names as types and values, you're going to scratch your head if you suddenly get a good old "TS2749: *YourType* refers to a value, but is being used as a type" error:

```
type PersonProps = {
  name: string;
};

function Person({ name }: PersonProps) {
  // ...
}

type PrintComponentProps = {
  collection: Person[];
  //           ^- 'Person' refers to a value,
  //              but is being used as a type
}
```

This is where TypeScript can get really confusing. What is a type, what is a value, why do we need to separate them, and why doesn't this work like in other programming languages? Suddenly, you are confronted with `typeof` calls or even the `InstanceType` helper type, because you realize that classes actually contribute two types (see Chapter 11).

Classes contribute a name to the type namespace, and since TypeScript is a structural type system, they allow values that have the same shape as an instance of a certain class. So this is allowed:

```
class Person {
  name: string;

  constructor(n: string) {
    this.name = n;
  }
}

function printPerson(person: Person) {
  console.log(person.name);
}

printPerson(new Person("Stefan")); // ok
printPerson({ name: "Stefan" }); // also ok
```

However, `instanceof` checks, which are working entirely in the value namespace and just have implications in the type namespace, would fail, as objects with the same shape may have the same properties but are not an actual *instance* of a class:

```
function checkPerson(person: Person) {
  return person instanceof Person;
}

checkPerson(new Person("Stefan")); // true
checkPerson({ name: "Stefan" }); // false
```

So it's useful to understand what contributes types and what contributes value. Table 2-1, adapted from the TypeScript docs, sums it up nicely.

Table 2-1. Type and value namespaces

Declaration type	Type	Value
Class	X	X
Enum	X	X
Interface	X	
Type Alias	X	
Function		X
Variable		X

If you stick with functions, interfaces (or type aliases, see Recipe 2.5), and variables at the beginning, you will get a feel for what you can use where. If you work with classes, think about the implications a bit longer.

CHAPTER 3

The Type System

In the previous chapter you learned about the basic building blocks that allow you to make your JavaScript code more expressive. But if you are experienced in JavaScript, you understand that TypeScript's fundamental types and annotations cover only a small set of its inherent flexibility.

TypeScript is supposed to make intentions in JavaScript clearer, and it wants to do so without sacrificing this flexibility, especially since it allowed developers to design fantastic APIs used and loved by millions. Think of TypeScript more as a way to formalize JavaScript, rather than restrict it. Enter TypeScript's type system.

In this chapter, you will develop a mental model for how to think about types. You will learn how to define sets of values as widely or as narrowly as you need, and how to change their scope throughout your control flow. You will also learn how to leverage a structural type system and when to break with the rules.

This chapter marks the line between TypeScript foundations and advanced type techniques. But whether you are an experienced TypeScript developer or just starting out, this mental model will be the baseline for everything to come.

3.1 Modeling Data with Union and Intersection Types

Problem

You have an elaborate data model you want to describe in TypeScript.

Solution

Use union and intersection types to model your data. Use literal types to define specific variants.

Discussion

Suppose you are creating a data model for a toy shop. Each item in this toy shop has some basic properties: name, quantity, and the recommended minimum age. Additional properties are relevant only for each particular type of toy, which requires you to create several derivations:

```
type BoardGame = {
  name: string;
  price: number;
  quantity: number;
  minimumAge: number;
  players: number;
};

type Puzzle = {
  name: string;
  price: number;
  quantity: number;
  minimumAge: number;
  pieces: number;
};

type Doll = {
  name: string;
  price: number;
  quantity: number;
  minimumAge: number;
  material: string;
};
```

For the functions you create, you need a type that is representative of all toys, a supertype that contains just the basic properties common to all toys:

```
type ToyBase = {
  name: string;
  price: number;
  quantity: number;
  minimumAge: number;
};

function printToy(toy: ToyBase) {
  /* ... */
}

const doll: Doll = {
  name: "Mickey Mouse",
  price: 9.99,
  quantity: 10000,
  minimumAge: 2,
  material: "plush",
```

```
};

printToy(doll); // works
```

This works, as you can print all dolls, board games, or puzzles with that function, but there's one caveat: you lose the information of the original toy within `printToy`. You can print only common properties, not specific ones.

For a type representing all possible toys, you can create a *union type*:

```
// Union Toy
type Toy = Doll | BoardGame | Puzzle;

function printToy(toy: Toy) {
  /* ... */
}
```

A good way to think of a type is as a set of compatible values. For each value, either annotated or not, TypeScript checks if this value is compatible with a certain type. For objects, this also includes values with more properties than defined in their type. Through inference, values with more properties are assigned a subtype in the structural type system. And values of subtypes are also part of the supertype set.

A union type is a union of sets. The number of compatible values gets broader, and there is also some overlap between types. For example, an object that has both `material` and `players` can be compatible with both `Doll` and `BoardGame`. This is a detail to look out for, and you can see a method to work with that detail in Recipe 3.2.

Figure 3-1 illustrates the concept of a union type in the form of a Venn diagram. Set theory analogies work well here, too.

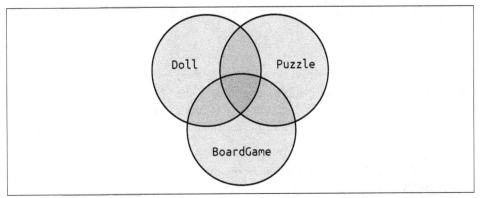

Figure 3-1. Visualization of a union type; each type represents a set of compatible values, and a union type represents the union sets

You can create union types everywhere, and with primitive types:

```
function takesNumberOrString(value: number | string) {
  /* ... */
}

takesNumberOrString(2); // ok
takesNumberOrString("Hello"); // ok
```

This allows you to widen the set of values as much as you like.

What you also see in the toy shop example is some redundancy: the ToyBase properties are repeated. It would be much nicer if we could use ToyBase as the basis of each union part. And we can, using intersection types:

```
type ToyBase = {
  name: string;
  price: number;
  quantity: number;
  minimumAge: number;
};

// Intersection of ToyBase and { players: number }
type BoardGame = ToyBase & {
  players: number;
};

// Intersection of ToyBase and { pieces: number }
type Puzzle = ToyBase & {
  pieces: number;
};

// Intersection of ToyBase and { material: string }
type Doll = ToyBase & {
  material: string;
};
```

Just like union types, *intersection types* resemble their counterparts from set theory. They tell TypeScript that compatible values need to be of type A *and* type B. The type now accepts a narrower set of values, one that includes all properties from both types, including their subtypes. Figure 3-2 shows a visualization of an intersection type.

Intersection types also work on primitive types, but they are of no good use. An intersection of string & number results in never, as no value satisfies both string and number properties.

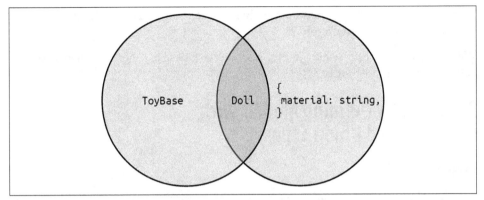

Figure 3-2. Visualization of an intersection type of two types; the set of possible values gets narrower

Instead of type aliases and intersection types you can also define your models with interfaces. In Recipe 2.5 we talk about the differences between them, and there are a few you need to look out for. So a `type BoardGame = ToyBase & { /* ... */ }` can easily be described as `interface BoardGame extends ToyBase { /* ... */ }`. However, you can't define an interface that is a union type. You can define a union of interfaces, though.

These are already great ways to model data within TypeScript, but we can do a little more. In TypeScript, literal values can be represented as a literal type. We can define a type that is just, for example, the number 1, and the only compatible value is 1:

```
type One = 1;
const one: One = 1; // nothing else can be assigned.
```

This is called a *literal type*, and while it doesn't seem to be quite useful alone, it is of great use when you combine multiple literal types to a union. For the `Doll` type, for example, we can explicitly set allowed values for `material`:

```
type Doll = ToyBase & {
  material: "plush" | "plastic";
};

function checkDoll(doll: Doll) {
  if (doll.material === "plush") {
    // do something with plush
  } else {
    // doll.material is "plastic", there are no other options
  }
}
```

This makes assigning any value other than "plush" or "plastic" impossible and makes our code much more robust.

With union types, intersection types, and literal types, it becomes much easier to define even elaborate models.

3.2 Explicitly Defining Models with Discriminated Union Types

Problem

Parts of your modeled union type have a huge overlap in their properties, so it becomes cumbersome to distinguish them in control flow.

Solution

Add a kind property to each union part with a string literal type, and check for its contents.

Discussion

Let's look at a data model similar to what we created in Recipe 3.1. This time, we want to define various shapes for a graphics software:

```
type Circle = {
  radius: number;
};

type Square = {
  x: number;
};

type Triangle = {
  x: number;
  y: number;
};

type Shape = Circle | Triangle | Square;
```

There are some similarities between the types but there is also still enough information to differentiate between them in an area function:

```
function area(shape: Shape) {
  if ("radius" in shape) {
    // shape is Circle
    return Math.PI * shape.radius * shape.radius;
  } else if ("y" in shape) {
    // shape is Triangle
    return (shape.x * shape.y) / 2;
```

```
  } else {
    // shape is Square
    return shape.x * shape.x;
  }
}
```

This works, but it comes with a few caveats. While `Circle` is the only type with a `radius` property, `Triangle` and `Square` share the x property. Since `Square` consists only of the x property, this makes `Triangle` a subtype of `Square`.

Given how we defined the control flow to check for the distinguishing subtype property y first, this is not an issue, but it's just too easy to check for x alone and create a branch in the control flow that computes the area for both `Triangle` and `Square` in the same manner, which is just wrong.

It is also hard to extend `Shape`. If we look at the required properties for a rectangle, we see that it contains the same properties as `Triangle`:

```
type Rectangle = {
  x: number;
  y: number;
};

type Shape = Circle | Triangle | Square | Rectangle;
```

There is no clear way to differentiate between each part of a union. To make sure each part of a union is distinguishable, we need to extend our models with an identifying property that makes absolutely clear what we are dealing with.

This can happen through the addition of a `kind` property. This property takes a string literal type identifying the part of the model.

As seen in Recipe 3.1, TypeScript allows you to subset primitive types like `string`, `number`, `bigint`, and `boolean` to concrete values. Which means that every value is also a type, a set that consists of exactly one compatible value.

So for our model to be clearly defined, we add a `kind` property to each model part and set it to an exact literal type identifying this part:

```
type Circle = {
  radius: number;
  kind: "circle";
};

type Square = {
  x: number;
  kind: "square";
};

type Triangle = {
  x: number;
```

```
    y: number;
    kind: "triangle";
  };

  type Shape = Circle | Triangle | Square;
```

Note that we don't set kind to string but to the *exact* literal type "circle" (or "square" and "triangle", respectively). This is a type, not a value, but the only compatible value is the literal string.

Adding the kind property with string literal types ensures there can't be any overlap between parts of the union, as the literal types are not compatible with one another. This technique is called *discriminated union types* and effectively tears away each set that's part of the union type Shape, pointing to an exact set.

This is fantastic for the area function, as we can effectively distinguish, for example, in a switch statement:

```
function area(shape: Shape) {
  switch (shape.kind) {
    case "circle": // shape is Circle
      return Math.PI * shape.radius * shape.radius;
    case "triangle": // shape is Triangle
      return (shape.x * shape.y) / 2;
    case "square": // shape is Square
      return shape.x * shape.x;
    default:
      throw Error("not possible");
  }
}
```

Not only does it become absolutely clear what we are dealing with, but it is also very future proof to upcoming changes, as we will see in Recipe 3.3.

3.3 Exhaustiveness Checking with the Assert never Technique

Problem

Your discriminated union types change over time, adding new parts to the union. It becomes difficult to track all occurrences in your code where you need to adapt to these changes.

Solution

Create exhaustiveness checks where you assert that all remaining cases can never happen with an assertNever function.

Discussion

Let's look at the full example from Recipe 3.2:

```
type Circle = {
  radius: number;
  kind: "circle";
};

type Square = {
  x: number;
  kind: "square";
};

type Triangle = {
  x: number;
  y: number;
  kind: "triangle";
};

type Shape = Circle | Triangle | Square;

function area(shape: Shape) {
  switch (shape.kind) {
    case "circle": // shape is Circle
      return Math.PI * shape.radius * shape.radius;
    case "triangle": // shape is Triangle
      return (shape.x * shape.y) / 2;
    case "square": // shape is Square
      return shape.x * shape.x;
    default:
      throw Error("not possible");
  }
}
```

Using discriminated unions, we can distinguish between each part of a union. The area function uses a switch-case statement to handle each case separately. Thanks to string literal types for the kind property, there can be no overlap between types.

Once all options are exhausted, in the default case we throw an error, indicating that we reached an invalid situation that should never occur. If our types are right throughout the codebase, this error should never be thrown.

Even the type system tells us that the default case is an impossible scenario. If we add shape in the default case and hover over it, TypeScript tells us that shape is of type never:

```
function area(shape: Shape) {
  switch (shape.kind) {
    case "circle": // shape is Circle
      return Math.PI * shape.radius * shape.radius;
    case "triangle": // shape is Triangle
```

```
      return (shape.x * shape.y) / 2;
    case "square": // shape is Square
      return shape.x * shape.x;
    default:
      console.error("Shape not defined:", shape); // shape is never
      throw Error("not possible");
  }
}
```

never is an interesting type. It's TypeScript *bottom type*, meaning that it's at the very end of the type hierarchy. Where any and unknown include every possible value, no value is compatible to never. It's the empty set, which explains the name. If one of your values happens to be of type never, you are in a situation that should *never* happen.

The type of shape in the default cases changes immediately if we extend the type Shape with, for example, a Rectangle:

```
type Rectangle = {
  x: number;
  y: number;
  kind: "rectangle";
};

type Shape = Circle | Triangle | Square | Rectangle;

function area(shape: Shape) {
  switch (shape.kind) {
    case "circle": // shape is Circle
      return Math.PI * shape.radius * shape.radius;
    case "triangle": // shape is Triangle
      return (shape.x * shape.y) / 2;
    case "square": // shape is Square
      return shape.x * shape.x;
    default:
      console.error("Shape not defined:", shape); // shape is Rectangle
      throw Error("not possible");
  }
}
```

This is control flow analysis at its best: TypeScript knows at exactly every point in time which types your values have. In the default branch, shape is of type Rectangle, but we are expected to deal with rectangles. Wouldn't it be great if TypeScript could tell us that we missed taking care of a potential type? With the change, we now run into it every time we calculate the shape of a rectangle. The default case was meant to handle (from the perspective of the type system) impossible situations; we'd like to keep it that way.

This is already bad in one situation, and it gets worse if you use the exhaustiveness checking pattern multiple times in your codebase. You can't tell for sure that you didn't miss one spot where your software will ultimately crash.

One technique to ensure that you handled all possible cases is to create a helper function that asserts that all options are exhausted. It should ensure that the only values possible are no values:

```
function assertNever(value: never) {
  console.error("Unknown value", value);
  throw Error("Not possible");
}
```

Usually, you see never as an indicator that you are in an impossible situation. Here, we use it as an explicit type annotation for a function signature. You might ask: which values are we supposed to pass? And the answer is: none! In the best case, this function will never get called.

However, if we substitute the original default case from our example with assert Never, we can use the type system to ensure that all possible values are compatible, even if there are no values:

```
function area(shape: Shape) {
  switch (shape.kind) {
    case "circle": // shape is Circle
      return Math.PI * shape.radius * shape.radius;
    case "triangle": // shape is Triangle
      return (shape.x * shape.y) / 2;
    case "square": // shape is Square
      return shape.x * shape.x;
    default: // shape is Rectangle
      assertNever(shape);
//      ^-- Error: Argument of type 'Rectangle' is not
//          assignable to parameter of type 'never'
  }
}
```

Great! We now get red squiggly lines whenever we forget to exhaust all options. TypeScript won't compile this code without an error, and it's easy to spot all occurrences in our codebase where we need to add the Rectangle case:

```
function area(shape: Shape) {
  switch (shape.kind) {
    case "circle": // shape is Circle
      return Math.PI * shape.radius * shape.radius;
    case "triangle": // shape is Triangle
      return (shape.x * shape.y) / 2;
    case "square": // shape is Square
      return shape.x * shape.x;
    case "rectangle":
      return shape.x * shape.y;
```

```
        default: // shape is never
            assertNever(shape); // shape can be passed to assertNever!
    }
}
```

Even though never has no compatible values and is used to indicate—for the type system—an impossible situation, we can use the type as type annotation to make sure we don't forget about *possible* situations. Seeing types as sets of compatible values that can get broader or narrower based on control flow leads us to techniques like assertNever, a very helpful little function that can strengthen our codebase's quality.

3.4 Pinning Types with Const Context

Problem

You can't assign object literals to your carefully modeled discriminated union types.

Solution

Pin the type of your literals using type assertions and *const context*.

Discussion

In TypeScript, it's possible to use each value as its own type. These are called literal types and allow you to subset bigger sets to just a couple of valid values.

Literal types in TypeScript are not only a nice trick to point to specific values but are also an essential part of how the type system works. This becomes obvious when you assign values of primitive types to different bindings via let or const.

If we assign the same value twice, once via let and once via const, TypeScript infers two different types. With the let binding, TypeScript will infer the broader primitive type:

```
let name = "Stefan"; // name is string
```

With a const binding, TypeScript will infer the exact literal type:

```
const name = "Stefan"; // name is "Stefan"
```

Object types behave slightly differently. let bindings still infer the broader set:

```
// person is { name: string }
let person = { name: "Stefan" };
```

But so do const bindings:

```
// person is { name: string }
const person = { name: "Stefan" };
```

The reasoning behind this is in JavaScript, while the binding itself is *constant*, which means I can't reassign person, the values of an object's property can change:

```
// person is { name: string }
const person = { name: "Stefan" };

person.name = "Not Stefan"; // works!
```

This behavior is correct in the sense that it mirrors the behavior of JavaScript, but it can cause problems when we are very exact with our data models.

In the previous recipes we modeled data using union and intersection types. We used *discriminated union types* to distinguish between types that are too similar.

The problem is that when we use literals for data, TypeScript will usually infer the broader set, which makes the values incompatible to the types defined. This produces a very lengthy error message:

```
type Circle = {
  radius: number;
  kind: "circle";
};

type Square = {
  x: number;
  kind: "square";
};

type Triangle = {
  x: number;
  y: number;
  kind: "triangle";
};

type Shape = Circle | Triangle | Square;

function area(shape: Shape) {
  /* ... */
}

const circle = {
  radius: 2,
  kind: "circle",
};

area(circle);
//     ^-- Argument of type '{ radius: number; kind: string; '
//         is not assignable to parameter of type 'Shape'.
//         Type '{ radius: number; kind: string; }' is not
//         assignable to type 'Circle'.
//         Types of property 'kind' are incompatible.
//         Type 'string' is not assignable to type '"circle"'.
```

There are several ways to solve this problem. First, we can use explicit annotations to ensure the type. As described in Recipe 2.1, each annotation is a type-check, which means the value on the righthand side is checked for compatibility. Since there is no inference, Typescript will look at the exact values to decide whether an object literal is compatible:

```
// Exact type
const circle: Circle = {
  radius: 2,
  kind: "circle",
};

area(circle); // Works!

// Broader set
const circle: Shape = {
  radius: 2,
  kind: "circle",
};

area(circle); // Also works!
```

Instead of type annotations, we can also do type assertions at the end of the assignment:

```
// Type assertion
const circle = {
  radius: 2,
  kind: "circle",
} as Circle;

area(circle); // Works!
```

Sometimes, however, annotations can limit us. This is true especially when we have to work with literals that contain more information and are used in different places with different semantics.

From the moment we annotate or assert as Circle, the binding will always be a circle, no matter which values circle actually carries.

But we can be much more fine-grained with assertions. Instead of asserting that the entire object is of a certain type, we can assert single properties to be of a certain type:

```
const circle = {
  radius: 2,
  kind: "circle" as "circle",
};

area(circle); // Works!
```

Another way to assert as exact values is to use *const context* with an as const type assertion; TypeScript locks the value in as literal type:

```
const circle = {
  radius: 2,
  kind: "circle" as const,
};

area(circle); // Works!
```

If we apply *const context* to the entire object, we also make sure that the values are read-only and won't be changed:

```
const circle = {
  radius: 2,
  kind: "circle",
} as const;

area2(circle); // Works!

circle.kind = "rectangle";
//      ^-- Cannot assign to 'kind' because
//          it is a read-only property.
```

Const context type assertions are a very handy tool if we want to pin values to their exact literal type and keep them that way. If there are a lot of object literals in your code base that are not supposed to change but need to be consumed in various occasions, *const context* can help!

3.5 Narrowing Types with Type Predicates

Problem

Based on certain conditions, you can assert that a value is of a narrower type than originally assigned, but TypeScript can't narrow it for you.

Solution

Add type predicates to a helper function's signature to indicate the impact of a Boolean condition for the type system.

Discussion

With literal types and union types, TypeScript allows you to define very specific sets of values. For example, we can define a die with six sides easily:

```
type Dice = 1 | 2 | 3 | 4 | 5 | 6;
```

While this notation is expressive, and the type system can tell you exactly which values are valid, it requires some work to get to this type.

Let's imagine we have some kind of game where users are allowed to input any number. If it's a valid number of dots, we are doing certain actions.

We write a conditional check to see if the input number is part of a set of values:

```
function rollDice(input: number) {
  if ([1, 2, 3, 4, 5, 6].includes(input)) {
    // `input` is still `number`, even though we know it
    // should be Dice
  }
}
```

The problem is that even though we do a check to make sure the set of values is known, TypeScript still handles input as number. There is no way for the type system to make the connection between your check and the change in the type system.

But you can help the type system. First, extract your check into its own helper function:

```
function isDice(value: number): boolean {
  return [1, 2, 3, 4, 5, 6].includes(value);
}
```

Note that this check returns a boolean. Either this condition is true or it's false. For functions that return a Boolean value, we can change the return type of the function signature to a type predicate.

We tell TypeScript that if this function returns true, we know more about the value that has been passed to the function. In our case, value is of type Dice:

```
function isDice(value: number): value is Dice {
  return [1, 2, 3, 4, 5, 6].includes(value);
}
```

With that, TypeScript gets a hint of what the actual types of your values are, allowing you to do more fine-grained operations on your values:

```
function rollDice(input: number) {
  if (isDice(input)) {
    // Great! `input` is now `Dice`
  } else {
    // input is still `number`
  }
}
```

TypeScript is restrictive and doesn't allow any assertion with type predicates. It needs to be a type that is narrower than the original type. For example, getting a string input and asserting a subset of number as output will error:

```
type Dice = 1 | 2 | 3 | 4 | 5 | 6;

function isDice(value: string): value is Dice {
  // Error: A type predicate's type must be assignable to
```

```
// its parameter's type. Type 'number' is not assignable to type 'string'.
  return ["1", "2", "3", "4", "5", "6"].includes(value);
}
```

This fail-safe mechanism gives you some guarantee on the type level, but there is a caveat: it won't check if your conditions make sense. The original check in `isDice` ensures that the value passed is included in an array of valid numbers.

The values in this array are your choice. If you include a wrong number, TypeScript will still think `value` is a valid `Dice`, even though your check does not line up:

```
// Correct on a type-level
// incorrect set of values on a value-level
function isDice(value: number): value is Dice {
  return [1, 2, 3, 4, 5, 7].includes(value);
}
```

This is easy to trip over. The condition in Example 3-1 is true for integer numbers but wrong if you pass a floating point number. For example, 3.1415 would be a valid `Dice` dot count!

Example 3-1. Incorrect logic for `isDice` for floating point numbers

```
// Correct on a type-level, incorrect logic
function isDice(value: number): value is Dice {
  return value >= 1 && value <= 6;
}
```

Actually, any condition works for TypeScript. Return `true` and TypeScript will think `value` is `Dice`:

```
function isDice(value: number): value is Dice {
  return true;
}
```

TypeScript puts type assertions in your hand. It is your duty to make sure those assertions are valid and sound. If you rely heavily on type assertions via type predicates, make sure that you test accordingly.

3.6 Understanding void

Problem

You know `void` as a concept from other programming languages, but in TypeScript it can behave a little bit differently.

Solution

Embrace `void` as a substitutable type for callbacks.

Discussion

You might know void from programming languages like Java or C#, where it indicates the absence of a return value. void also exists in TypeScript, and at first glance it does the same thing: if your functions or methods aren't returning something, the return type is void.

---

void in JavaScript

void also exists as an operator in JavaScript and has a very special behavior. It evaluates the expression next to it but guarantees to return undefined:

```
let i = void 2; // i === undefined
```

What are the use cases for void? First, in ECMAScript 3, you could override undefined and give it an actual value. void always returned the *real* undefined.

Second, it's a nice way to call immediately invoked functions:

```
// executes immediately.
void function() {
  console.log('Hey');
}();
```

All without polluting the global namespace:

```
void function aRecursion(i) {
  if(i > 0) {
    console.log(i--);
    aRecursion(i);
  }
}(3);

console.log(typeof aRecursion); // undefined
```

Since void always returns undefined and void always evaluates the expression next to it, you have a very terse way of returning from a function without returning a value but still calling a callback, for example:

```
// returning something else than undefined would crash the app
function middleware(nextCallback) {
  if(conditionApplies()) {
    return void nextCallback();
  }
}
```

Which brings me to the most important use case of void: it's a security gate for your app. When your function is always supposed to return undefined, you can make sure that this is always the case:

```
button.onclick = () => void doSomething();
```

At second glance, however, the behavior of void is a bit more nuanced, and so is its position in the type system. void in TypeScript is a subtype of undefined. Functions in JavaScript always return something. Either a function explicitly returns a value, or it implicitly returns undefined:

```
function iHaveNoReturnValue(i) {
  console.log(i);
}

let check = iHaveNoReturnValue(2);
// check is undefined
```

If we created a type for iHaveNoReturnValue, it would show a function type with void as return type:

```
function iHaveNoReturnValue(i) {
  console.log(i);
}

type Fn = typeof iHaveNoReturnValue;
// type Fn = (i: any) => void
```

void as type can also be used for parameters and all other declarations. The only value that can be passed is undefined:

```
function iTakeNoParameters(x: void): void { }

iTakeNoParameters(); // works
iTakeNoParameters(undefined); // works
iTakeNoParameters(void 2); // works
```

void and undefined are pretty much the same. There's one significant difference though: void as a return type can be substituted with different types, to allow for advanced callback patterns. Let's create a fetch function, for example. Its task is to get a set of numbers and pass the results to a callback function, provided as a parameter:

```
function fetchResults(
  callback: (statusCode: number, results: number[]) => void
) {
  // get results from somewhere ...
  callback(200, results);
}
```

The callback function has two parameters in its signature—a status code and the results—and the return type is void. We can call fetchResults with callback functions that match the exact type of callback:

```
function normalHandler(statusCode: number, results: number[]): void {
  // do something with both parameters
}

fetchResults(normalHandler);
```

But if a function type specifies return type void, functions with a different, more specific return type are also accepted:

```
function handler(statusCode: number): boolean {
  // evaluate the status code ...
  return true;
}
```

```
fetchResults(handler); // compiles, no problem!
```

The function signatures don't match exactly, but the code still compiles. First, it's OK to provide functions with a shorter argument list in their signature. JavaScript can call functions with excess parameters, and if they aren't specified in the function, they're simply ignored. No need to carry more parameters than you actually need.

Second, the return type is boolean, but TypeScript will still pass this function along. This is useful when declaring a void return type. The original caller fetchResults does not expect a return value when calling the callback. So for the type system, the return value of callback is still undefined, even though it could be something else.

As long as the type system won't allow you to work with the return value, your code should be safe:

```
function fetchResults(
  callback: (statusCode: number, results: number[]) => void
) {
  // get results from somewhere ...
  const didItWork = callback(200, results);
  // didItWork is `undefined` in the type system,
  // even though it would be a boolean with `handler`.
}
```

That's why we can pass callbacks with any return type. Even if the callback returns something, this value isn't used and goes into the void.

The power lies within the calling function, which knows best what to expect from the callback function. And if the calling function doesn't require a return value at all from the callback, anything goes!

TypeScript calls this feature *substitutability*: the ability to substitute one thing for another, wherever it makes sense. This might seem odd at first. But especially when you work with libraries that you didn't author, you will find this feature to be very valuable.

3.7 Dealing with Error Types in catch Clauses

Problem

You can't annotate explicit error types in try-catch blocks.

Solution

Annotate with `any` or `unknown` and use type predicates (see Recipe 3.5 to narrow to specific error types).

Discussion

When you are coming from languages like Java, C++, or C#, you are used to doing your error handling by throwing exceptions and subsequently catching them in a cascade of `catch` clauses. There are arguably better ways to do error handling, but this one has been around for ages and, given history and influences, has found its way into JavaScript.[1]

"Throwing" errors and "catching" them is a valid way to handle errors in JavaScript and TypeScript, but there is a big difference when it comes to specifying your `catch` clauses. When you try to catch a specific error type, TypeScript will error.

Example 3-2 uses the popular data-fetching library Axios (*https://axios-http.com*) to show the problem.

Example 3-2. Catching explicit error types does not work

```
try {
  // something with the popular fetching library Axios, for example
} catch(e: AxiosError) {
//         ^^^^^^^^^^ Error 1196: Catch clause variable
//                    type annotation must be 'any' or
//                    'unknown' if specified.
}
```

There are a few reasons for this:

Any type can be thrown

In JavaScript, you are allowed to throw every expression. Of course, you can throw "exceptions" (or errors, as we call them in JavaScript), but it's also possible to throw any other value:

```
throw "What a weird error"; // OK
throw 404; // OK
throw new Error("What a weird error"); // OK
```

Since any valid value can be thrown, the possible values to catch are already broader than your usual subtype of `Error`.

---

1 For example, the Rust Programming Language has been lauded for its error handling.

There is only one catch clause in JavaScript

JavaScript has only one catch clause per try statement. In the past there have been proposals for multiple catch clauses (*https://oreil.ly/NMn8O*) and even conditional expressions, but due to the lack of interest in JavaScript in the early 2000s, they never manifested.

Instead, you should use this one catch clause and do instanceof and typeof checks, as proposed on MDN (*https://oreil.ly/ipzoR*).

This example is also the only correct way to narrow types for catch clauses in TypeScript:

```
try {
  myroutine(); // There's a couple of errors thrown here
} catch (e) {
  if (e instanceof TypeError) {
    // A TypeError
  } else if (e instanceof RangeError) {
    // Handle the RangeError
  } else if (e instanceof EvalError) {
    // you guessed it: EvalError
  } else if (typeof e === "string") {
    // The error is a string
  } else if (axios.isAxiosError(e)) {
    // axios does an error check for us!
  } else {
    // everything else
    logMyErrors(e);
  }
}
```

Since all possible values can be thrown, and we only have one catch clause per try statement to handle them, the type range of e is exceptionally broad.

Any exception can happen

Since you know about every error that can happen, wouldn't a proper union type with all possible "throwables" work just as well? In theory, yes. In practice, there is no way to tell which types the exception will have.

Next to all your user-defined exceptions and errors, the system might throw errors when something is wrong with the memory when it encountered a type mismatch or one of your functions has been undefined. A simple function call could exceed your call stack and cause the infamous stack overflow.

The broad set of possible values, the single catch clause, and the uncertainty of errors that happen allow only two types for e: any and unknown.

All reasons apply if you reject a `Promise`. The only thing TypeScript allows you to specify is the type of a fulfilled `Promise`. A rejection can happen on your behalf or through a system error:

```
const somePromise = () =>
  new Promise((fulfil, reject) => {
    if (someConditionIsValid()) {
      fulfil(42);
    } else {
      reject("Oh no!");
    }
  });

somePromise()
  .then((val) => console.log(val)) // val is number
  .catch((e) => console.log(e)); // can be anything, really;
```

It becomes clearer if you call the same `Promise` in an `async/await` flow:

```
try {
  const z = await somePromise(); // z is number
} catch(e) {
  // same thing, e can be anything!
}
```

If you want to define your own errors and catch accordingly, you can either write error classes and do instance of checks or create helper functions that check for certain properties and tell the correct type via type predicates. Axios is again a good example for that:

```
function isAxiosError(payload: any): payload is AxiosError {
  return payload !== null
    && typeof payload === 'object'
    && payload.isAxiosError;
}
```

Error handling in JavaScript and TypeScript can be a "false friend" if you come from other programming languages with similar features. Be aware of the differences and trust the TypeScript team and type-checker to give you the correct control flow to make sure your errors are handled effectively.

3.8 Creating Exclusive Or Models with Optional never

Problem

Your model requires you to have mutually exclusive parts of a union, but your API can't rely on the `kind` property to differentiate.

Solution

Use the *optional never* technique to exclude certain properties.

Discussion

You want to write a function that handles the result of a select operation in your application. This select operation gives you the list of possible options as well as the list of selected options. This function can deal with calls from a select operation that produces only a single value as well as from a select operation that results in multiple values.

Since you need to adapt to an existing API, your function should be able to handle both and decide for the single and multiple cases within the function.

 Of course there are better ways to model APIs, and we can talk endlessly about that. But sometimes you have to deal with existing APIs that are not that great to begin with. TypeScript gives you techniques and methods to correctly type your data in scenarios like this.

Your model mirrors that API, as you can pass either a single `value` or multiple `values`:

```
type SelectBase = {
  options: string[];
};

type SingleSelect = SelectBase & {
  value: string;
};

type MultipleSelect = SelectBase & {
  values: string[];
};

type SelectProperties = SingleSelect | MultipleSelect;

function selectCallback(params: SelectProperties) {
  if ("value" in params) {
    // handle single cases
  } else if ("values" in params) {
    // handle multiple cases
  }
}

selectCallback({
  options: ["dracula", "monokai", "vscode"],
  value: "dracula",
```

```
  });

  selectCallback({
    options: ["dracula", "monokai", "vscode"],
    values: ["dracula", "vscode"],
  });
```

This works as intended, but remember the structural type system features of Type-Script. Defining `SingleSelect` as a type allows also for values of all subtypes, which means that objects that have both the `value` property and the `values` property are also compatible to `SingleSelect`. The same goes for `MultipleSelect`. Nothing keeps you from using the `selectCallback` function with an object that contains both:

```
  selectCallback({
    options: ["dracula", "monokai", "vscode"],
    values: ["dracula", "vscode"],
    value: "dracula",
  }); // still works! Which one to choose?
```

The value you pass here is valid, but it doesn't make sense in your application. You couldn't decide whether this is a multiple select operation or a single select operation.

In cases like this we again need to separate the two sets of values just enough so our model becomes clearer. We can do this by using the optional `never` technique.[2] It involves taking the properties that are exclusive to each branch of a union and adding them as optional properties of type `never` to the other branches:

```
  type SelectBase = {
    options: string[];
  };

  type SingleSelect = SelectBase & {
    value: string;
    values?: never;
  };

  type MultipleSelect = SelectBase & {
    value?: never;
    values: string[];
  };
```

You tell TypeScript that this property is optional in this branch, and when it's set, there is no compatible value for it. With that, all objects that contain both properties are invalid to `SelectProperties`:

```
  selectCallback({
    options: ["dracula", "monokai", "vscode"],
```

---

2 Shout-out to Dan Vanderkam who was first to call this technique "optional never" on his fantastic *Effective TypeScript* blog (*https://effectivetypescript.com*).

```
    values: ["dracula", "vscode"],
    value: "dracula",
});
// ^ Argument of type '{ options: string[]; values: string[]; value: string; }'
//   is not assignable to parameter of type 'SelectProperties'.
```

The union types are separated again, without the inclusion of a kind property. This works great for models where the discriminating properties are just a few. If your model has too many distinct properties, and you can afford to add a kind property, use *discriminated union types* as shown in Recipe 3.2.

3.9 Effectively Using Type Assertions

Problem

Your code produces the correct results, but the types are way too wide. You know better!

Solution

Use type assertions to narrow to a smaller set using the `as` keyword, indicating an unsafe operation.

Discussion

Think of rolling a die and producing a number between one and six. The JavaScript function is one line, using the Math library. You want to work with a narrowed type, a union of six literal number types indicating the results. However, your operation produces a number, and number is a type too wide for your results:

```
type Dice = 1 | 2 | 3 | 4 | 5 | 6;

function rollDice(): Dice {
  let num = Math.floor(Math.random() * 6) + 1;
  return num;
//^ Type 'number' is not assignable to type 'Dice'.(2322)
}
```

Since number allows for more values than Dice, TypeScript won't allow you to narrow the type just by annotating the function signature. This works only if the type is wider, a supertype:

```
// All dice are numbers
function asNumber(dice: Dice): number {
  return dice;
}
```

Instead, just like with type predicates from Recipe 3.5, we can tell TypeScript that we know better, by asserting that the type is narrower than expected:

```
type Dice = 1 | 2 | 3 | 4 | 5 | 6;

function rollDice(): Dice {
  let num = Math.floor(Math.random() * 6) + 1;
  return num as Dice;
}
```

Just like type predicates, type assertions work only within the supertypes and subtypes of an assumed type. We can either set the value to a wider supertype or change it to a narrower subtype. TypeScript won't allow us to switch sets:

```
function asString(num: number): string {
  return num as string;
//       ^- Conversion of type 'number' to type 'string' may
//          be a mistake because neither type sufficiently
//          overlaps with the other.
//          If this was intentional, convert the expression to 'unknown' first.
}
```

Using the `as Dice` syntax is quite handy. It indicates a type change that we as developers are responsible for. This means that if something turns out wrong, we can easily scan our code for the `as` keyword and find possible culprits.

 In everyday language, people tend to call type assertions *type casts*. This arguably comes from similarity to actual, explicit type casts in C, Java, and the like. However, a type assertion is very different from a type cast. A type cast not only changes the set of compatible values but also changes the memory layout and even the values themselves. Casting a floating point number to an integer will cut off the mantissa. A type assertion in TypeScript, on the other hand, changes only the set of compatible values. The value stays the same. It's called a *type assertion* because you assert that the type is something either narrower or wider, giving more hints to the type system. So if you are in a discussion on changing types, call them assertions, not casts.

Assertions are also often used when you assemble the properties of an object. You know that the shape is going to be of, for example, `Person`, but you need to set the properties first:

```
type Person = {
  name: string;
  age: number;
};

function createDemoPerson(name: string) {
```

```
    const person = {} as Person;
    person.name = name;
    person.age = Math.floor(Math.random() * 95);
    return person;
}
```

A type assertion tells TypeScript that the empty object is supposed to be `Person` at the end. Subsequently, TypeScript allows you to set properties. It's also an *unsafe* operation, because you might forget that you set a property and TypeScript would not complain. Even worse, `Person` might change and get more properties, and you would get no indication at all that you are missing properties:

```
type Person = {
  name: string;
  age: number;
  profession: string;
};

function createDemoPerson(name: string) {
  const person = {} as Person;
  person.name = name;
  person.age = Math.floor(Math.random() * 95);
  // Where's Profession?
  return person;
}
```

In situations like this, it's better to opt for a *safe* object creation. Nothing keeps you from annotating and making sure that you set all the required properties with the assignment:

```
type Person = {
  name: string;
  age: number;
};

function createDemoPerson(name: string) {
  const person: Person = {
    name,
    age: Math.floor(Math.random() * 95),
  };
  return person;
}
```

While type annotations are safer than type assertions, in situations like `rollDice` there is no better choice. In other TypeScript scenarios you do have a choice but might want to prefer type assertions, even if you could annotate.

When we use the `fetch` API, for example, getting JSON data from a backend, we can call `fetch` and assign the results to an annotated type:

```
type Person = {
  name: string;
```

```
  age: number;
};
```

```
const ppl: Person[] = await fetch("/api/people").then((res) => res.json());
```

`res.json()` results in any, and everything that is any can be changed to any other type through a type annotation. There is no guarantee that the results are actually `Person[]`. We can write the same line differently, by asserting that the result is a `Person[]`, narrowing any to something more specific:

```
const ppl = await fetch("/api/people").then((res) => res.json()) as Person[];
```

For the type system, this is the same thing, but we can easily scan situations where there might be problems. What if the model in "/api/people" changes? It's harder to spot errors if we are just looking for annotations. An assertion here is an indicator of an *unsafe* operation.

What really helps is to think of creating a set of models that works within your application boundaries. The moment you rely on something from the outside, like APIs, or the correct calculation of a number, type assertions can indicate that you've crossed the boundary.

Just like using type predicates (see Recipe 3.5), type assertions put the responsibility of a correct type in your hands. Use them wisely.

3.10 Using Index Signatures

Problem

You want to work with objects where you know the type of the values, but you don't know all the property names up front.

Solution

Use index signatures to define an open set of keys but with defined value types.

Discussion

There is a style in web APIs where you get collections in the form of a JavaScript object, where the property name is roughly equivalent to a unique identifier and the values have the same shape. This style is great if you are mostly concerned about *keys*, as a simple `Object.keys` call gives you all relevant IDs, allowing you to quickly filter and index the values you are looking for.

Let's think of a performance review across all your websites, where you gather relevant performance metrics and group them by the domain's name:

```
const timings = {
  "fettblog.eu": {
    ttfb: 300,
    fcp: 1000,
    si: 1200,
    lcp: 1500,
    tti: 1100,
    tbt: 10,
  },
  "typescript-book.com": {
    ttfb: 400,
    fcp: 1100,
    si: 1100,
    lcp: 2200,
    tti: 1100,
    tbt: 0,
  },
};
```

If we want to find the domain with the lowest timing for a given metric, we can create a function where we loop over all keys, index each metrics entry, and compare:

```
function findLowestTiming(collection, metric) {
  let result = {
    domain: "",
    value: Number.MAX_VALUE,
  };
  for (const domain in collection) {
    const timing = collection[domain];
    if (timing[metric] < result.value) {
      result.domain = domain;
      result.value = timing[metric];
    }
  }
  return result.domain;
}
```

As we are good programmers, we want to type our function accordingly so that we make sure we don't pass any data that doesn't match our idea of a metric collection. Typing the value for the metrics on the righthand side is pretty straightforward:

```
type Metrics = {
  // Time to first byte
  ttfb: number;
  // First contentful paint
  fcp: number;
  // Speed Index
  si: number;
  // Largest contentful paint
  lcp: number;
  // Time to interactive
  tti: number;
  // Total blocking time
```

```
  tbt: number;
};
```

Defining a shape that has a yet-to-be-defined set of keys is trickier, but TypeScript has a tool for that: index signatures. We can tell TypeScript that we don't know which property names there are, but we know they will be of type string and they will point to Metrics:

```
type MetricCollection = {
  [domain: string]: Timings;
};
```

And that's all we need to type findLowestTiming. We annotate collection with Metric Collection and make sure we only pass keys of Metrics for the second parameter:

```
function findLowestTiming(
  collection: MetricCollection,
  key: keyof Metrics
): string {
  let result = {
    domain: "",
    value: Number.MAX_VALUE,
  };
  for (const domain in collection) {
    const timing = collection[domain];
    if (timing[key] < result.value) {
      result.domain = domain;
      result.value = timing[key];
    }
  }
  return result.domain;
}
```

This is great, but there are some caveats. TypeScript allows you to read properties of any string, but it does not do any checks if the property is actually available, so be aware:

```
const emptySet: MetricCollection = {};
let timing = emptySet["typescript-cookbook.com"].fcp * 2; // No type errors!
```

Changing your index signature type to be either Metrics or undefined is a more realistic representation. It says you can index with all possible strings, but there might be no value; this results in a couple more safeguards but is ultimately the right choice:

```
type MetricCollection = {
  [domain: string]: Metrics | undefined;
};

function findLowestTiming(
  collection: MetricCollection,
  key: keyof Metrics
```

```
  ): string {
    let result = {
      domain: "",
      value: Number.MAX_VALUE,
    };
    for (const domain in collection) {
      const timing = collection[domain]; // Metrics | undefined
      // extra check for undefined values
      if (timing && timing[key] < result.value) {
        result.domain = domain;
        result.value = timing[key];
      }
    }
    return result.domain;
  }

  const emptySet: MetricCollection = {};
  // access with optional chaining and nullish coalescing
  let timing = (emptySet["typescript-cookbook.com"]?.fcp ?? 0) * 2;
```

The value being either `Metrics` or `undefined` is not exactly like a missing property, but it's close enough and good enough for this use case. You can read about the nuance between missing properties and undefined values in Recipe 3.11. To set the property keys as optional, you tell TypeScript that `domain` is not the entire set of `string` but a subset of `string` with a so-called *mapped type*:

```
type MetricCollection = {
  [domain in string]?: Metrics;
};
```

You can define index signatures for everything that is a valid property key: `string`, number, or symbol, and with *mapped types* also everything that is a subset of those. For example, you can define a type to index only valid faces of a die:

```
type Throws = {
  [x in 1 | 2 | 3 | 4 | 5 | 6]: number;
};
```

You can also add properties to your type. Take this `ElementCollection`, for example, which allows you to index items via a number but also has additional properties for get and filter functions as well as a `length` property:

```
type ElementCollection = {
  [y: number]: HTMLElement | undefined;
  get(index: number): HTMLElement | undefined;
  length: number;
  filter(callback: (element: HTMLElement) => boolean): ElementCollection;
};
```

If you combine your index signatures with other properties, you need to make sure that the broader set of your index signature includes the types from the specific properties. In the previous example there is no overlap between the number index signature and the string keys of your other properties, but if you define an index signature of strings that maps to `string` and want to have a `count` property of type `number` next to it, TypeScript will error:

```
type StringDictionary = {
  [index: string]: string;
  count: number;
  // Error: Property 'count' of type 'number' is not assignable
  // to 'string' index type 'string'.(2411)
};
```

And it makes sense: if all string keys point to a string, why would `count` point to something else? There's ambiguity, and TypeScript won't allow this. You would have to widen the type of your index signature to make sure that the smaller set is part of the bigger set:

```
type StringOrNumberDictionary = {
  [index: string]: string | number;
  count: number; // works
};
```

Now `count` subsets both the type from the index signature and the type of the property's value.

Index signatures and mapped types are powerful tools that allow you to work with web APIs as well as data structures that allow for flexible access to elements. Something that we know and love from JavaScript is now securely typed in TypeScript.

3.11 Distinguishing Missing Properties and Undefined Values

Problem

Missing properties and undefined values are not the same! You will run into situations where this difference matters.

Solution

Activate `exactOptionalPropertyTypes` in *tsconfig* to enable stricter handling of optional properties.

Discussion

Our software has user settings where we can define the user's language and their preferred color overrides. It's an additional theme, which means that the basic colors are already set in a `"default"` style. This means that the user setting for `theme` is optional: either it is available or it isn't. We use TypeScript's optional properties for that:

```
type Settings = {
  language: "en" | "de" | "fr";
  theme?: "dracula" | "monokai" | "github";
};
```

With `strictNullChecks` active, accessing `theme` somewhere in your code widens the number of possible values. You have not only the three theme overrides but also the possibility of `undefined`:

```
function applySettings(settings: Settings) {
  // theme is "dracula" | "monokai" | "github" | undefined
  const theme = settings.theme;
}
```

This is great behavior, as you really want to make sure that this property is set; otherwise, it could result in runtime errors. TypeScript adding `undefined` to the list of possible values of optional properties is good, but it doesn't entirely mirror the behavior of JavaScript. *Optional properties* means that this key is missing from the object, which is subtle but important. For example, a missing key would return `false` in property checks:

```
function getTheme(settings: Settings) {
  if ('theme' in settings) { // only true if the property is set!
    return settings.theme;
  }
  return 'default';
}

const settings: Settings = {
  language: "de",
};

const settingsUndefinedTheme: Settings = {
  language: "de",
  theme: undefined,
};

console.log(getTheme(settings)) // "default"
console.log(getTheme(settingsUndefinedTheme)) // undefined
```

Here, we get entirely different results even though the two settings objects seem similar. What's worse is that an `undefined` theme is a value we don't consider valid. TypeScript doesn't lie to us, though, as it's fully aware that an `in` check only tells us if the property is available. The possible return values of `getTheme` include `undefined` as well:

```
type Fn = typeof getTheme;
// type Fn = (settings: Settings)
//   => "dracula" | "monokai" | "github" | "default" | undefined
```

And there are arguably better checks to see if the correct values are here. With *nullish coalescing* the preceding code becomes:

```
function getTheme(settings: Settings) {
  return settings.theme ?? "default";
}

type Fn = typeof getTheme;
// type Fn = (settings: Settings)
//   => "dracula" | "monokai" | "github" | "default"
```

Still, in checks are valid and used by developers, and the way TypeScript interprets optional properties can cause ambiguity. Reading undefined from an optional property is correct, but setting optional properties to undefined isn't. By switching on exactOptionalPropertyTypes, TypeScript changes this behavior:

```
// exactOptionalPropertyTypes is true
const settingsUndefinedTheme: Settings = {
  language: "de",
  theme: undefined,
};

// Error: Type '{ language: "de"; theme: undefined; }' is
// not assignable to type 'Settings' with 'exactOptionalPropertyTypes: true'.
// Consider adding 'undefined' to the types of the target's properties.
// Types of property 'theme' are incompatible.
// Type 'undefined' is not assignable to type
// '"dracula" | "monokai" | "github"'.(2375)
```

exactOptionalPropertyTypes aligns TypeScript's behavior even more to JavaScript. This flag is not within strict mode, however, so you need to set it yourself if you encounter problems like this.

3.12 Working with Enums

Problem

TypeScript enums are a nice abstraction, but they seem to behave very differently compared to the rest of the type system.

Solution

Use them sparingly, prefer const enums, know their caveats, and maybe choose union types instead.

Discussion

Enums in TypeScript allow a developer to define a set of named constants, which makes it easier to document intent or create a set of distinct cases.

They're defined using the enum keyword:

```
enum Direction {
  Up,
  Down,
  Left,
  Right,
};
```

Like classes, they contribute to the value and type namespaces, which means you can use Direction when annotating types or in your JavaScript code as values:

```
// used as type
function move(direction: Direction) {
  // ...
}

// used as value
move(Direction.Up);
```

They are a syntactic extension to JavaScript, which means they not only work on a type system level but also emit JavaScript code:

```
var Direction;
(function (Direction) {
    Direction[Direction["Up"] = 0] = "Up";
    Direction[Direction["Down"] = 1] = "Down";
    Direction[Direction["Left"] = 2] = "Left";
    Direction[Direction["Right"] = 3] = "Right";
})(Direction || (Direction = {}));
```

When you define your enum as a const enum, TypeScript tries to substitute the usage with the actual values, getting rid of the emitted code:

```
const enum Direction {
  Up,
  Down,
  Left,
  Right,
};

// When having a const enum, TypeScript
// transpiles move(Direction.Up) to this:
move(0 /* Direction.Up */);
```

TypeScript supports both string and numeric enums, and both variants behave very differently.

TypeScript enums are by default numeric, which means that every variant of that enum has a numeric value assigned, starting at 0. The starting point and actual values of enum variants can be a default or user defined:

```
// Default
enum Direction {
    Up, // 0
    Down, // 1
    Left, // 2
    Right, // 3
};

enum Direction {
    Up = 1,     // 1
    Down,       // 2
    Left,       // 3
    Right = 5, // 5
};
```

In a way, numeric enums define the same set as a union type of numbers:

```
type Direction = 0 | 1 | 2 | 3;
```

But there are significant differences. Where a union type of numbers allows only a strictly defined set of values, a numeric enum allows for every value to be assigned:

```
function move(direction: Direction) { /* ... */ }

move(30);// This is   ok!
```

The reason is that there is a use case of implementing flags with numeric enums:

```
// Possible traits of a person, can be multiple
enum Traits {
    None,                  // 0000
    Friendly = 1,          // 0001 or 1 << 0
    Mean      = 1 << 1, // 0010
    Funny     = 1 << 2, // 0100
    Boring    = 1 << 3, // 1000
}

// (0010 | 0100) === 0110
let aPersonsTraits = Traits.Mean | Traits.Funny;

if ((aPersonsTraits & Traits.Mean) === Traits.Mean) {
    // Person is mean, amongst other things
}
```

Enums provide syntactic sugar for this scenario. To make it easier for the compiler to see which values are allowed, TypeScript expands compatible values for numeric enums to the entire set of number.

Enum variants can also be initialized with strings instead of numbers, effectively creating a string enum. If you choose to write a string enum, you have to define each variant, as strings can't be incremented:

```
enum Status {
  Admin = "Admin",
  User = "User",
  Moderator = "Moderator",
};
```

String enums are more restrictive than numeric enums. They only allow you to pass actual variants of the enum rather than the entire set of strings. However, they don't allow you to pass the string equivalent:

```
function closeThread(threadId: number, status: Status): {
  // ...
}

closeThread(10, "Admin");
//                 ^-- Argument of type '"Admin"' is not assignable to
//                     parameter of type 'Status'


closeThread(10, Status.Admin); // This works
```

Unlike every other type in TypeScript, string enums are *nominal* types. This also means two enums with the same set of values are not compatible with each other:

```
enum Roles {
  Admin = "Admin",
  User = "User",
  Moderator = "Moderator",
};

closeThread(10, Roles.Admin);
//                 ^-- Argument of type 'Roles.Admin' is not
//                     assignable to parameter of type 'Status'
```

This can be a source of confusion and frustration, especially when values come from another source that doesn't have knowledge of your enums but does have the correct string values.

Use enums wisely and know their caveats. Enums are great for feature flags and a set of named constants where you intentionally want people to use the data structure instead of just values.

 Since TypeScript 5.0, the interpretation of number enums has become much stricter; now they behave, like string enums, as nominal types and don't include the entire set of numbers as values. You still might find codebases that rely on the unique features of pre-5.0 number enums, so be aware!

Also try to prefer const enums wherever possible, as non-const enums can add size to your codebase that might be redundant. I have seen projects with more than two thousand flags in a non-const enum, resulting in huge tooling overhead, compile time overhead, and subsequently, runtime overhead.

Or, don't use them at all. A simple union type works similarly and is much more aligned with the rest of the type system:

```
type Status = "Admin" | "User" | "Moderator";

function closeThread(threadId: number, status: Status) {
  // ...
}

closeThread(10, "Admin"); // All good
```

You get all the benefits from enums such as proper tooling and type safety without going the extra round and risking outputting code that you don't want. It also becomes clearer what you need to pass and where to get the value from.

If you want to write your code enum-style, with an object and a named identifier, a const object with a Values helper type might just give you the desired behavior and is *much* closer to JavaScript. The same technique is also applicable to string unions:

```
const Direction = {
  Up: 0,
  Down: 1,
  Left: 2,
  Right: 3,
} as const;

// Get to the const values of Direction
type Direction = (typeof Direction)[keyof typeof Direction];

// (typeof Direction)[keyof typeof Direction] yields 0 | 1 | 2 | 3
function move(direction: Direction) {
  // ...
}

move(30); // This breaks!

move(0); //This works!

move(Direction.Left); // This also works!
```

This line is particularly interesting:

```
// = 0 | 1 | 2 | 3
type Direction = (typeof Direction)[keyof typeof Direction];
```

A few things happen that are not that usual:

- We declare a type with the same name as a value. This is possible because Type-Script has distinct value and type namespaces.
- Using the `typeof` operator, we grab the type from `Direction`. As `Direction` is in *const context*, we get the literal type.
- We index the type of `Direction` with its own keys, leaving us all the values on the righthand side of the object: 0, 1, 2, and 3. In short: a union type of numbers.

Using union types leaves no surprises:

- You *know* what code you end up with within the output.
- You don't end up with changed behavior because somebody decides to go from a string enum to a numeric enum.
- You have type safety where you need it.
- You give your colleagues and users the same conveniences as provided by enums.

But to be fair, a simple string union type does just what you need: type safety, auto-complete, and predictable behavior.

3.13 Defining Nominal Types in a Structural Type System

Problem

Your application has several types that are aliases for the same primitive type but with entirely different semantics. Structural typing treats them the same, but it shouldn't!

Solution

Use wrapping classes or create an intersection of your primitive type with a literal object type and use this to differentiate two integers.

Discussion

TypeScript's type system is structural. This means that if two types have a similar shape, values of this type are compatible with each other:

```
type Person = {
  name: string;
  age: number;
};

type Student = {
  name: string;
  age: number;
};
```

```
function acceptsPerson(person: Person) {
  // ...
}

const student: Student = {
  name: "Hannah",
  age: 27,
};

acceptsPerson(student); // all ok
```

JavaScript relies heavily on object literals, and TypeScript tries to infer the type or *shape* of those literals. A structural type system makes a lot of sense in this scenario, as values can come from anywhere and need to be compatible with interface and type definitions.

However, there are situations where you need to be more definitive with your types. For object types, we learned about techniques like *discriminated unions* with the kind property in Recipe 3.2, or *exclusive or* with "optional never" in Recipe 3.8. string enums are also nominal, as we see in Recipe 3.12.

Those measurements are good enough for object types and enums, but they don't solve the problem if you have two independent types that use the same set of values as primitive types. What if your eight-digit account number and your balance all point to the number type and you mix them up? Getting an eight-figure number on your balance sheet is a nice surprise, but it's likely not correct.

Or perhaps you need to validate user input strings and want to make sure that you carry around only the validated user input in your program, not falling back to the original, probably unsafe, string.

TypeScript allows you to mimic nominal types within the type system to get more security. The trick is also to separate the sets of possible values with distinct properties just enough to ensure the same values don't fall into the same set.

One way to achieve this would be wrapping classes. Instead of working with the values directly, we wrap each value in a class. With a private kind property we make sure they don't overlap:

```
class Balance {
  private kind = "balance";
  value: number;

  constructor(value: number) {
    this.value = value;
  }
}

class AccountNumber {
```

```
    private kind = "account";
    value: number;

    constructor(value: number) {
      this.value = value;
    }
  }
}
```

What's interesting here is that since we use `private` properties, TypeScript will differentiate between the two classes. Right now, both `kind` properties are of type `string`. Even though they feature a different value, they can be changed internally. But classes work differently. If `private` or `protected` members are present, TypeScript considers two types compatible if they originate from the same declaration. Otherwise, they aren't considered compatible.

This allows us to refine this pattern with a more general approach. Instead of defining a `kind` member and setting it to a value, we define a `_nominal` member in each class declaration that is of type `void`. This separates both classes just enough but keeps us from using `_nominal` in just any way. `void` only allows us to set `_nominal` to `undefined`, and `undefined` is a falsy, and thus highly useless:

```
class Balance {
  private _nominal: void = undefined;
  value: number;

  constructor(value: number) {
    this.value = value;
  }
}

class AccountNumber {
  private _nominal: void = undefined;
  value: number;

  constructor(value: number) {
    this.value = value;
  }
}

const account = new AccountNumber(12345678);
const balance = new Balance(10000);

function acceptBalance(balance: Balance) {
  // ...
}

acceptBalance(balance); // ok
acceptBalance(account);
// ^ Argument of type 'AccountNumber' is not
//   assignable to parameter of type 'Balance'.
```

```
//   Types have separate declarations of a
//     private property '_nominal'.(2345)
```

We can now differentiate between two types that would have the same set of values. The only downside to this approach is that we wrap the original type, which means that every time we want to work with the original value, we need to unwrap it.

A different way to mimic nominal types is to intersect the primitive type with a branded object type with a kind property. This way, we retain all the operations from the original type, but we need to require type assertions to tell TypeScript that we want to use those types differently.

As we learned in Recipe 3.9, we can safely assert another type if it is a subtype or supertype of the original:

```
type Credits = number & { _kind: "credits" };

type AccountNumber = number & { _kind: "accountNumber" };

const account = 12345678 as AccountNumber;
let balance = 10000 as Credits;
const amount = 3000 as Credits;

function increase(balance: Credits, amount: Credits): Credits {
  return (balance + amount) as Credits;
}

balance = increase(balance, amount);
balance = increase(balance, account);
// ^ Argument of type 'AccountNumber' is not
//   assignable to parameter of type 'Credits'.
//   Type 'AccountNumber' is not assignable to type '{ _kind: "credits"; }'.
//   Types of property '_kind' are incompatible.
//   Type '"accountNumber"' is not assignable to type '"credits"'.(2345)
```

Also note that the addition of balance and amount still works as originally intended but produces a number again. This is why we need to add another assertion:

```
const result = balance + amount; // result is number
const credits = (balance + amount) as Credits; // credits is Credits
```

Both approaches have their advantages and disadvantages, and whether you prefer one or the other mostly depends on your scenario. Both approaches are workarounds and techniques developed by the community based on their understanding of the type system's behavior.

There are discussions on the TypeScript issue tracker on GitHub (*https://oreil.ly/XxmUV*) about opening the type system for nomimal types, and the possibility is constantly under investigation. One idea is to use the unique keyword from Symbols to differentiate:

```
// Hypothetical code, this does not work!
type Balance = unique number;
type AccountNumber = unique number;
```

As time of writing, this idea—and many others—remains a future possibility.

3.14 Enabling Loose Autocomplete for String Subsets

Problem

Your API allows for any string to be passed, but you still want to show a couple of string values for autocomplete.

Solution

Add `string & {}` to your union type of string literals.

Discussion

Let's say you define an API for access to a content management system. There are predefined content types like `post`, `page`, and `asset`, but developers can define their own.

You create a `retrieve` function with a single parameter, the content type, that allows entries to be loaded:

```
type Entry = {
    // tbd.
};

function retrieve(contentType: string): Entry[] {
    // tbd.
}
```

This works well enough, but you want to give your users a hint on the default options for content type. A possibility is to create a helper type that lists all predefined content types as string literals in a union with `string`:

```
type ContentType = "post" | "page" | "asset" | string;

function retrieve(content: ContentType): Entry[] {
  // tbd
}
```

This describes your situation very well but comes with a downside: `post`, `page`, and `asset` are subtypes of `string`, so putting them in a union *with* `string` effectively swallows the detailed information into the broader set.

This means you don't get statement completion hints via your editor, as you can see in Figure 3-3.

Figure 3-3. TypeScript widens `ContentType` to the entire set of `string`, thus swallowing autocomplete information

To retain autocomplete information and preserve the literal types, we need to intersect `string` with the empty object type `{}`:

```
type ContentType = "post" | "page" | "asset" | string & {};
```

The effect of this change is more subtle. It doesn't alter the number of compatible values to `ContentType`, but it will set TypeScript into a mode that prevents subtype reduction and preserves the literal types.

You can see the effect in Figure 3-4, where `ContentType` is not reduced to `string`, and therefore all literal values are available for statement completion in the text editor.

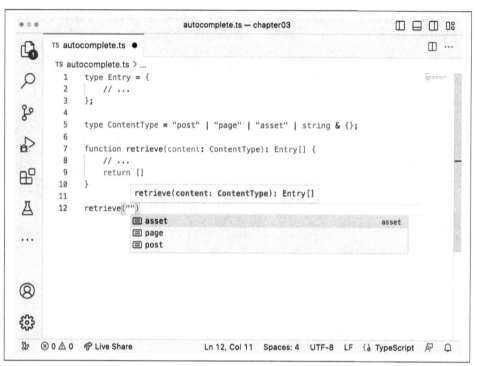

Figure 3-4. Intersecting string with the empty object retains statement completion hints

Still, every string is a valid `ContentType`; it just changes the developer experience of your API and gives hints where needed.

This technique is used by popular libraries like CSSType (*https://oreil.ly/lwtC5*) or the Definitely Typed type definitions for React (*https://oreil.ly/epbLV*).

CHAPTER 4
Generics

Until now, our main goal was to take the inherent flexibility of JavaScript and find a way to formalize it through the type system. We added static types for a dynamically typed language, to communicate intent, get tooling, and catch bugs before they happen.

Some parts in JavaScript don't really care about static types, though. For example, an `isKeyAvailableInObject` function should only check if a key is available in an object; it doesn't need to know about the concrete types. To properly formalize a function like this we can use TypeScript's structural type system and describe either a very wide type for the price of information or a very strict type for the price of flexibility.

But we don't want to pay any price. We want both flexibility and information. Generics in TypeScript are just the silver bullet we need. We can describe complex relationships and formalize structure for data that has not been defined yet.

Generics, along with its gang of mapped types, type maps, type modifiers, and helper types, open the door to metatyping, where we can create new types based on old ones and keep relationships between types intact while the newly generated types challenge our original code for possible bugs.

This is the entrance to advanced TypeScript concepts. But fear not, *there shan't be dragons*, unless we define them.

4.1 Generalizing Function Signatures

Problem

You have two functions that work the same, but on different and largely incompatible types.

Solution

Generalize their behavior using generics.

Discussion

You are writing an application that stores several language files (for example, subtitles) in an object. The keys are the language codes, and the values are URLs. You load language files by selecting them via a language code, which comes from some API or user interface as `string`. To make sure the language code is correct and valid, you add an `isLanguageAvailable` function that does an `in` check and sets the correct type using a type predicate:

```
type Languages = {
  de: URL;
  en: URL;
  pt: URL;
  es: URL;
  fr: URL;
  ja: URL;
};

function isLanguageAvailable(
  collection: Languages,
  lang: string
): lang is keyof Languages {
  return lang in collection;
}

function loadLanguage(collection: Languages, lang: string) {
  if (isLanguageAvailable(collection, lang)) {
    // lang is keyof Languages
    collection[lang]; // access ok!
  }
}
```

Same application, different scenario, entirely different file. You load media data into an HTML element: either audio, video, or a combination with certain animations in a `canvas` element. All elements exist in the application already, but you need to select the right one based on input from an API. Again, the selection comes as `string`, and you write an `isElementAllowed` function to ensure that the input is actually a valid key of your `AllowedElements` collection:

```
type AllowedElements = {
  video: HTMLVideoElement;
  audio: HTMLAudioElement;
  canvas: HTMLCanvasElement;
};

function isElementAllowed(
  collection: AllowedElements,
  elem: string
): elem is keyof AllowedElements {
  return elem in collection;
}

function selectElement(collection: AllowedElements, elem: string) {
  if (isElementAllowed(collection, elem)) {
    // elem is keyof AllowedElements
    collection[elem]; // access ok
  }
}
```

You don't need to look too closely to see that both scenarios are very similar. The type guard functions especially catch our eye. If we strip away all the type information and align the names, they are identical:

```
function isAvailable(obj, key) {
  return key in obj;
}
```

The two of them exist because of the type information we get. Not because of the input parameters, but because of the type predicates. In both scenarios we can tell more about the input parameters by asserting a specific `keyof` type.

The problem is that both input types for the collection are entirely different and have no overlap. Except for the empty object, for which we don't get that much valuable information if we create a `keyof` type. `keyof {}` is actually `never`.

But there is some type information here that we can generalize. We know the first input parameter is an object. And the second one is a property key. If this check evaluates to `true`, we know that the first parameter is a key of the second parameter.

To generalize this function, we can add a *generic type parameter* to `isAvailable` called `Obj`, put in angle brackets. This is a placeholder for an actual type that will be substituted once `isAvailable` is used. We can use this *generic type parameter* like we would use `AllowedElements` or `Languages` and can add a type predicate. Since `Obj` can be substituted for *every* type, `key` needs to include all possible property keys—`string`, `symbol`, and `number`:

```
function isAvailable<Obj>(
  obj: Obj,
  key: string | number | symbol
): key is keyof Obj {
  return key in obj;
}

function loadLanguage(collection: Languages, lang: string) {
  if (isAvailable(collection, lang)) {
    // lang is keyof Languages
    collection[lang]; // access ok!
  }
}

function selectElement(collection: AllowedElements, elem: string) {
  if (isAvailable(collection, elem)) {
    // elem is keyof AllowedElements
    collection[elem]; // access ok
  }
}
```

And there you have it: one function that works in both scenarios, no matter which types we substitute Obj for. Just like JavaScript works! We still get the same functionality, and we get the right type information. Index access becomes safe, without sacrificing flexibility.

The best part? We can use isAvailable just like we would use an untyped JavaScript equivalent. This is because TypeScript infers types for generic type parameters through usage. And this comes with some neat side effects. You can read more about that in Recipe 4.3.

4.2 Creating Related Function Arguments

Problem

You write functions where the second parameter is dependent on the first one.

Solution

Annotate each parameter with a generic type and create a relationship between them through generic constraints.

Discussion

Similar to Recipe 4.1, our application stores a list of subtitles in an object of type Languages. Languages has a set of keys describing the language code and a URL as the value:

```
type Languages = {
  de: URL;
  en: URL;
  pt: URL;
  es: URL;
  fr: URL;
  ja: URL;
};
```

```
const languages: Languages = { /* ... */ };
```

There are several lists like this in our application, and we can abstract them in a type
called URLList, whose index signatures allow for any string key:

```
type URLList = {
  [x: string]: URL;
};
```

URLList is a supertype of Languages: every value of type Languages is a URLList, but
not every URLList is Languages. Still, we can use URLList to write a function called
fetchFile, where we load a specific entry from this list:

```
function fetchFile(urls: URLList, key: string) {
  return fetch(urls[key]).then((res) => res.json());
}
```

```
const de = fetchFile(languages, "de");
const it = fetchFile(languages, "it");
```

The problem is that type string for key allows for way too many entries. For example, no Italian subtitles are defined, but fetchFile doesn't keep us from loading "it"
as a language code anyway. When we load items from a specific URLList, it would be
great to also know which keys we can access.

We can solve this by substituting the broader type for a generic and setting a *generic
constraint* to make sure we pass a subtype of URLList. This way, the function signature behaves very similarly to before, but we can work with the subtituted types much
better. We define a *generic type parameter* List which is a subtype of URLList and set
key to keyof List:

```
function fetchFile<List extends URLList>(urls: List, key: keyof List) {
  return fetch(urls[key]).then((res) => res.json());
}
```

```
const de = fetchFile(languages, "de");
const it = fetchFile(languages, "it");
//                                  ^
// Argument of type '"it"' is not assignable to
// parameter of type 'keyof Languages'.(2345)
```

The moment we call `fetchFile`, `List` will be substituted for an actual type, and we know that `"it"` is not part of the keys of `Languages`. TypeScript will show us when we made a typo or selected elements that aren't part of our data types.

This also works if we are loading many keys. The same constraints, the same effect:

```
function fetchFiles<List extends URLList>(urls: List, keys: (keyof List)[]) {
  const els = keys.map((el) =>
    fetch(urls[el])
      .then((res) => res.json())
      .then((data) => [el, data])
  );
  return els;
}

const de_and_fr = fetchFiles(languages, ["de", "fr"]); // Promise<any[]≥[]
const de_and_it = fetchFiles(languages, ["de", "it"]);
//                                                 ^
// Type '"it"' is not assignable to type 'keyof Languages'.(2322)
```

We store the results in a tuple with the language key as first element and the data as the second element. However, when we get the result, it's an array of `Promise`s that resolve to an `any[]`. This is understandable, as `fetch` does not tell us anything about the data loaded, and with `data` being of type `any` and thus having the broadest type, it just swallows `el`, which is `keyof List`.

But we know more at this stage. We know, for example, that `[el, data]` is not an array but a tuple. There is a subtle but important difference, as shown in Recipe 2.4. If we annotate the result with a tuple type, we get more information from our return values:

```
function fetchFiles<List extends URLList>(urls: List, keys: (keyof List)[]) {
  const els = keys.map((el) =>
    fetch(urls[el])
      .then((res) => res.json())
      .then((data) => {
        const entry: [keyof List, any] = [el, data];
        return entry;
      })
  );
  return els;
}

const de_and_fr = fetchFiles(languages, ["de", "fr"]);
```

`fetchFiles` now returns an array of `Promise`s of `[keyof List, any]`. So the moment we substitute `List` for `Languages`, we know that the only possible keys can be language codes.

However, there's still one caveat. As the preceding code sample shows, the only languages available in de_and_fr are German and French, but the compiler doesn't warn us that we check for English later on. The compiler should be able to do that, because this condition will always return false:

```
for (const result of de_and_fr) {
  if (result[0] === "en") {
    // English?
  }
}
```

The problem is that we are dealing again with a type that is way too broad. Yes, keyof List is already a lot narrower than string, but we can substitute all keys for a smaller set as well.

We need to repeat the same process:

1. Create a new generic type parameter.

2. Set the broader type as a constraint of the newly created generic type parameter.

3. Use the parameter in the function signature to be substituted for an actual type.

And just like that, we can also substitute keyof List with a subtype: "de" | "fr":

```
function fetchFiles<List extends URLList, Keys extends keyof List>(
  urls: List,
  keys: Keys[]
) {
  const els = keys.map((el) =>
    fetch(urls[el])
      .then((res) => res.json())
      .then((data) => {
        const entry: [Keys, any] = [el, data];
        return entry;
      })
  );
  return els;
}
```

```
const de_and_fr = fetchFiles(languages, ["de", "fr"]);
```

What's nice about this is that we can set relationships between generic type parameters. The second type parameter can be constrained by something from the first generic type parameter. This allows us to narrow very specifically, until we substitute with real values. The effect? We know about possible values of our types anywhere in our code. So we won't check for English language if we can already say that we never requested to load English:

```
for (const entry of de_and_fr) {
  const result = await entry;
  if (result[0] === "en") {
```

```
    // This condition will always return 'false' since the types
    //. '"de" | "fr"' and '"en"' have no overlap.(2367)
  }
}
```

One check that we didn't get rid of is to see which language is at position 0.

One thing that we didn't take into account is *generic instantiation*. We let type parameters be substituted for real values through usage, just like type inference. But we also could substitute them explicitly through annotations:

```
const de_and_ja = fetchFiles<Languages, "ja" | "de">(languages, ["de"]);
```

Here the types tell us there might be Japanese subtitles as well, even though we can see from usage that we load only German ones. Let this be a reminder, and get more insights in Recipe 4.4.

4.3 Getting Rid of any and unknown

Problem

Generic type parameters, any, and unknown all seem to describe very wide sets of values. When should you use what?

Solution

Use generic type parameters when you get to the actual type eventually; refer to Recipe 2.2 on the decision between any and unknown.

Discussion

When we are using generics, they might seem like a substitute for any and unknown. Take an identity function—its only job is to return the value passed as input parameter:

```
function identity(value: any): any {
  return value;
}

let a = identity("Hello!");
let b = identity(false);
let c = identity(2);
```

It takes values of every type, and the return type of it can also be anything. We can write the same function using unknown if we want to safely access properties:

```
function identity(value: unknown): unknown {
  return value;
}
```

```
let a = identity("Hello!");
let b = identity(false);
let c = identity(2);
```

We can even mix and match any and unknown, but the result is always the same: Type information is lost. The type of the return value is what we define it to be.

Now let's write the same function with generics instead of any or unknown. Its type annotations say that the generic type is also the return type:

```
function identity<T>(t: T): T {
  return t;
}
```

We can use this function to pass in any value and see which type TypeScript infers:

```
let a = identity("Hello!"); // a is string
let b = identity(2000);     // b is number
let c = identity({ a: 2 }); // c is { a: number }
```

Assigning to a binding with const instead of let gives slightly different results:

```
const a = identity("Hello!"); // a is "Hello!"
const b = identity(2000);     // b is 2000
const c = identity({ a: 2 }); // c is { a: number }
```

For primitive types, TypeScript substitutes the generic type parameter with the actual type. We can make great use of this in more advanced scenarios.

With TypeScript's generics, it's also possible to *annotate* the generic type parameter:

```
const a = identity<string>("Hello!"); // a is string
const b = identity<number>(2000);     // b is number
const c = identity<{ a: 2 }>({ a: 2 }); // c is { a: 2 }
```

If this behavior reminds you of annotation and inference described in Recipe 3.4, you are absolutely right. It's very similar but with generic type parameters in functions.

When using generics without constraints, we can write functions that work with values of any type. Inside, they behave like unknown, which means we can do type guards to narrow the type. The biggest difference is that once we use the function, we substitute our generics with real types, not losing any information on typing at all.

This allows us to be a bit clearer with our types than just allowing everything. This pairs function takes two arguments and creates a tuple:

```
function pairs(a: unknown, b: unknown): [unknown, unknown] {
  return [a, b];
}

const a = pairs(1, "1"); // [unknown, unknown]
```

With generic type parameters, we get a nice tuple type:

```
function pairs<T, U>(a: T, b: U): [T, U] {
  return [a, b];
}

const b = pairs(1, "1"); // [number, string]
```

Using the same generic type parameter, we can make sure we get tuples only where each element is of the same type:

```
function pairs<T>(a: T, b: T): [T, T] {
  return [a, b];
}

const c = pairs(1, "1");
//                    ^
// Argument of type 'string' is not assignable to parameter of type 'number'
```

So, should you use generics everywhere? Not necessarily. This chapter includes many solutions that rely on getting the right type information at the right time. When you are happy with a wider set of values and can rely on subtypes being compatible, you don't need to use generics at all. If you have any and unknown in your code, think whether you need the actual type at some point. Adding a generic type parameter instead might help.

4.4 Understanding Generic Instantiation

Problem

You understand how generics are substituted for real types, but sometimes errors like "Foo is assignable to the constraint of type Bar, but could be instantiated with a different subtype of constraint Baz" confuse you.

Solution

Remember that values of a generic type can be—explicitly and implicitly—substituted with a variety of subtypes. Write subtype-friendly code.

Discussion

You create a filter logic for your application. You have different filter rules that you can combine using "and" | "or" combinators. You can also chain regular filter rules with the outcome of *combinatorial filters*. You create your types based on this behavior:

```
type FilterRule = {
  field: string;
  operator: string;
  value: any;
```

```
};

type CombinatorialFilter = {
  combinator: "and" | "or";
  rules: FilterRule[];
};

type ChainedFilter = {
  rules: (CombinatorialFilter | FilterRule)[];
};

type Filter = CombinatorialFilter | ChainedFilter;
```

Now you want to write a `reset` function that, based on an already provided filter, resets all rules. You use type guards to distinguish between `CombinatorialFilter` and `ChainedFilter`:

```
function reset(filter: Filter): Filter {
  if ("combinator" in filter) {
    // filter is CombinatorialFilter
    return { combinator: "and", rules: [] };
  }
  // filter is ChainedFilter
  return { rules: [] };
}

const filter: CombinatorialFilter = { rules: [], combinator: "or" };
const resetFilter = reset(filter); // resetFilter is Filter
```

The behavior is what you are after, but the return type of `reset` is too wide. When we pass a `CombinatorialFilter`, we should be sure that the reset filter is also a `CombinatorialFilter`. Here it's the union type, just like our function signature indicates. But you want to make sure that if you pass a filter of a certain type, you also get the same return type. So you replace the broad union type with a generic type parameter that is constrained to `Filter`. The return type works as intended, but the implementation of your function throws errors:

```
function reset<F extends Filter>(filter: F): F {
  if ("combinator" in filter) {
    return { combinator: "and", rules: [] };
//  ^ '{ combinator: "and"; rules: never[]; }' is assignable to
//      the constraint of type 'F', but 'F' could be instantiated
//      with a different subtype of constraint 'Filter'.
  }
  return { rules: [] };
//^ '{ rules: never[]; }' is assignable to the constraint of type 'F',
//    but 'F' could be instantiated with a different subtype of
//    constraint 'Filter'.
}

const resetFilter = reset(filter); // resetFilter is CombinatorialFilter
```

While you want to differentiate between two parts of a union, TypeScript thinks more broadly. It knows that you might pass in an object that is *structurally compatible* with `Filter`, but it has more properties and is therefore a subtype.

This means you can call `reset` with F instantiated to a subtype, and your program would happily override all excess properties. This is wrong, and TypeScript tells you that:

```
const onDemandFilter = reset({
  combinator: "and",
  rules: [],
  evaluated: true,
  result: false,
});
/* filter is {
    combinator: "and";
    rules: never[];
    evaluated: boolean;
    result: boolean;
}; */
```

Overcome this by writing subtype-friendly code. Clone the input object (still type F), set the properties that need to be changed accordingly, and return something that is still of type F:

```
function reset<F extends Filter>(filter: F): F {
  const result = { ...filter }; // result is F
  result.rules = [];
  if ("combinator" in result) {
    result.combinator = "and";
  }
  return result;
}

const resetFilter = reset(filter); // resetFilter is CombinatorialFilter
```

Generic types can be one of many in a union, but they can be much, much more. TypeScript's structural type system allows you to work on a variety of subtypes, and your code needs to reflect that.

Here's a different scenario but with a similar outcome. You want to create a tree data structure and write a recursive type that stores all tree items. This type can be subtyped, so you write a `createRootItem` function with a generic type parameter since you want to instantiate it with the correct subtype:

```
type TreeItem = {
  id: string;
  children: TreeItem[];
  collapsed?: boolean;
};
```

```
function createRootItem<T extends TreeItem>(): T {
  return {
    id: "root",
    children: [],
  };
// '{ id: string; children: never[]; }' is assignable to the constraint
//   of type 'T', but 'T' could be instantiated with a different subtype
//   of constraint 'TreeItem'.(2322)
}
```

```
const root = createRootItem(); // root is TreeItem
```

We get a similar error as before, since we can't possibly say that the return value will be compatible with all the subtypes. To solve this problem, get rid of the generic! We know how the return type will look—it's a TreeItem:

```
function createRootItem(): TreeItem {
  return {
    id: "root",
    children: [],
  };
}
```

The simplest solutions are often the better ones. But now you want to extend your software by being able to attach children of type or subtype TreeItem to a newly created root. We don't add any generics yet and are somewhat dissatisfied:

```
function attachToRoot(children: TreeItem[]): TreeItem {
  return {
    id: "root",
    children,
  };
}
```

```
const root = attachToRoot([]); // TreeItem
```

root is of type TreeItem, but we lose any information about the subtyped children. Even if we add a generic type parameter just for the children, constrained to Tree Item, we don't retain this information on the go:

```
function attachToRoot<T extends TreeItem>(children: T[]): TreeItem {
  return {
    id: "root",
    children,
  };
}
```

```
const root = attachToRoot([
  {
    id: "child",
    children: [],
    collapsed: false,
```

```
    marked: true,
  },
]); // root is TreeItem
```

When we start adding a generic type as a return type, we run into the same problems as before. To solve this issue, we need to split the root item type from the children item type, by opening up `TreeItem` to be a generic, where we can set `Children` to be a subtype of `TreeItem`.

Since we want to avoid any circular references, we need to set `Children` to a default `BaseTreeItem`, so we can use `TreeItem` both as a constraint for `Children` and for `attachToRoot`:

```
type BaseTreeItem = {
  id: string;
  children: BaseTreeItem[];
};

type TreeItem<Children extends TreeItem = BaseTreeItem> = {
  id: string;
  children: Children[];
  collapsed?: boolean;
};

function attachToRoot<T extends TreeItem>(children: T[]): TreeItem<T> {
  return {
    id: "root",
    children,
  };
}

const root = attachToRoot([
  {
    id: "child",
    children: [],
    collapsed: false,
    marked: true,
  },
]);
/*
root is TreeItem<{
    id: string;
    children: never[];
    collapsed: false;
    marked: boolean;
}>
*/
```

Again, we write subtype friendly and treat our input parameters as their own, instead of making assumptions.

4.5 Generating New Object Types

Problem

You have a type in your application that is related to your model. Every time the model changes, you need to change your types as well.

Solution

Use generic mapped types to create new object types based on the original type.

Discussion

Let's go back to the toy shop from Recipe 3.1. Thanks to union types, intersection types, and discriminated union types, we were able to model our data quite nicely:

```
type ToyBase = {
  name: string;
  description: string;
  minimumAge: number;
};

type BoardGame = ToyBase & {
  kind: "boardgame";
  players: number;
};

type Puzzle = ToyBase & {
  kind: "puzzle";
  pieces: number;
};

type Doll = ToyBase & {
  kind: "doll";
  material: "plush" | "plastic";
};

type Toy = Doll | Puzzle | BoardGame;
```

Somewhere in our code, we need to group all toys from our model in a data structure that can be described by a type called GroupedToys. GroupedToys has a property for each category (or "kind") and a Toy array as value. A groupToys function takes an unsorted list of toys and groups them by kind:

```
type GroupedToys = {
  boardgame: Toy[];
  puzzle: Toy[];
  doll: Toy[];
};
```

```
function groupToys(toys: Toy[]): GroupedToys {
  const groups: GroupedToys = {
    boardgame: [],
    puzzle: [],
    doll: [],
  };
  for (let toy of toys) {
    groups[toy.kind].push(toy);
  }
  return groups;
}
```

There are already some niceties in this code. First, we use an explicit type annotation when declaring groups. This ensures we are not forgetting any category. Also, since the keys of GroupedToys are the same as the union of "kind" types in Toy, we can easily index access groups by toy.kind.

Months and sprints pass, and we need to touch our model again. The toy shop is now selling original or maybe alternate vendors of interlocking toy bricks. We wire the new type Bricks up to our Toy model:

```
type Bricks = ToyBase & {
  kind: "bricks",
  pieces: number;
  brand: string;
}


type Toy = Doll | Puzzle | BoardGame | Bricks;
```

Since groupToys needs to deal with Bricks, too, we get a nice error because Grouped Toys has no clue about a "bricks" kind:

```
function groupToys(toys: Toy[]): GroupedToys {
  const groups: GroupedToys = {
    boardgame: [],
    puzzle: [],
    doll: [],
  };
  for (let toy of toys) {
    groups[toy.kind].push(toy);
//  ^- Element implicitly has an 'any' type because expression
//     of type '"boardgame" | "puzzle" | "doll" | "bricks"' can't
//     be used to index type 'GroupedToys'.
//     Property 'bricks' does not exist on type 'GroupedToys'.(7053)
  }
  return groups;
}
```

This is desired behavior in TypeScript: knowing when types don't match anymore. This should draw our attention. Let's give GroupedToys and groupToys an update:

```
type GroupedToys = {
  boardgame: Toy[];
  puzzle: Toy[];
  doll: Toy[];
  bricks: Toy[];
};

function groupToys(toys: Toy[]): GroupedToys {
  const groups: GroupedToys = {
    boardgame: [],
    puzzle: [],
    doll: [],
    bricks: [],
  };
  for (let toy of toys) {
    groups[toy.kind].push(toy);
  }
  return groups;
}
```

There is one bothersome thing: the task of grouping toys is always the same. No matter how much our model changes, we will always select by kind and push into an array. We would need to maintain groups with every change, but if we change how we think about groups, we can optimize for change. First, we change the type GroupedToys to feature optional properties. Second, we initialize each group with an empty array if there hasn't been any initialization yet:

```
type GroupedToys = {
  boardgame?: Toy[];
  puzzle?: Toy[];
  doll?: Toy[];
  bricks?: Toy[];
};


function groupToys(toys: Toy[]): GroupedToys {
  const groups: GroupedToys = {};
  for (let toy of toys) {
    // Initialize when not available
    groups[toy.kind] = groups[toy.kind] ?? [];
    groups[toy.kind]?.push(toy);
  }
  return groups;
}
```

We don't need to maintain groupToys anymore. The only thing that needs maintenance is the type GroupedToys. If we look closely at GroupedToys, we see that there is an implicit relation to Toy. Each property key is part of Toy["kind"]. Let's make this relation *explicit*. With a *mapped type*, we create a new object type based on each type in Toy["kind"].

Toy["kind"] is a union of string literals: "boardgame" | "puzzle" | "doll" | "bricks". Since we have a very reduced set of strings, each element of this union will be used as its own property key. Let that sink in for a moment: we can use a *type* to be a *property key* of a newly generated type. Each property has an optional type modifier and points to a Toy[]:

```
type GroupedToys = {
  [k in Toy["kind"]]?: Toy[];
};
```

Fantastic! Every time we change Toy, we immediately change Toy[]. Our code needs no change at all; we can still group by kind as we did before.

This is a pattern we have the potential to generalize. Let's create a Group type that takes a collection and groups it by a specific selector. We want to create a generic type with two type parameters:

- The Collection can be anything.

- The Selector, a key of Collection, so it can create the respective properties.

Our first attempt would be to take what we had in GroupedToys and replace the concrete types with type parameters. This creates what we need but also causes an error:

```
// How to use it
type GroupedToys = Group<Toy, "kind">;

type Group<Collection, Selector extends keyof Collection> = {
  [x in Collection[Selector]]?: Collection[];
//       ^ Type 'Collection[Selector]' is not assignable
//         to type 'string | number | symbol'.
//         Type 'Collection[keyof Collection]' is not
//         assignable to type 'string | number | symbol'.
//         Type 'Collection[string] | Collection[number]
//          | Collection[symbol]' is not assignable to
//         type 'string | number | symbol'.
//         Type 'Collection[string]' is not assignable to
//         type 'string | number | symbol'.(2322)
};
```

TypeScript warns us that Collection[string] | Collection[number] | Collection[symbol] could result in anything, not just things that can be used as a key. That's true, and we need to prepare for that. We have two options.

First, use a type constraint on Collection that points to Record<string, any>. Record is a utility type that generates a new object where the first parameter gives you all keys and the second parameter gives you the types:

```
// This type is built-in!
type Record<K extends string | number | symbol, T> = { [P in K]: T; };
```

This elevates Collection to a wildcard object, effectively disabling the type-check from Groups. This is OK because if something would be an unusable type for a property key, TypeScript will throw it away anyway. So the final Group has two constrained type parameters:

```
type Group<
  Collection extends Record<string, any>,
  Selector extends keyof Collection
> = {
  [x in Collection[Selector]]: Collection[];
};
```

The second option is to do a check for each key to see if it is a valid string key. We can use a *conditional type* to see if Collection[Selector] is in fact a valid type for a key. Otherwise, we would remove this type by choosing never. Conditional types are their own beast, and we tackle this in Recipe 5.4 extensively:

```
type Group<Collection, Selector extends keyof Collection> = {
  [k in Collection[Selector] extends string
    ? Collection[Selector]
    : never]?: Collection[];
};
```

Note that we did remove the optional type modifier. We do this because making keys optional is not the task of grouping. We have another type for that: Partial<T>, another mapped type that makes every property in an object type optional:

```
// This type is built-in!
type Partial<T> = { [P in keyof T]?: T[P] };
```

No matter which Group helper you create, you can now create a GroupedToys object by telling TypeScript that you want a Partial (changing everything to optional properties) of a Group of Toys by "kind":

```
type GroupedToys = Partial<Group<Toy, "kind">>;
```

Now that reads nicely.

4.6 Modifying Objects with Assertion Signatures

Problem

After a certain function execution in your code, you know the type of a value has changed.

Solution

Use assertion signatures to change types independently of if and switch statements.

Discussion

JavaScript is a very flexible language. Its dynamic typing features allow you to change objects at runtime, adding new properties on the fly. And developers use this. There are situations where you, for example, run over a collection of elements and need to assert certain properties. You then store a checked property and set it to true, just so you know that you passed a certain mark:

```
function check(person: any) {
  person.checked = true;
}

const person = {
  name: "Stefan",
  age: 27,
};

check(person); // person now has the checked property

person.checked; // this is true!
```

You want to mirror this behavior in the type system; otherwise, you would need to constantly do extra checks if certain properties are in an object, even though you can be sure that they exist.

One way to assert that certain properties exist are, well, type assertions. We say that at a certain point in time, this property has a different type:

```
(person as typeof person & { checked: boolean }).checked = true;
```

Good, but you would need to do this type assertion over and over again, as they don't change the original type of person. Another way to assert that certain properties are available is to create type predicates, like those shown in Recipe 3.5:

```
function check<T>(obj: T): obj is T & { checked: true } {
  (obj as T & { checked: boolean }).checked = true;
  return true;
}

const person = {
  name: "Stefan",
  age: 27,
};

if (check(person)) {
  person.checked; // checked is true!
}
```

This situation is a bit different, though, which makes the check function feel clumsy: you need to do an extra condition and return true in the predicate function. This doesn't feel right.

Thankfully, TypeScript has another technique we can leverage in situations like this: assertion signatures. Assertion signatures can change the type of a value in control flow, without the need for conditionals. They have been modeled for the Node.js `assert` function, which takes a condition, and it throws an error if it isn't true. This means that, after calling `assert`, you might have more information than before. For example, if you call `assert` and check if a value has a type of `string`, you know that after this `assert` function the value should be `string`:

```
function assert(condition: any, msg?: string): asserts condition {
  if (!condition) {
    throw new Error(msg);
  }
}

function yell(str: any) {
  assert(typeof str === "string");
  // str is string
  return str.toUpperCase();
}
```

Please note that the function short-circuits if the condition is false. It throws an error, the `never` case. If this function passes, you can really assert the condition.

While assertion signatures have been modeled for the Node.js assert function, you can assert any type you like. For example, you can have a function that takes any value for an addition, but you assert that the values need to be `number` to continue:

```
function assertNumber(val: any): asserts val is number {
  if (typeof val !== "number") {
    throw Error("value is not a number");
  }
}

function add(x: unknown, y: unknown): number {
  assertNumber(x); // x is number
  assertNumber(y); // y is number
  return x + y;
}
```

All the examples you find on assertion signatures are based after assertions and short-circuit with errors. But we can take the same technique to tell TypeScript that more properties are available. We write a function that is very similar to check in the predicate function before, but this time we don't need to return `true`. We set the property, and since objects are passed by value in JavaScript, we can assert that after calling this function whatever we pass has a property `checked`, which is `true`:

```
function check<T>(obj: T): asserts obj is T & { checked: true } {
  (obj as T & { checked: boolean }).checked = true;
}
```

```
const person = {
  name: "Stefan",
  age: 27,
};
```

```
check(person);
```

And with that, we can modify a value's type on the fly. It's a little-known technique that can help you a lot.

4.7 Mapping Types with Type Maps

Problem

You write a factory function that creates an object of a specific subtype based on a string identifier, and there are a lot of possible subtypes.

Solution

Store all subtypes in a type map, widen with index access, and use mapped types like `Partial<T>`.

Discussion

Factory functions are great if you want to create variants of complex objects based on some basic information. One scenario that you might know from browser JavaScript is the creation of elements. The `document.createElement` function accepts an element's tag name, and you get an object where you can modify all necessary properties.

You want to spice up this creation with a neat factory function you call `create Element`. Not only does it take the element's tag name, but it also makes a list of properties so you don't need to set each property individually:

```
// Using create Element

// a is HTMLAnchorElement
const a = createElement("a", { href: "https://fettblog.eu" });
// b is HTMLVideoElement
const b = createElement("video", { src: "/movie.mp4", autoplay: true });
// c is HTMLElement
const c = createElement("my-element");
```

You want to create good types for this, so you need to take care of two things:

- Make sure you create only valid HTML elements.
- Provide a type that accepts a subset of an HTML element's properties.

Let's take care of the valid HTML elements first. There are around 140 possible HTML elements, which is a lot. Each of those elements has a tag name, which can be represented as a string, and a respective prototype object in the DOM. Using the *dom* lib in your *tsconfig.json*, TypeScript has information on those prototype objects in the form of types. And you can figure out all 140 element names.

A good way to provide a mapping between element tag names and prototype objects is to use a *type map*. A type map is a technique where you take a type alias or interface and let keys point to the respective type variants. You can then get the correct type variant using index access of a string literal type:

```
type AllElements = {
  a: HTMLAnchorElement;
  div: HTMLDivElement;
  video: HTMLVideoElement;
  //... and ~140 more!
};

// HTMLAnchorElement
type A = AllElements["a"];
```

It looks like accessing a JavaScript object's properties using index access, but remember that we're still working on a type level. This means index access can be broad:

```
type AllElements = {
  a: HTMLAnchorElement;
  div: HTMLDivElement;
  video: HTMLVideoElement;
  //... and ~140 more!
};

// HTMLAnchorElement | HTMLDivElement
type AandDiv = AllElements["a" | "div"];
```

Let's use this map to type the `createElement` function. We use a generic type parameter constrained to all keys of `AllElements`, which allows us to pass only valid HTML elements:

```
function createElement<T extends keyof AllElements>(tag: T): AllElements[T] {
  return document.createElement(tag as string) as AllElements[T];
}

// a is HTMLAnchorElement
const a = createElement("a");
```

Use generics here to pin a string literal to a literal type, which we can use to index the right HTML element variant from the type map. Also note that using `document.createElement` requires two type assertions. One makes the set wider (`T` to `string`), and one makes the set narrower (`HTMLElement` to `AllElements[T]`). Both assertions indicate that we have to deal with an API outside our control, as established in Recipe 3.9. We will deal with the assertions later on.

Now we want to provide the option to pass extra properties for said HTML elements, to set an `href` to an `HTMLAnchorElement`, and so forth. All properties are already in the respective `HTMLElement` variants, but they're required, not optional. We can make all properties optional with the built-in type `Partial<T>`. It's a mapped type that takes all properties of a certain type and adds a type modifier:

```
type Partial<T> = { [P in keyof T]?: T[P] };
```

We extend our function with an optional argument `props` that is a `Partial` of the indexed element from `AllElements`. This way, we know that if we pass an `"a"`, we can only set properties that are available in `HTMLAnchorElement`:

```
function createElement<T extends keyof AllElements>(
  tag: T,
  props?: Partial<AllElements[T]>
): AllElements[T] {
  const elem = document.createElement(tag as string) as AllElements[T];
  return Object.assign(elem, props);
}

const a = createElement("a", { href: "https://fettblog.eu" });
const x = createElement("a", { src: "https://fettblog.eu" });
//                                ^--
// Argument of type '{ src: string; }' is not assignable to parameter
// of type 'Partial<HTMLAnchorElement>'.
// Object literal may only specify known properties, and 'src' does not
// exist in type 'Partial<HTMLAnchorElement>'.(2345)
```

Fantastic! Now it's up to you to figure out all 140 HTML elements. Or not. Somebody already did the work and put `HTMLElementTagNameMap` into *lib.dom.ts*. So let's use this instead:

```
function createElement<T extends keyof HTMLElementTagNameMap>(
  tag: T,
  props?: Partial<HTMLElementTagNameMap[T]>
): HTMLElementTagNameMap[T] {
  const elem = document.createElement(tag);
  return Object.assign(elem, props);
}
```

This is also the interface used by `document.createElement`, so there is no friction between your factory function and the built-in one. No extra assertions necessary.

There is only one caveat. You are restricted to the 140 elements provided by `HTMLElementTagNameMap`. What if you want to create SVG elements, or web components that can have fully customized element names? Your factory function suddenly is too constrained.

To allow for more—as `document.createElement` does—we would need to add all possible strings to the mix again. `HTMLElementTagNameMap` is an interface. So we can use *declaration merging* to extend the interface with an *indexed signature*, where we map all remaining strings to `HTMLUnknownElement`:

```
interface HTMLElementTagNameMap {
  [x: string]: HTMLUnknownElement;
};

function createElement<T extends keyof HTMLElementTagNameMap>(
  tag: T,
  props?: Partial<HTMLElementTagNameMap[T]>
): HTMLElementTagNameMap[T] {
  const elem = document.createElement(tag);
  return Object.assign(elem, props);
}

// a is HTMLAnchorElement
const a = createElement("a", { href: "https://fettblog.eu" });
// b is HTMLUnknownElement
const b = createElement("my-element");
```

Now we have everything we want:

- A great factory function to create typed HTML elements
- The possibility to set element properties with just one configuration object .
- The flexibility to create more elements than defined

The last is great, but what if you only want to allow for web components? Web components have a convention; they need to have a *dash* in their tag name. We can model this using a mapped type on a *string template literal type*. You will learn all about string template literal types in Chapter 6.

For now, the only thing you need to know is that we create a set of strings where the pattern is *any string* followed by a *dash* followed by *any string*. This is enough to ensure we only pass correct element names.

Mapped types work only with type aliases, not interface declarations, so we need to define an `AllElements` type again:

```
type AllElements = HTMLElementTagNameMap &
  {
    [x in `${string}-${string}`]: HTMLElement;
  };

function createElement<T extends keyof AllElements>(
  tag: T,
  props?: Partial<AllElements[T]>
): AllElements[T] {
```

```
    const elem = document.createElement(tag as string) as AllElements[T];
    return Object.assign(elem, props);
}

const a = createElement("a", { href: "https://fettblog.eu" }); // OK
const b = createElement("my-element"); // OK


const c = createElement("thisWillError");
//                       ^
// Argument of type '"thisWillError"' is not
// assignable to parameter of type '`${string}-${string}`
// | keyof HTMLElementTagNameMap'.(2345)
```

Fantastic. With the AllElements type we also get type assertions back, which we don't
like that much. In that case, instead of asserting, we can also use a function overload,
defining two declarations: one for our users, and one for us to implement the function. You can learn more about this function overload technique in Recipes 2.6 and
12.7:

```
function createElement<T extends keyof AllElements>(
  tag: T,
  props?: Partial<AllElements[T]>
): AllElements[T];
function createElement(tag: string, props?: Partial<HTMLElement>): HTMLElement {
  const elem = document.createElement(tag);
  return Object.assign(elem, props);
}
```

We are all set. We defined a *type map* with *mapped types* and *index signatures*, using
generic type parameters to be very explicit about our intentions. A great combination
of multiple tools in our TypeScript tool belt.

4.8 Using ThisType to Define this in Objects

Problem

Your app requires complex configuration objects with methods, where this has a different context depending on usage.

Solution

Use the built-in generic ThisType<T> to define the correct this.

Discussion

Frameworks like VueJS (*https://vuejs.org*) rely a lot on factory functions, where you pass a comprehensive configuration object to define initial data, computed properties, and methods for each instance. You want to create a similar behavior for components of your app. The idea is to provide a configuration object with three properties:

A data *function*
> The return value is the initial data for the instance. You should not have access to any other properties from the configuration object in this function.

A computed *property*
> This is for computed properties, which are based on the initial data. Computed properties are declared using functions. They can access initial data just like normal properties.

A methods *property*
> Methods can be called and can access computed properties as well as the initial data. When methods access computed properties, they access it like they would access normal properties: no need to call the function.

Looking at the configuration object in use, there are three different ways to interpret this. In data, this doesn't have any properties at all. In computed, each function can access the return value of data via this just like it would be part of their object. In methods, each method can access computed properties and data via this in the same way:

```
const instance = create({
  data() {
    return {
      firstName: "Stefan",
      lastName: "Baumgartner",
    };
  },
  computed: {
    fullName() {
      // has access to the return object of data
      return this.firstName + " " + this.lastName;
    },
  },
  methods: {
    hi() {
      // use computed properties just like normal properties
      alert(this.fullName.toLowerCase());
    },
  },
});
```

This behavior is special but not uncommon. And with a behavior like that, we definitely want to rely on good types.

 In this lesson we will focus only on the types, not on the actual implementation, as that would exceed this chapter's scope.

Let's create types for each property. We define a type Options, which we are going to refine step by step. First is the data function. data can be user defined, so we want to specify data using a generic type parameter. The data we are looking for is specified by the return type of the data function:

```
type Options<Data> = {
  data(this: {})?: Data;
};
```

So once we specify an actual return value in the data function, the Data placeholder gets substituted with the real object's type. Note that we also define this to point to the empty object, which means that we don't get access to any other property from the configuration object.

Next, we define computed. computed is an object of functions. We add another generic type parameter called Computed and let the value of Computed be typed through usage. Here, this changes to all the properties of Data. Since we can't set this like we do in the data function, we can use the built-in helper type ThisType and set it to the generic type parameter Data:

```
type Options<Data, Computed> = {
  data(this: {})?: Data;
  computed?: Computed & ThisType<Data>;
};
```

This allows us to access, for example, this.firstName, like in the previous example. Last but not least, we want to specify methods. methods is again special, as you are getting access not only to Data via this but also to all methods and to all computed properties as properties.

Computed holds all computed properties as functions. We would need their value, though—more specifically, their return value. If we access fullName via property access, we expect it to be a string.

For that, we create a helper type called `MapFnToProp`. It takes a type that is an object of functions and maps it to the return values' types. The built-in `ReturnType` helper type is perfect for this scenario:

```
// An object of functions ...
type FnObj = Record<string, () => any>;

// ... to an object of return types
type MapFnToProp<FunctionObj extends FnObj> = {
  [K in keyof FunctionObj]: ReturnType<FunctionObj[K]>;
};
```

We can use `MapFnToProp` to set `ThisType` for a newly added generic type parameter called `Methods`. We also add `Data` and `Methods` to the mix. To pass the `Computed` generic type parameter to `MapFnToProp`, it needs to be constrained to `FnObj`, the same constraint of the first parameter `FunctionObj` in `MapFnToProp`:

```
type Options<Data, Computed extends FnObj, Methods> = {
  data(this: {})?: Data;
  computed?: Computed & ThisType<Data>;
  methods?: Methods & ThisType<Data & MapFnToProp<Computed> & Methods>;
};
```

And that's the type! We take all generic type properties and add them to the `create` factory function:

```
declare function create<Data, Computed extends FnObj, Methods>(
  options: Options<Data, Computed, Methods>
): any;
```

Through usage, all generic type parameters will be substituted. And the way `Options` is typed, we get all the autocomplete necessary to ensure we don't run into troubles, as seen in Figure 4-1.

This example shows wonderfully how TypeScript can be used to type elaborate APIs where a lot of object manipulation is happening underneath.[1]

---

1 Special thanks to the creators of Type Challenges (*https://oreil.ly/pHc9j*) for this beautiful example.

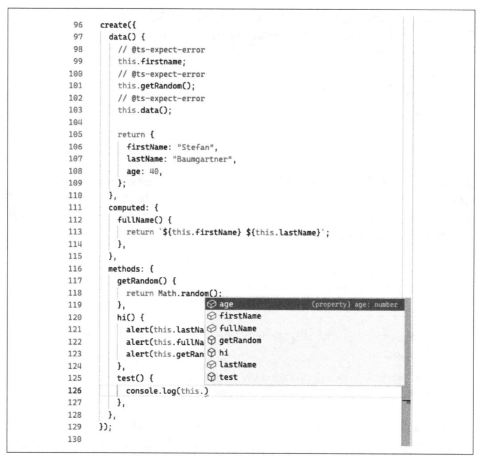

```
 96    create({
 97      data() {
 98        // @ts-expect-error
 99        this.firstname;
100        // @ts-expect-error
101        this.getRandom();
102        // @ts-expect-error
103        this.data();
104
105        return {
106          firstName: "Stefan",
107          lastName: "Baumgartner",
108          age: 40,
109        };
110      },
111      computed: {
112        fullName() {
113          return `${this.firstName} ${this.lastName}`;
114        },
115      },
116      methods: {
117        getRandom() {
118          return Math.random();
119        },
120        hi() {
121          alert(this.lastNa  ⊘ age              (property) age: number
122          alert(this.fullNa  ⊘ firstName
123          alert(this.getRan  ⊘ fullName
124        },                   ⊘ getRandom
125        test() {             ⊘ hi
126          console.log(this.) ⊘ lastName
127        },                   ⊘ test
128      },
129    });
130
```

Figure 4-1. The methods configuration in the factory function having all the access to the correct properties

4.9 Adding Const Context to Generic Type Parameters

Problem

When you pass complex, literal values to a function, TypeScript widens the type to something more general. While this is desired behavior in a lot of cases, in some you want to work on the literal types rather than the widened type.

Solution

Add a const modifier in front of your generic type parameter to keep the passed values in *const context*.

Discussion

Single-page application (SPA) frameworks tend to reimplement a lot of browser functionality in JavaScript. For example, features like the History API (*https://oreil.ly/ KMBgj*) made it possible to override the regular navigation behavior, which SPA frameworks use to switch between pages without a real page reload, by swapping the content of the page and changing the URL in the browser.

Imagine working on a minimalistic SPA framework that uses a so-called router to navigate between pages. Pages are defined as *components*, and a `ComponentConstructor` interface knows how to instantiate and render new elements on your website:

```
interface ComponentConstructor {
  new(): Component;
}

interface Component {
  render(): HTMLElement;
}
```

The *router* should take a list of components and associated paths, stored as `string`. When creating a router through the `router` function, it should return an object that lets you `navigate` the desired path:

```
type Route = {
  path: string;
  component: ComponentConstructor;
};

function router(routes: Route[]) {
  return {
    navigate(path: string) {
      // ...
    },
  };
}
```

How the actual navigation is implemented is of no concern to us right now; instead, we want to focus on the typings of the function interface.

The router works as intended; it takes an array of `Route` objects and returns an object with a `navigate` function, which allows us to trigger the navigation from one URL to the other and renders the new component:

```
const rtr = router([
  {
    path: "/",
    component: Main,
  },
  {
    path: "/about",
```

```
    component: About,
  },
])

rtr.navigate("/faq");
```

What you immediately see is that the types are way too broad. If we allow navigating to every `string` available, nothing keeps us from using bogus routes that lead nowhere. We would need to implement some sort of error handling for information that is already ready and available. So why not use it?

Our first idea would be to replace the concrete type with a generic type parameter. The way TypeScript deals with generic substitution is that if we have a literal type, TypeScript will subtype accordingly. Introducing `T` for `Route` and using `T["path"]` instead of `string` comes close to what we want to achieve:

```
function router<T extends Route>(routes: T[]) {
  return {
    navigate(path: T["path"]) {
      // ...
    },
  };
}
```

In theory, this should work. If we remind ourselves what TypeScript does with literal, primitives types in that case, we would expect the value to be narrowed to the literal type:

```
function getPath<T extends string>(route: T): T {
  return route;
}

const path = getPath("/"); // "/"
```

You can read more on that in Recipe 4.3. One important detail is that `path` in the previous example is in a *const context*, because the returned value is immutable.

The only problem is that we are working with objects and arrays, and TypeScript tends to widen types in objects and arrays to something more general to allow for the mutability of values. If we look at a similar example, but with a nested object, we see that TypeScript takes the broader type instead:

```
type Routes = {
  paths: string[];
};

function getPaths<T extends Routes>(routes: T): T["paths"] {
  return routes.paths;
}

const paths = getPaths({ paths: ["/", "/about"] }); // string[]
```

For objects, the *const context* for `paths` is only for the binding of the variable, not for its contents. This eventually leads to losing some of the information we need to correctly type `navigate`.

A way to work around this limitation is to manually apply *const context*, which needs us to redefine the input parameter to be `readonly`:

```
function router<T extends Route>(routes: readonly T[]) {
  return {
    navigate(path: T["path"]) {
      history.pushState({}, "", path);
    },
  };
}

const rtr = router([
  {
    path: "/",
    component: Main,
  },
  {
    path: "/about",
    component: About,
  },
] as const);

rtr.navigate("/about");
```

This works but also requires that we not forget a very important detail when coding. And actively remembering workarounds is always a recipe for disaster.

Thankfully, TypeScript allows us to request *const context* from generic type parameters. Instead of applying it to the value, we substitute the generic type parameter for a concrete value *but* in *const context* by adding the const modifier to the generic type parameter:

```
function router<const T extends Route>(routes: T[]) {
  return {
    navigate(path: T["path"]) {
      // tbd
    },
  };
}
```

We can then use our router just as we are accustomed to and even get autocomplete for possible paths:

```
const rtr = router([
  {
    path: "/",
    component: Main,
  },
```

```
      {
        path: "/about",
        component: About,
      },
    ])

    rtr.navigate("/about");
```

Even better, we get proper errors when we pass in something bogus:

```
    const rtr = router([
      {
        path: "/",
        component: Main,
      },
      {
        path: "/about",
        component: About,
      },
    ])

    rtr.navigate("/faq");
    //              ^
    // Argument of type '"/faq"' is not assignable to
    // parameter of type '"/" | "/about"'.(2345)
```

The beautiful thing: it's all hidden in the function's API. What we expect becomes clearer, the interface tells us the constraints, and we don't have to do anything extra when using router to ensure type safety.

CHAPTER 5

Conditional Types

In this chapter, we will take a good look at a feature that is unique to TypeScript: *conditional types*. Conditional types allow us to select types based on subtype checks, allowing us to move around in the type space and get even more flexibility in how we want to design interfaces and function signatures.

Conditional types are a powerful tool that allows you to make up types on the fly. It makes TypeScript's type system turing complete, as shown in this GitHub issue (*https://oreil.ly/igPhB*), which is both outstanding but also a bit frightening. With so much power in your hands, it's easy to lose focus on which types you actually need, leading you into dead ends or crafting types that are too hard to read. Throughout this book, we will discuss the usage of conditional types thoroughly, always reassessing that what we do actually leads to our desired goal.

Note that this chapter is much shorter than others. This is not because there's not a lot to say about conditional types: quite the contrary. It's more because we will see good use of conditional types in the subsequent chapters. Here, we want to focus on the fundamentals and establish terminology that you can use and refer to whenever you need some type magic.

5.1 Managing Complex Function Signatures

Problem

You are creating a function with varying parameters and return types. Managing all variations using function overloads gets increasingly complex.

Solution

Use conditional types to define a set of rules for parameter and return types.

Discussion

You create software that presents certain attributes as labels based on user-defined input. You distinguish between StringLabel and NumberLabel to allow for different kinds of filter operations and searches:

```
type StringLabel = {
  name: string;
};

type NumberLabel = {
  id: number;
};
```

User input is either a string or a number. The createLabel function takes the input as a primitive type and produces either a StringLabel or NumberLabel object:

```
function createLabel(input: number | string): NumberLabel | StringLabel {
  if (typeof input === "number") {
    return { id: input };
  } else {
    return { name: input };
  }
}
```

With the basic functionality done, you see that your types are way too broad. If you enter a number, the return type of createLabel is still NumberLabel | StringLabel, when it can only be NumberLabel. The solution? Adding function overloads to explicitly define type relationships, like we learned in Recipe 2.6:

```
function createLabel(input: number): NumberLabel;
function createLabel(input: string): StringLabel;
function createLabel(input: number | string): NumberLabel | StringLabel {
  if (typeof input === "number") {
    return { id: input };
  } else {
    return { name: input };
  }
}
```

The way function overloads work is that the overloads themselves define types for usage, whereas the last function declaration defines the types for the implementation of the function body. With createLabel, we are able to pass in a string and get a StringLabel or pass in a number and get a NumberLabel, as those are the types available to the outside.

This is problematic in cases where we couldn't narrow the input type beforehand. We lack a function type to the outside that allows us to pass in input that is either number or string:

```
function inputToLabel(input: string | number) {
  return createLabel(input);
  //                   ^
  // No overload matches this call. (2769)
}
```

To circumvent this, we add another overload that mirrors the implementation function signature for very broad input types:

```
function createLabel(input: number): NumberLabel;
function createLabel(input: string): StringLabel;
function createLabel(input: number | string): NumberLabel | StringLabel;
function createLabel(input: number | string): NumberLabel | StringLabel {
  if (typeof input === "number") {
    return { id: input };
  } else {
    return { name: input };
  }
}
```

What we see here is that we already need three overloads and four function signature declarations total to describe the most basic behavior for this functionality. And from there on, it just gets worse.

We want to extend our function to be able to copy existing StringLabel and Number Label objects. This ultimately means more overloads:

```
function createLabel(input: number): NumberLabel;
function createLabel(input: string): StringLabel;
function createLabel(input: StringLabel): StringLabel;
function createLabel(input: NumberLabel): NumberLabel;
function createLabel(input: string | StringLabel): StringLabel;
function createLabel(input: number | NumberLabel): NumberLabel;
function createLabel(
  input: number | string | StringLabel | NumberLabel
): NumberLabel | StringLabel;
function createLabel(
  input: number | string | StringLabel | NumberLabel
): NumberLabel | StringLabel {
  if (typeof input === "number") {
    return { id: input };
  } else if (typeof input === "string") {
    return { name: input };
  } else if ("id" in input) {
    return { id: input.id };
  } else {
    return { name: input.name };
  }
}
```

Truth be told, depending on how expressive we want our type hints to be, we can write fewer but also a lot more function overloads. The problem is still apparent: more variety results in more complex function signatures.

One tool in TypeScript's toolbelt can help with situations like this: conditional types. Conditional types allow us to select a type based on certain subtype checks. We ask if a generic type parameter is of a certain subtype and, if so, return the type from the true branch, or otherwise return the type from the false branch.

For example, the following type returns the input parameter if T is a subtype of string (which means all strings or very specific ones). Otherwise, it returns never:

```
type IsString<T> = T extends string ? T : never;

type A = IsString<string>; // string
type B = IsString<"hello" | "world">; // string
type C = IsString<1000>; // never
```

TypeScript borrows this syntax from JavaScript's ternary operator. And just like JavaScript's ternary operator, it checks if certain conditions are valid. But instead of having the typical set of conditions you know from a programming language, TypeScript's type system checks only if the values of the input type are included in the set of values we check against.

With that tool, we are able to write a conditional type called GetLabel<T>. We check if the input is either of string or StringLabel. If so, we return StringLabel; else, we know that it must be a NumberLabel:

```
type GetLabel<T> = T extends string | StringLabel ? StringLabel : NumberLabel;
```

This type only checks if the inputs string, StringLabel, number, and NumberLabel are in the else branch. If we want to be on the safe side, we would also include a check against possible inputs that produce a NumberLabel by nesting conditional types:

```
type GetLabel<T> = T extends string | StringLabel
  ? StringLabel
  : T extends number | NumberLabel
  ? NumberLabel
  : never;
```

Now it's time to wire up our generics. We add a new generic type parameter T to createLabel that is constrained to all possible input types. This T parameter serves as input for GetLabel<T>, where it will produce the respective return type:

```
function createLabel<T extends number | string | StringLabel | NumberLabel>(
  input: T
): GetLabel<T> {
  if (typeof input === "number") {
    return { id: input } as GetLabel<T>;
```

```
    } else if (typeof input === "string") {
      return { name: input } as GetLabel<T>;
    } else if ("id" in input) {
      return { id: input.id } as GetLabel<T>;
    } else {
      return { name: input.name } as GetLabel<T>;
    }
  }
```

Now we are ready to handle all possible type combinations and will still get the correct return type from getLabel, all in just one line of code.

If you look closely, you will see that we needed to work around type-checks for the return type. Unfortunately, TypeScript is not able to do proper control flow analysis when working with generics and conditional types. A little type assertion tells TypeScript that we are dealing with the right return type.

Another workaround would be to think of the function signature with conditional types as an overload to the original broadly typed function:

```
function createLabel<T extends number | string | StringLabel | NumberLabel>(
  input: T
): GetLabel<T>;
function createLabel(
  input: number | string | StringLabel | NumberLabel
): NumberLabel | StringLabel {
  if (typeof input === "number") {
    return { id: input };
  } else if (typeof input === "string") {
    return { name: input };
  } else if ("id" in input) {
    return { id: input.id };
  } else {
    return { name: input.name };
  }
}
```

This way, we have a flexible type for the outside world that tells exactly what output we get based on our input. And for implementation, you have the full flexibility you know from a broad set of types.

Does this mean you should prefer conditional types over function overloads in all scenarios? Not necessarily. In Recipe 12.7 we look at situations where function overloads are the better choice.

5.2 Filtering with never

Problem

You have a union of various types but you just want to have all subtypes of string.

Solution

Use a distributive conditional type to filter for the right type.

Discussion

Let's say you have some legacy code in your application where you tried to re-create frameworks like *jQuery*. You have your own kind of ElementList that has helper functions to add and remove class names to objects of type HTMLElement, or to bind event listeners to events.

Additionally, you can access each element of your list through index access. A type for such an ElementList can be described using an index access type for number index access, together with regular string property keys:

```
type ElementList = {
  addClass: (className: string) => ElementList;
  removeClass: (className: string) => ElementList;
  on: (event: string, callback: (ev: Event) => void) => ElementList;
  length: number;
  [x: number]: HTMLElement;
};
```

This data structure has been designed to have a fluent interface. Meaning that if you call methods like addClass or removeClass, you get the same object back so you can chain your method calls.

A sample implementation of these methods could look like this:

```
// begin excerpt
  addClass: function (className: string): ElementList {
    for (let i = 0; i < this.length; i++) {
      this[i].classList.add(className);
    }
    return this;
  },
  removeClass: function (className: string): ElementList {
    for (let i = 0; i < this.length; i++) {
      this[i].classList.remove(className);
    }
    return this;
  },
  on: function (event: string, callback: (ev: Event) => void): ElementList {
    for (let i = 0; i < this.length; i++) {
      this[i].addEventListener(event, callback);
    }
    return this;
  },
// end excerpt
```

As an extension of a built-in collection like `Array` or `NodeList`, changing things on a set of `HTMLElement` objects becomes really convenient:

```
declare const myCollection: ElementList;

myCollection
  .addClass("toggle-off")
  .removeClass("toggle-on")
  .on("click", (e) => {});
```

Let's say you need to maintain your *jQuery* substitute and figure out that direct element access has proven to be somewhat unsafe. When parts of your application can change things directly, it becomes harder for you to figure out where changes come from, if not from your carefully designed `ElementList` data structure:

```
myCollection[1].classList.toggle("toggle-on");
```

Since you can't change the original library code (too many departments depend on it), you decide to wrap the original `ElementList` in a `Proxy`.

`Proxy` objects take an original target object and a handler object that defines how to handle access. The following implementation shows a `Proxy` that allows only read access, and only if the property key is of type `string` and not a string that is a string representation of a number:

```
const safeAccessCollection = new Proxy(myCollection, {
  get(target, property) {
    if (
      typeof property === "string" &&
      property in target &&
      "" + parseInt(property) !== property
    ) {
      return target[property as keyof typeof target];
    }
    return undefined;
  },
});
```

> Handler objects in `Proxy` objects receive only string or symbol properties. If you do index access with a number—for example, `0`—JavaScript converts this to the string `"0"`.

This works great in JavaScript, but our types don't match anymore. The return type of the `Proxy` constructor is `ElementList` again, which means that the number index access is still intact:

```
// Works in TypeScript throws in JavaScript
safeAccessCollection[0].classList.toggle("toggle-on");
```

We need to tell TypeScript that we are now dealing with an object with no number index access by defining a new type.

Let's look at the keys of `ElementList`. If we use the `keyof` operator, we get a union type of all possible access methods for objects of type `ElementList`:

```
// resolves to "addClass" | "removeClass" | "on" | "length" | number
type ElementListKeys = keyof ElementList;
```

It contains four strings as well as all possible numbers. Now that we have this union, we can create a conditional type that gets rid of everything that isn't a string:

```
type JustStrings<T> = T extends string ? T : never;
```

`JustStrings<T>` is what we call a *distributive conditional type*. Since T is on its own in the condition—not wrapped in an object or array—TypeScript will treat a conditional type of a union as a union of conditional types. Effectively, TypeScript does the same conditional check for every member of the union T.

In our case, it goes through all members of `keyof ElementList`:

```
type JustElementListStrings =
  | "addClass" extends string ? "addClass" : never
  | "removeClass" extends string ? "removeClass" : never
  | "on" extends string ? "on" : never
  | "length" extends string ? "length" : never
  | number extends string ? number : never;
```

The only condition that hops into the `false` branch is the last one, where we check if `number` is a subtype of `string`, which it isn't. If we resolve every condition, we end up with a new union type:

```
type JustElementListStrings =
  | "addClass"
  | "removeClass"
  | "on"
  | "length"
  | never;
```

A union with `never` effectively drops `never`. If you have a set with no possible value and you join it with a set of values, the values remain:

```
type JustElementListStrings =
  | "addClass"
  | "removeClass"
  | "on"
  | "length";
```

This is exactly the list of keys we consider safe to access! By using the `Pick` helper type, we can create a type that is effectively a supertype of `ElementList` by picking all keys that are of type `string`:

```
type SafeAccess = Pick<ElementList, JustStrings<keyof ElementList>>;
```

If we hover over it, we see that the resulting type is exactly what we were looking for:

```
type SafeAccess = {
  addClass: (className: string) => ElementList;
  removeClass: (className: string) => ElementList;
  on: (event: string, callback: (ev: Event) => void) => ElementList;
  length: number;
};
```

Let's add the type as an annotation to `safeAccessCollection`. Since it's possible to assign to a supertype, TypeScript will treat `safeAccessCollection` as a type with no number index access from that moment on:

```
const safeAccessCollection: Pick<
  ElementList,
  JustStrings<keyof ElementList>
> = new Proxy(myCollection, {
  get(target, property) {
    if (
      typeof property === "string" &&
      property in target &&
      "" + parseInt(property) !== property
    ) {
      return target[property as keyof typeof target];
    }
    return undefined;
  },
});
```

When we now try to access elements from `safeAccessCollection`, TypeScript will greet us with an error:

```
safeAccessCollection[1].classList.toggle("toggle-on");
// ^ Element implicitly has an 'any' type because expression of
// type '1' can't be used to index type
// 'Pick<ElementList, "addClass" | "removeClass" | "on" | "length">'.
```

And that's exactly what we need. The power of distributive conditional types is that we change members of a union. We will see another example in Recipe 5.3, where we work with built-in helper types.

5.3 Grouping Elements by Kind

Problem

Your Group type from Recipe 4.5 works fine, but the type for each entry of the group is too broad.

Solution

Use the `Extract` helper type to pick the right member from a union type.

Discussion

Let's go back to the toy shop example from Recipes 3.1 and 4.5. We started with a thoughtfully crafted model, with discriminated union types allowing us to get exact information about every possible value:

```
type ToyBase = {
  name: string;
  description: string;
  minimumAge: number;
};

type BoardGame = ToyBase & {
  kind: "boardgame";
  players: number;
};

type Puzzle = ToyBase & {
  kind: "puzzle";
  pieces: number;
};

type Doll = ToyBase & {
  kind: "doll";
  material: "plush" | "plastic";
};

type Toy = Doll | Puzzle | BoardGame;
```

We then found a way to *derive* another type called `GroupedToys` from `Toy`, where we take the union type members of the `kind` property as property keys for a mapped type, where each property is of type `Toy[]`:

```
type GroupedToys = {
  [k in Toy["kind"]]?: Toy[];
};
```

Thanks to generics, we were able to define a helper type `Group<Collection, Selector>` to reuse the same pattern for different scenarios:

```
type Group<
  Collection extends Record<string, any>,
  Selector extends keyof Collection
> = {
  [K in Collection[Selector]]: Collection[];
};

type GroupedToys = Partial<Group<Toy, "kind">>;
```

The helper type works great, but there's one caveat. If we hover over the generated type, we see that while Group<Collection, Selector> is able to pick the discriminant of the Toy union type correctly, all properties point to a very broad Toy[]:

```
type GroupedToys = {
  boardgame?: Toy[] | undefined;
  puzzle?: Toy[] | undefined;
  doll?: Toy[] | undefined;
};
```

But shouldn't we know more? For example, why does boardgame point to a Toy[] when the only realistic type should be BoardGame[]. Same for puzzles and dolls, and all the subsequent toys we want to add to our collection. The type we are expecting should look more like this:

```
type GroupedToys = {
  boardgame?: BoardGame[] | undefined;
  puzzle?: Puzzle[] | undefined;
  doll?: Doll[] | undefined;
};
```

We can achieve this type by *extracting* the respective member from the Collection union type. Thankfully, there is a helper type for that: Extract<T, U>, where T is the collection, U is part of T.

Extract<T, U> is defined as:

```
type Extract<T, U> = T extends U ? T : never;
```

As T in the condition is a naked type, T is a *distributive conditional type*, which means TypeScript checks if each member of T is a subtype of U, and if this is the case, it keeps this member in the union type. How would this work for picking the right group of toys from Toy?

Let's say we want to pick Doll from Toy. Doll has a couple of properties, but the kind property separates distinctly from the rest. So for a type to look only for Doll would mean that we extract *from* Toy every type where { kind: "doll" }:

```
type ExtractedDoll = Extract<Toy, { kind: "doll" }>;
```

With distributive conditional types, a conditional type of a union is a union of conditional types, so each member of T is checked against U:

```
type ExtractedDoll =
  BoardGame extends { kind: "doll" } ? BoardGame : never |
  Puzzle extends { kind: "doll" } ? Puzzle : never |
  Doll extends { kind: "doll" } ? Doll : never;
```

Both BoardGame and Puzzle are not subtypes of { kind: "doll" }, so they resolve to never. But Doll *is* a subtype of { kind: "doll" }, so it resolves to Doll:

```
type ExtractedDoll = never | never | Doll;
```

In a union with never, never just disappears. So the resulting type is `Doll`:

```
type ExtractedDoll = Doll;
```

This is exactly what we are looking for. Let's get that check into our `Group` helper type. Thankfully, we have all parts available to extract a specific type from a group's collection:

- The `Collection` itself, a placeholder that eventually is substituted with `Toy`
- The discriminant property in `Selector`, which eventually is substituted with `"kind"`
- The discriminant type we want to extract, which is a string type and coincidentally also the property key we map out in `Group`: K

So the generic version of `Extract<Toy, { kind: "doll" }>` within `Group<Collection, Selector>` is this:

```
type Group<
  Collection extends Record<string, any>,
  Selector extends keyof Collection
> = {
  [K in Collection[Selector]]: Extract<Collection, { [P in Selector]: K }>[];
};
```

If we substitute `Collection` with `Toy` and `Selector` with `"kind"`, the type reads as follows:

`[K in Collection[Selector]]`
Take each member of `Toy["kind"]`—in that case, `"boardgame"`, `"puzzle"`, and `"doll"`—as a property key for a new object type.

`Extract<Collection, …>`
Extract from the `Collection`, the union type `Toy`, each member that is a subtype of…

`{ [P in Selector]: K }`
Go through each member of `Selector`—in our case, it's just `"kind"`—and create an object type that points to `"boardgame"` when the property key is `"boardgame"`, `"puzzle"` when the property key is `"puzzle"`, and so on.

That's how we pick for each property key the right member of `Toy`. The result is as expected:

```
type GroupedToys = Partial<Group<Toy, "kind">>;
// resolves to:
type GroupedToys = {
  boardgame?: BoardGame[] | undefined;
  puzzle?: Puzzle[] | undefined;
```

```
    doll?: Doll[] | undefined;
};
```

Fantastic! The type is now a lot clearer, and we can make sure that we don't need to deal with puzzles when we selected board games. But some new problems have popped up.

Since the types of each property are much more refined and don't point to the very broad Toy type, TypeScript struggles a bit with resolving each collection in our group correctly:

```
function groupToys(toys: Toy[]): GroupedToys {
  const groups: GroupedToys = {};
  for (let toy of toys) {
    groups[toy.kind] = groups[toy.kind] ?? [];
//  ^ Type 'BoardGame[] | Doll[] | Puzzle[]' is not assignable to
//    type '(BoardGame[] & Puzzle[] & Doll[]) | undefined'. (2322)
    groups[toy.kind]?.push(toy);
//                    ^
//  Argument of type 'Toy' is not assignable to
//  parameter of type 'never'. (2345)
  }
  return groups;
}
```

The problem is that TypeScript still thinks of toy as potentially being all toys, whereas each property of group points to some very specific ones. There are three ways to solve this issue.

First, we could again check for each member individually. Since TypeScript thinks of toy as a very broad type, narrowing makes the relationship clear again:

```
function groupToys(toys: Toy[]): GroupedToys {
  const groups: GroupedToys = {};
  for (let toy of toys) {
    switch (toy.kind) {
      case "boardgame":
        groups[toy.kind] = groups[toy.kind] ?? [];
        groups[toy.kind]?.push(toy);
        break;
      case "doll":
        groups[toy.kind] = groups[toy.kind] ?? [];
        groups[toy.kind]?.push(toy);
        break;
      case "puzzle":
        groups[toy.kind] = groups[toy.kind] ?? [];
        groups[toy.kind]?.push(toy);
        break;
    }
  }
  return groups;
}
```

That works, but there's lots of duplication and repetition we want to avoid.

Second, we can use a type assertion to widen the type of groups[toy.kind] so Type-Script can ensure index access:

```
function groupToys(toys: Toy[]): GroupedToys {
  const groups: GroupedToys = {};
  for (let toy of toys) {
    (groups[toy.kind] as Toy[]) = groups[toy.kind] ?? [];
    (groups[toy.kind] as Toy[])?.push(toy);
  }
  return groups;
}
```

This effectively works like before our change to GroupedToys, and the type assertion tells us that we intentionally changed the type here to get rid of type errors.

Third, we can work with a little indirection. Instead of adding toy directly to a group, we use a helper function **assign** where we work with generics:

```
function groupToys(toys: Toy[]): GroupedToys {
  const groups: GroupedToys = {};
  for (let toy of toys) {
    assign(groups, toy.kind, toy);
  }
  return groups;
}

function assign<T extends Record<string, K[]>, K>(
  groups: T,
  key: keyof T,
  value: K
) {
  // Initialize when not available
  groups[key] = groups[key] ?? [];
  groups[key]?.push(value);
}
```

Here, we narrow the right member of the Toy union by using TypeScript's generic substitution:

- groups is T, a Record<string, K[]>. K[] can be potentially broad.
- key is in relation to T: a property key of T.
- value is of type K.

All three function parameters are in relation to one another, and the way we designed the type relations allows us to safely access groups[key] and push value to the array.

Also, the types of each parameter when we call `assign` fulfill the generic type constraints we just set. If you want to know more about this technique, check out Recipe 12.6.

5.4 Removing Specific Object Properties

Problem

You want to create a generic helper type for objects, where you select properties based on their type rather than the property's name.

Solution

Filter with conditional types and type assertions when mapping property keys.

Discussion

TypeScript allows you to create types based on other types, so you can keep them up to date without maintaining every one of their derivates. We've seen examples in earlier items, like Recipe 4.5. In the following scenario, we want to adapt an existing object type based on the types of its properties. Let's look at a type for `Person`:

```
type Person = {
  name: string;
  age: number;
  profession?: string;
};
```

It consists of two strings—`profession` and `name`—and a number: `age`. We want to create a type that consists only of string type properties:

```
type PersonStrings = {
  name: string;
  profession?: string;
};
```

TypeScript already has certain helper types to deal with filtering property names. For example, the mapped type `Pick<T>` takes a subset of an object's keys to create a new object that contains only those keys:

```
type Pick<T, K extends keyof T> = {
  [P in K]: T[P];
}

// Only includes "name"
type PersonName = Pick<Person, "name">;

// Includes "name" and "profession"
type PersonStrings = Pick<Person, "name" | "profession">;
```

If we want to remove certain properties, we can use `Omit<T>`, which works just like `Pick<T>` with the small difference that we map through a slightly altered set of properties, one where we remove property names that we don't want to include:

```
type Omit<T, K extends string | number | symbol> = {
  [P in Exclude<keyof T, K>]: T[P];
}

// Omits age, thus includes "name" and "profession"
type PersonWithoutAge = Omit<Person, "age">;
```

To select the right properties based on their type, rather than their name, we would need to create a similar helper type, one where we map a dynamically generated set of property names that point only to the types we are looking for. We know from Recipe 5.2 that when using conditional types over a union type, we can use `never` to filter elements from this union.

So a first possibility could be that we map all property keys of `Person` and check if `Person[K]` is a subset of our desired type. If so, we return the type; otherwise, we return `never`:

```
// Not there yet
type PersonStrings = {
  [K in keyof Person]: Person[K] extends string ? Person[K] : never;
};
```

This is good, but it comes with a caveat: the types we are checking are not in a union but are types from a mapped type. So instead of filtering property keys, we would get properties that point to type `never`, meaning that we would forbid certain properties to be set at all.

Another idea would be to set the type to `undefined`, treating the property as sort of optional but, as we learned in Recipe 3.11, missing properties and undefined values are not the same.

What we actually want to do is drop the property keys that point to a certain type. This can be achieved by putting the condition not on the righthand side of the object but on the lefthand side, where the properties are created.

Just like with the `Omit` type, we need to make sure that we map over a specific set of properties. When mapping `keyof Person`, it is possible to change the type of the property key with a type assertion. Just like with regular type assertions, there is a sort of fail-safe mechanism, meaning you just can't assert it to be anything: it has to be within the boundaries of a property key.

We want to assert that K part of the set if `Person[K]` is of type `string`. If this is true, we keep K; otherwise, we filter the element of the set with `never`. With `never` being on the lefthand side of the object, the property gets dropped:

```
type PersonStrings = {
  [K in keyof Person as Person[K] extends string ? K : never]: Person[K];
};
```

And with that, we select only property keys that point to string values. There is one catch: optional string properties have a broader type than regular strings, as undefined is also included as a possible value. Using a union type ensures that optional properties are also kept:

```
type PersonStrings = {
  [K in keyof Person as Person[K] extends string | undefined
    ? K
    : never]: Person[K];
};
```

The next step is making this type generic. We create a type Select<O, T> by replacing Person with O and string with T:

```
type Select<O, T> = {
  [K in keyof O as O[K] extends T | undefined ? K : never]: O[K];
};
```

This new helper type is versatile. We can use it to select properties of a certain type from our own object types:

```
type PersonStrings = Select<Person, string>;
type PersonNumbers = Select<Person, number>;
```

But we can also figure out, for example, which functions in the string prototype return a number:

```
type StringFnsReturningNumber = Select<String, (...args: any[]) => number>;
```

An inverse helper type Remove<O, T>, where we want to remove property keys of a certain type, is very similar to Select<O, T>. The only difference is to switch the condition and return never in the true branch:

```
type Remove<O, T> = {
  [K in keyof O as O[K] extends T | undefined ? never : K]: O[K];
};
```

```
type PersonWithoutStrings = Remove<Person, string>;
```

This is especially helpful if you create a serializable version of your object types:

```
type User = {
  name: string;
  age: number;
  profession?: string;
  posts(): string[];
  greeting(): string;
};
```

```
type SerializeableUser = Remove<User, Function>;
```

By knowing that you can do conditional types while mapping out keys, you suddenly have access to a wide range of potential helper types. More about that in Chapter 8.

5.5 Inferring Types in Conditionals

Problem

You want to create a class for object serialization, which removes all unserializable properties of an object like functions. If your object has a `serialize` function, the serializer takes the return value of the function instead of serializing the object on its own. How can you type that?

Solution

Use a recursive conditional type to modify the existing object type. For objects that implement `serialize`, use the `infer` keyword to pin the generic return type to a concrete type.

Discussion

Serialization is the process of converting data structures and objects into a format that can be stored or transferred. Think of taking a JavaScript object and storing its data on disk, just to pick it up later by deserializing it again into JavaScript.

JavaScript objects can hold any type of data: primitive types like strings or numbers, as well as compound types like objects, and even functions. Functions are interesting as they don't contain data but behavior: something that can't be serialized well. One approach to serializing JavaScript objects is to get rid of functions entirely. And this is what we want to implement in this lesson.

We start with a simple object type `Person`, which contains the usual subjects of data we want to store: a person's name and age. It also has a `hello` method, which produces a string:

```
type Person = {
  name: string;
  age: number;
  hello: () => string;
};
```

We want to serialize objects of this type. A `Serializer` class contains an empty constructor and a generic function `serialize`. Note that we add the generic type parameter to `serialize` and not to the class. That way, we can reuse `serialize` for different object types. The return type points to a generic type `Serialize<T>`, which will be the result of the serialization process:

```
class Serializer {
  constructor() {}
  serialize<T>(obj: T): Serialize<T> {
    // tbd...
  }
}
```

We will take care of the implementation later. For now let's focus on the `Serialize<T>` type. The first idea that comes to mind is to just drop properties that are functions. We already defined a `Remove<O, T>` type in Recipe 5.4 that comes in handy, as it does exactly that—removes properties that are of a certain type:

```
type Remove<O, T> = {
  [K in keyof O as O[K] extends T | undefined ? never : K]: O[K];
};

type Serialize<T> = Remove<T, Function>;
```

The first iteration is done, and it works for simple, one-level-deep objects. Objects can be complex, however. For example, `Person` could nest other objects, which in turn also could have functions:

```
type Person = {
  name: string;
  age: number;
  profession: {
    title: string;
    level: number;
    printProfession: () => void;
  };
  hello: () => string;
};
```

To solve this, we need to check each property if it is another object, and if so, use the `Serialize<T>` type again. A mapped type called `NestSerialization` checks in a conditional type if each property is of type `object` and returns a serialized version of that type in the `true` branch and the type itself in the `false` branch:

```
type NestSerialization<T> = {
  [K in keyof T]: T[K] extends object ? Serialize<T[K]> : T[K];
};
```

We redefine `Serialize<T>` by wrapping the original `Remove<T, Function>` type of `Serialize<T>` in `NestSerialization`, effectively creating a *recursive type*: `Serialize<T>` uses `NestSerialization<T>` uses `Serialize<T>`, and so on:

```
type Serialize<T> = NestSerialization<Remove<T, Function>>;
```

TypeScript can handle type recursion to a certain degree. In this case, it can see that there is literally a condition to break out of type recursion in `NestSerialization`.

And that's serialization type! Now for the implementation of the function, which is curiously a straight translation of our type declaration in JavaScript. We check for every property if it's an object. If so, we call `serialize` again. If not, we carry over the property only if it isn't a function:

```
class Serializer {
  constructor() {}
  serialize<T>(obj: T): Serialize<T> {
    const ret: Record<string, any> = {};

    for (let k in obj) {
      if (typeof obj[k] === "object") {
        ret[k] = this.serialize(obj[k]);
      } else if (typeof obj[k] !== "function") {
        ret[k] = obj[k];
      }
    }
    return ret as Serialize<T>;
  }
}
```

Note that since we are generating a new object within `serialize`, we start out with a very broad `Record<string, any>`, which allows us to set any string property key to basically anything, and assert at the end that we created an object that fits our return type. This pattern is common when you create new objects, but it ultimately requires you to be 100% sure that you did everything right. Please test this function extensively.

With the first implementation done, we can create a new object of type `Person` and pass it to our newly generated serializer:

```
const person: Person = {
  name: "Stefan",
  age: 40,
  profession: {
    title: "Software Developer",
    level: 5,
    printProfession() {
      console.log(`${this.title}, Level ${this.level}`);
    },
  },
  hello() {
    return `Hello ${this.name}`;
  },
};

const serializer = new Serializer();
const serializedPerson = serializer.serialize(person);
console.log(serializedPerson);
```

The result is as expected: the type of `serializedPerson` lacks all information on methods and functions. And if we log `serializedPerson`, we also see that all methods and functions are gone. The type matches the implementation result:

```
[LOG]: {
  "name": "Stefan",
  "age": 40,
  "profession": {
    "title": "Software Developer",
    "level": 5
  }
}
```

But we are not done yet. The serializer has a special feature. Objects can implement a `serialize` method, and if they do, the serializer takes the output of this method instead of serializing the object on its own. Let's extend the `Person` type to feature a `serialize` method:

```
type Person = {
  name: string;
  age: number;
  profession: {
    title: string;
    level: number;
    printProfession: () => void;
  };
  hello: () => string;
  serialize: () => string;
};

const person: Person = {
  name: "Stefan",
  age: 40,
  profession: {
    title: "Software Developer",
    level: 5,
    printProfession() {
      console.log(`${this.title}, Level ${this.level}`);
    },
  },
  hello() {
    return `Hello ${this.name}`;
  },
  serialize() {
    return `${this.name}: ${this.profession.title} L${this.profession.level}`;
  },
};
```

We need to adapt the `Serialize<T>` type. Before running `NestSerialization`, we check in a conditional type if the object implements a `serialize` method. We do so by asking if T is a subtype of a type that contains a `serialize` method. If so, we need to get to the return type, because that's the result of serialization.

This is where the `infer` keyword comes into play. It allows us to take a type from a condition and use it as a type parameter in the `true` branch. We tell TypeScript, if this condition is true, take the type that you found there and make it available to us:

```
type Serialize<T> = T extends { serialize(): infer R }
  ? R
  : NestSerialization<Remove<T, Function>>;
```

Think of R as being any at first. If we check `Person` against `{ serialize(): any }` we hop into the `true` branch, as `Person` has a `serialize` function, making it a valid subtype. But any is broad, and we are interested in the specific type at the position of any. The `infer` keyword can pick that exact type. So `Serialize<T>` now reads:

- If T contains a `serialize` method, get its return type and return it.
- Otherwise, start serialization by deeply removing all properties that are of type `Function`.

We want to mirror that type's behavior in our JavaScript implementation as well. We do a couple of type-checks (checking if `serialize` is available and if it's a function) and ultimately call it. TypeScript requires us to be explicit with type guards, to be absolutely sure that this function exists:

```
class Serializer {
  constructor() {}
  serialize<T>(obj: T): Serialize<T> {
    if (
      // is an object
      typeof obj === "object" &&
      // not null
      obj &&
      // serialize is available
      "serialize" in obj &&
      // and a function
      typeof obj.serialize === "function"
    ) {
      return obj.serialize();
    }

    const ret: Record<string, any> = {};

    for (let k in obj) {
      if (typeof obj[k] === "object") {
        ret[k] = this.serialize(obj[k]);
      } else if (typeof obj[k] !== "function") {
```

```
        ret[k] = obj[k];
      }
    }
    return ret as Serialize<T>;
  }
}
```

With this change, the type of serializedPerson is string, and the result is as expected:

```
[LOG]: "Stefan: Software Developer L5"
```

This powerful tool helps greatly with object generation. And there's beauty in the fact that we create a type using a declarative metalanguage that is TypeScript's type system, to ultimately see the same process imperatively written in JavaScript.

CHAPTER 6

String Template Literal Types

In TypeScript's type system, every value is also a type. We call them literal types, and in union with other literal types, you can define a type that is very clear about which values it can accept. Let's take subsets of `string` as an example. You can define exactly which strings should be part of your set and rule out a ton of errors. The other end of the spectrum would be the entire set of strings again.

But what if there is something between? What if we can define types that check if certain string patterns are available, and let the rest be more flexible? *String template literal types* do exactly that. They allow us to define types where certain parts of a string are predefined; the rest is open and flexible for a variety of uses.

But even more, in conjunction with conditional types, it's possible to split strings into bits and pieces and reuse the same bits for new types. This is an incredibly powerful tool, especially if you think about how much code in JavaScript relies on patterns within strings.

In this chapter, we look at a variety of use cases for *string template literal types*. From following simple string patterns to extracting parameters and types based on format strings, you will see the enabling power of parsing strings as types.

But we keep it real. Everything you see here comes from real-world examples. What you can accomplish with string template literal types seems endless. People push the usage of string template literal types to the extreme by writing spell checkers (*https://oreil.ly/63z2Y*) or implementing SQL parsers (*https://oreil.ly/foSvx*); there seems to be no limit to what you can do with this mind-blowing feature.

6.1 Defining a Custom Event System

Problem

You are creating a custom event system and want to make sure every event name follows a convention and starts with "on".

Solution

Use string template literal types to describe string patterns.

Discussion

It's common in JavaScript event systems to have some sort of prefix that indicates a particular string is an event. Usually, event or event handler strings start with on, but depending on the implementation, this can be different.

You want to create your own event system and want to honor this convention. With TypeScript's string types it is possible to either accept all possible strings or subset to a union type of string literal types. While one is too broad, the other one is not flexible enough for our needs. We don't want to define every possible event name up front; we want to adhere to a pattern.

Thankfully, a type called *string template literal type* or just *template literal type* is exactly what we are looking for. Template literal types allow us to define string literals but leave certain parts flexible.

For example, a type that accepts all strings that start with on could look like this:

```
type EventName = `on${string}`;
```

Syntactically, template literal types borrow from JavaScript's *template strings*. They start and end with a backtick, followed by any string.

Using the specific syntax ${} allows adding JavaScript expressions, like variables, function calls, and the like to strings:

```
function greet(name: string) {
  return `Hi, ${name}!`;
}

greet("Stefan"); // "Hi, Stefan!"
```

Template literal types in TypeScript are very similar. Instead of JavaScript expressions, they allow us to add a set of values in the form of types. A type defining the string representation of all available heading elements in HTML could look like this:

```
type Levels = 1 | 2 | 3 | 4 | 5 | 6;

// resolves to "H1" | "H2" | "H3" | "H4" | "H5" | "H6"
type Headings = `H${Levels}`;
```

Levels is a subset of number, and Headings reads as "starts with H, followed by a value compatible with Levels." You can't put every type in here, only ones that have a string representation.

Let's go back to EventName:

```
type EventName = `on${string}`;
```

Defined like this, EventName reads like "starts with "on", followed by any string." This includes the empty string. Let's use EventName to create a simple event system. In the first step, we only want to collect callback functions.

For that, we define a Callback type that is a function type with one parameter: an EventObject. The EventObject is a generic type that contains the value with the event information:

```
type EventObject<T> = {
  val: T;
};

type Callback<T = any> = (ev: EventObject<T>) => void;
```

Furthermore, we need a type to store all registered event callbacks, Events:

```
type Events = {
  [x: EventName]: Callback[] | undefined;
};
```

We use EventName as index access as it is a valid subtype of string. Each index points to an array of callbacks. With our types defined, we set up an EventSystem class:

```
class EventSystem {
  events: Events;
  constructor() {
    this.events = {};
  }

  defineEventHandler(ev: EventName, cb: Callback): void {
    this.events[ev] = this.events[ev] ?? [];
    this.events[ev]?.push(cb);
  }

  trigger(ev: EventName, value: any) {
    let callbacks = this.events[ev];
```

```
      if (callbacks) {
        callbacks.forEach((cb) => {
          cb({ val: value });
        });
      }
    }
  }
}
```

The constructor creates a new events storage, and `defineEventHandler` takes an `EventName` and `Callback` and stores them in said events storage. Also, `trigger` takes an `EventName` and, if callbacks are registered, executes every registered callback with an `EventObject`.

The first step is done. We now have type safety when defining events:

```
const system = new EventSystem();
system.defineEventHandler("click", () => {});
// ^ Argument of type '"click"' is not assignable to parameter
//. of type '`on${string}`'.(2345)
system.defineEventHandler("onClick", () => {});
system.defineEventHandler("onchange", () => {});
```

In Recipe 6.2 we will look at how we can use string manipulation types and key remapping to enhance our system.

6.2 Creating Event Callbacks with String Manipulation Types and Key Remapping

Problem

You want to provide a `watch` function that takes any object and adds watcher functions for each property, allowing you to define event callbacks.

Solution

Use *key remapping* to create new string property keys. Use *string manipulation types* to have proper camel casing for watcher functions.

Discussion

Our event system from Recipe 6.1 is taking shape. We are able to register event handlers and trigger events. Now we want to add watch functionality. The idea is to extend valid objects with methods for registering callbacks that are executed every time a property changes. For example, when we define a `person` object, we should be able to listen to `onAgeChanged` and `onNameChanged` events:

```
let person = {
  name: "Stefan",
```

```
    age: 40,
};

const watchedPerson = system.watch(person);

watchedPerson.onAgeChanged((ev) => {
  console.log(ev.val, "changed!!");
});

watchedPerson.age = 41; // triggers callbacks
```

So for each property, there will be a method that starts with `on`, ends with `Changed`, and accepts callback functions with event object parameters.

To define the new event handler methods, we create a helper type called `Watched Object<T>`, where we add bespoke methods:

```
type WatchedObject<T> = {
  [K in string & keyof T as `on${K}Changed`]: (
    ev: Callback<T[K]>
  ) => void;
};
```

There's a lot to unpack. Let's go through it step by step:

1. We define a *mapped type* by iterating over all keys from `T`. Since we care only about `string` property keys, we use the intersection `string & keyof T` to get rid of potential symbols or numbers.

2. Next, we *remap* this key to a new string, defined by a *string template literal type*. It starts with `on`, then takes the key `K` from our mapping process, and appends `Changed`.

3. The property key points to a function that accepts a callback. The callback itself has an event object as an argument, and by correctly substituting its generics, we can make sure this event object contains the original type of our watched object. This means when we call `onAgeChanged`, the event object will actually contain a `number`.

This is already fantastic but lacks significant detail. When we use `WatchedObject` on `person` like that, all generated event handler methods lack an uppercase character after `on`. To solve this, we can use one of the built-in *string manipulation types* to capitalize string types:

```
type WatchedObject<T> = {
  [K in string & keyof T as `on${Capitalize<K>}Changed`]: (
    ev: Callback<T[K]>
  ) => void;
};
```

Next to `Capitalize`, `Lowercase`, `Uppercase`, and `Uncapitalize` are also available. If we hover over `WatchedObject<typeof person>`, we can see what the generated type looks like:

```
type WatchedPerson = {
  onNameChanged: (ev: Callback<string>) => void;
  onAgeChanged: (ev: Callback<number>) => void;
};
```

With our types set up, we start with the implementation. First, we create two helper functions:

```
function capitalize(inp: string) {
  return inp.charAt(0).toUpperCase() + inp.slice(1);
}

function handlerName(name: string): EventName {
  return `on${capitalize(name)}Changed` as EventName;
}
```

We need both helper functions to mimic TypeScript's behavior of remapping and manipulating strings. `capitalize` changes the first letter of a string to its uppercase equivalent, and `handlerName` adds a prefix and suffix to it. With `handlerName` we need a little type assertion to signal TypeScript that the type has changed. With the many ways we can transform strings in JavaScript, TypeScript can't figure out that this will result in a capitalized version.

Next, we implement the `watch` functionality in the event system. We create a generic function that accepts any object and returns an object that contains both the original properties and the watcher properties.

To successfully implement triggering of event handlers on property change, we use Proxy objects to intercept `get` and `set` calls:

```
class EventSystem {
  // cut for brevity
  watch<T extends object>(obj: T): T & WatchedObject<T> {
    const self = this;
    return new Proxy(obj, {
      get(target, property) {
        // (1)
        if (
          typeof property === "string" &&
          property.startsWith("on") &&
          property.endsWith("Changed")
        ) {
          // (2)
          return (cb: Callback) => {
            self.defineEventHandler(property as EventName, cb);
          };
        }
```

```
      // (3)
      return target[property as keyof T];
    },
    // set to be done ...
  }) as T & WatchedObject<T>;
 }
}
```

The `get` calls we want to intercept are whenever we access the properties of `WatchedObject<T>`:

- They start with `on` and end with `Changed`.
- If that's the case, we return a function that accepts callbacks. The function itself adds callbacks to the event storage via `defineEventHandler`.
- In all other cases we do regular property access.

Now, every time we set a value of the original object, we want to trigger stored events. This is why we modify all `set` calls:

```
class EventSystem {
  // ... cut for brevity
  watch<T extends object>(obj: T): T & WatchedObject<T> {
    const self = this;
    return new Proxy(obj, {
      // get from above ...
      set(target, property, value) {
        if (property in target && typeof property === "string") {
          // (1)
          target[property as keyof T] = value;
          // (2)
          self.trigger(handlerName(property), value);
          return true;
        }
        return false;
      },
    }) as T & WatchedObject<T>;
  }
}
```

The process is as follows:

1. Set the value. We need to update the object anyway.
2. Call the `trigger` function to execute all registered callbacks.

Please note that we need a couple of type assertions to nudge TypeScript in the right direction. We are creating new objects, after all.

And that's it! Try the example from the beginning to see your event system in action:

```
let person = {
  name: "Stefan",
  age: 40,
};

const watchedPerson = system.watch(person);

watchedPerson.onAgeChanged((ev) => {
  console.log(ev.val, "changed!!");
});

watchedPerson.age = 41; // logs "41 changed!!"
```

String template literal types along with string manipulation types and key remapping allow us to create types for new objects on the fly. These powerful tools make the use of advanced JavaScript object creation more robust.

6.3 Writing a Formatter Function

Problem

You want to create typings for a function that takes a format string and substitutes placeholders with actual values.

Solution

Create a conditional type that infers the placeholder name from a string template literal type.

Discussion

Your application has a way of defining format strings by defining placeholders with curly braces. A second parameter takes an object with substitutions, so for each placeholder defined in the format string, there is one property key with the respective value:

```
format("Hello {world}. My name is {you}.", {
  world: "World",
  you: "Stefan",
});
```

Let's create typings for this function, where we make sure that your users don't forget to add the required properties. As a first step, we define the function interface with some very broad types. The format string is of type string, and the formatting parameters are in a Record of string keys and literally any value. We focus on the types first; the function body's implementation comes later:

```
function format(fmtString: string, params: Record<string, any>): string {
  throw "unimplemented";
}
```

As a next step, we want to lock function arguments to concrete values or literal types by adding generics. We change the type of fmtString to be of a generic type T, which is a subtype of string. This allows us to still pass strings to the function, but the moment we pass a literal string, we can analyze the literal type and look for patterns (see Recipe 4.3 for more details):

```
function format<T extends string>(
  fmtString: T,
  params: Record<string, any>
): string {
  throw "unimplemented";
}
```

Now that we locked in T, we can pass it as a type parameter to a generic type Format Keys. This is a conditional type that will scan our format string for curly braces:

```
type FormatKeys<
  T extends string
> = T extends `${string}{${string}}${string}`
  ? T
  : never;
```

Here, we check if the format string:

- Starts with a string; this can also be an empty string

- Contains a {, followed by any string, followed by a }

- Is followed again by any string

This effectively means that we check if there is exactly one placeholder in the format string. If so, we return the entire format string, and if not, we return never:

```
type A = FormatKeys<"Hello {world}">; // "Hello {world}"
type B = FormatKeys<"Hello">; // never
```

FormatKeys can tell us if the strings we pass in are format strings or not, but we are actually much more interested in a specific part of the format string: the piece between the curly braces. Using TypeScript's infer keyword, we can tell TypeScript that, if the format string matches this pattern, then grab whatever literal type you find between the curly braces and put it in a type variable:

```
type FormatKeys<
  T extends string
> = T extends `${string}{${infer Key}}${string}`
  ? Key
  : never;
```

That way, we can extract substrings and reuse them for our needs:

```
type A = FormatKeys<"Hello {world}">; // "world"
type B = FormatKeys<"Hello">; // never
```

Fantastic! We extracted the first placeholder name. Now on to the rest. Since there might be placeholders following, we take everything *after* the first placeholder and store it in a type variable called `Rest`. This condition will be always true, because either `Rest` is the empty string or it contains an actual string that we can analyze again.

We take the `Rest` and in the `true` branch call `FormatKeys<Rest>` in a union type of `Key`:

```
type FormatKeys<
  T extends string
> = T extends `${string}{${infer Key}}${infer Rest}`
  ? Key | FormatKeys<Rest>
  : never;
```

This is a *recursive conditional type*. The result will be a union of placeholders, which we can use as keys for the formatting object:

```
type A = FormatKeys<"Hello {world}">; // "world"
type B = FormatKeys<"Hello {world}. I'm {you}.">; // "world" | "you"
type C = FormatKeys<"Hello">; // never
```

Now it's time to wire up `FormatKeys`. Since we already locked in T, we can pass it as an argument to `FormatKeys`, which we can use as an argument for `Record`:

```
function format<T extends string>(
  fmtString: T,
  params: Record<FormatKeys<T>, any>
): string {
  throw "unimplemented";
}
```

And with that, our typings are all ready. On to the implementation! The implementation is beautifully inverted to how we defined our types. We go over all keys from `params` and replace all occurrences within curly braces with the respective value:

```
function format<T extends string>(
  fmtString: T,
  params: Record<FormatKeys<T>, any>
): string {
  let ret: string = fmtString;
  for (let k in params) {
    ret = ret.replaceAll(`{${k}}`, params[k as keyof typeof params]);
  }
  return ret;
}
```

Notice two particular typings:

- We need to annotate ret with string. fmtString is with T, a subtype of string; thus ret would also be T. This would mean we couldn't change values because the type of T would change. Annotating it to a broader string type helps us modify ret.

- We also need to assert that the object key k is actually a key of params. This is an unfortunate workaround that is due to some fail-safe mechanisms of TypeScript. Read more on this topic in Recipe 9.1.

With the information from Recipe 9.1, we can redefine format to get rid of some type assertions to reach our final version of the format function:

```
function format<T extends string, K extends Record<FormatKeys<T>, any>>(
  fmtString: T,
  params: K
): string {
  let ret: string = fmtString;
  for (let k in params) {
    ret = ret.replaceAll(`{${k}}`, params[k]);
  }
  return ret;
}
```

Being able to split strings and extract property keys is extremely powerful. TypeScript developers all over the world use this pattern to strengthen types, for example, for web servers like Express (*https://expressjs.com*). We will see more examples of how we can use this tool to get better types.

6.4 Extracting Format Parameter Types

Problem

You want to extend the formatting function from Recipe 6.3 with the ability to define types for your placeholders.

Solution

Create a nested conditional type and look up types with a type map.

Discussion

Let's extend the example from the previous lesson. We now want to not only know all placeholders but also be able to define a certain set of types with the placeholders. Types should be optional, be indicated with a colon after the placeholder name, and be one of JavaScript's primitive types. We expect to get type errors when we pass in a value that is of the wrong type:

```
format("Hello {world:string}. I'm {you}, {age:number} years old.", {
  world: "World",
  age: 40,
  you: "Stefan",
});
```

For reference, let's look at the original implementation from Recipe 6.3:

```
type FormatKeys<
  T extends string
> = T extends `${string}{${infer Key}}${infer Rest}`
  ? Key | FormatKeys<Rest>
  : never;


function format<T extends string>(
  fmtString: T,
  params: Record<FormatKeys<T>, any>
): string {
  let ret: string = fmtString;
  for (let k in params) {
    ret = ret.replace(`{${k}}`, params[k as keyof typeof params]);
  }
  return ret;
}
```

To achieve this, we need to do two things:

1. Change the type of params from Record<FormatKeys<T>, any> to an actual object type that has proper types associated with each property key.

2. Adapt the string template literal type within FormatKeys to be able to extract primitive JavaScript types.

For the first step, we introduce a new type called FormatObj<T>. It works just as For matKeys did, but instead of simply returning string keys, it maps out the same keys to a new object type. This requires us to chain the recursion using intersection types instead of a union type (we add more properties with each recursion) and to change the breaking condition from never to {}. If we did an intersection with never, the entire return type becomes never. This way, we don't add any new properties to the return type:

```
type FormatObj<
  T extends string
> = T extends `${string}{${infer Key}}${infer Rest}`
  ? { [K in Key]: any } & FormatObj<Rest>
  : {};
```

FormatObj<T> works the same way as Record<FormatKeys<T>, any>. We still didn't extract any placeholder type, but we made it easy to set the type for each placeholder now that we are in control of the entire object type.

As a next step, we change the parsing condition in `FormatObj<T>` to also look out for colon delimiters. If we find a : character, we infer the subsequent string literal type in Type and use it as the type for the mapped-out key:

```
type FormatObj<
  T extends string
> = T extends `${string}{${infer Key}:${infer Type}}${infer Rest}`
  ? { [K in Key]: Type } & FormatObj<Rest>
  : {};
```

We are very close; there's just one caveat. We infer a *string* literal type. This means that if we, for example, parse {age:number}, the type of age would be the literal string "number". We need to convert this string to an actual type. We could do another conditional type or use a map type as a lookup:

```
type MapFormatType = {
  string: string;
  number: number;
  boolean: boolean;
  [x: string]: any;
};
```

That way, we can simply check which type is associated with which key and have a fantastic fallback for all other strings:

```
type A = MapFormatType["string"]; // string
type B = MapFormatType["number"]; // number
type C = MapFormatType["notavailable"]; // any
```

Let's wire `MapFormatType` up to `FormatObj<T>`:

```
type FormatObj<
  T extends string
> = T extends `${string}{${infer Key}:${infer Type}}${infer Rest}`
  ? { [K in Key]: MapFormatType[Type] } & FormatObj<Rest>
  : {};
```

We are almost there! The problem now is that we expect every placeholder to also define a type. We want to make types optional. But our parsing condition explicitly asks for : delimiters, so every placeholder that doesn't define a type doesn't produce a property, either.

The solution is to do the check for types *after* we check for placeholder:

```
type FormatObj<
  T extends string
> = T extends `${string}{${infer Key}}${infer Rest}`
  ? Key extends `${infer KeyPart}:${infer TypePart}`
    ? { [K in KeyPart]: MapFormatType[TypePart] } & FormatObj<Rest>
    : { [K in Key]: any } & FormatObj<Rest>
  : {};
```

The type reads as follows:

1. Check if there is a placeholder available.

2. If a placeholder is available, check if there is a type annotation. If so, map the key to a format type; otherwise, map the original key to any.

3. In all other cases, return the empty object.

And that's it. There is one fail-safe guard that we can add. Instead of allowing any type for placeholders without a type definition, we can at least expect that the type implements toString(). This ensures we always get a string representation:

```
type FormatObj<
  T extends string
> = T extends `${string}{${infer Key}}${infer Rest}`
  ? Key extends `${infer KeyPart}:${infer TypePart}`
    ? { [K in KeyPart]: MapFormatType[TypePart] } & FormatObj<Rest>
    : { [K in Key]: { toString(): string } } & FormatObj<Rest>
  : {};
```

And with that, let's apply the new type to format and change the implementation:

```
function format<T extends string, K extends FormatObj<T>>(
  fmtString: T,
  params: K
): string {
  let ret: string = fmtString;
  for (let k in params) {
    let val = `${params[k]}`;
    let searchPattern = new RegExp(`{${k}:?.*?}`, "g");
    ret = ret.replaceAll(searchPattern, val);
  }
  return ret;
}
```

We help ourselves with a regular expression to replace names with potential type annotations. There is no need to check types within the function. TypeScript should be enough to help in this case.

What we've seen is that conditional types in combination with string template literal types and other tools like recursion and type lookups allow us to specify complex relationships with a couple of lines of code. Our types get better, our code gets more robust, and it's a joy for developers to use APIs like this.

6.5 Dealing with Recursion Limits

Problem

You craft an elaborate string template literal type that converts any string to a valid property key. With your setup of helper types, you run into recursion limits.

Solution

Use the accumulation technique to enable tail-call optimization.

Discussion

TypeScript's string template literal types in combination with conditional types allow you to create new string types on the fly, which can serve as property keys or check your program for valid strings.

They work using recursion, which means that just like a function, you can call the same type over and over again, up to a certain limit.

For example, this type Trim<T> removes whitespaces at the start and end of your string type:

```
type Trim<T extends string> =
  T extends ` ${infer X}` ? Trim<X> :
  T extends `${infer X} ` ? Trim<X> :
  T;
```

It checks if there's a whitespace at the beginning, infers the rest, and does the same check over again. Once all whitespaces at the beginning are gone, the same checks happen for whitespaces at the end. Once all whitespaces at the beginning and end are gone, it is finished and hops into the last branch—returning the remaining string:

```
type Trimmed = Trim<"    key    ">; // "key"
```

Calling the type over and over is recursion, and writing it like that works reasonably well. TypeScript can see from the type that the recursive calls stand on their own, and it can evaluate them as tail-call optimized, which means it can evaluate the next step of the recursion within the same call stack frame.

 If you want to know more about the call stack in JavaScript, Thomas Hunter's book *Distributed Systems with Node.js* (O'Reilly) gives a great introduction.

We want to use TypeScript's feature to recursively call conditional types to create a valid string identifier out of any string, by removing whitespace and invalid characters.

First, we write a helper type similar to Trim<T> that gets rid of any whitespace it finds:

```
type RemoveWhiteSpace<T extends string> = T extends `${infer A} ${infer B}`
  ? RemoveWhiteSpace<`${Uncapitalize<A>}${Capitalize<B>}`>
  : T;
```

It checks if there is a whitespace, infers the strings in front of the whitespace and after the whitespace (which can be empty strings), and calls the same type again with a newly formed string type. It also uncapitalizes the first inference and capitalizes the second inference to create a camel-case-like string identifier.

It does so until all whitespaces are gone:

```
type Identifier = RemoveWhiteSpace<"Hello World!">; // "helloWorld!"
```

Next, we want to check if the remaining characters are valid. We again use recursion to take a string of valid characters, split them into single string types with only one character, and create a capitalized and uncapitalized version:

```
type StringSplit<T extends string> = T extends `${infer Char}${infer Rest}`
  ? Capitalize<Char> | Uncapitalize<Char> | StringSplit<Rest>
  : never;

type Chars = StringSplit<"abcdefghijklmnopqrstuvwxyz">;
// "a" | "A" | "b" | "B" | "c" | "C" | "d" | "D" | "e" | "E" |
// "f" | "F" | "g" | "G" | "h" | "H" | "i" | "I" | "j" | "J" |
// "k" | "K" | "l" | "L" | "m" | "M" | "n" | "N" | "o" | "O" |
// "p" | "P" | "q" | "Q" | "r" | "R" | "s" | "S" | "t" | "T" |
// "u" | "U" | "v" | "V" | "w" | "W" | "x" | "X" | "y" | "Y" |
// "z" | "Z"
```

We shave off the first character we find, capitalize it, uncapitalize it, and do the same with the rest until no more strings are left. Note that this recursion can't be tail-call optimized, as we put the recursive call in a union type with the results from each recursion step. Here we would reach a recursion limit when we hit 50 characters (a hard limit from the TypeScript compiler). With basic characters, we are fine!

But we hit the first limits when we are doing the next step, the creation of the Identifier. Here we check for valid characters. First, we call the RemoveWhiteSpace<T> type, which allows us to get rid of whitespaces and camel-cases the rest. Then we check the result against valid characters.

Just like in StringSplit<T>, we shave off the first character but do another type-check within inference. We see if the character we just shaved off is one of the valid characters. Then we get the rest. We combine the same string again but do a recursive check with the remaining string. If the first character isn't valid, then we call CreateIdentifier<T> with the rest:

```
type CreateIdentifier<T extends string> =
  RemoveWhiteSpace<T> extends `${infer A extends Chars}${infer Rest}`
  ? `${A}${CreateIdentifier<Rest>}`
// ^ Type instantiation is excessively deep and possibly infinite.(2589)_.
  : RemoveWhiteSpace<T> extends `${infer A}${infer Rest}`
  ? CreateIdentifier<Rest>
  : T;
```

And here we hit the first recursion limit. TypeScript warns us—with an error—that this type instantiation is possibly infinite and excessively deep. It seems that if we use the recursive call within a string template literal type, this might result in call stack errors and blow up. So TypeScript breaks. It can't do tail-call optimization here.

 `CreateIdentifier<T>` might still produce correct results, even though TypeScript errors when you write your type. Those are hard-to-spot bugs because they might hit you when you don't expect them. Be sure to not let TypeScript produce any results when errors happen.

There's one way to work around it. To activate tail-call optimization, the recursive call needs to stand alone. We can achieve this by using the so-called *accumulator technique*. Here, we pass a second type parameter called `Acc`, which is of a type `string` and is instantiated with the empty string. We use this as an accumulator where we store the intermediate result, passing it over and over again to the next call:

```
type CreateIdentifier<T extends string, Acc extends string = ""> =
  RemoveWhiteSpace<T> extends `${infer A extends Chars}${infer Rest}`
  ? CreateIdentifier<Rest, `${Acc}${A}`>
  : RemoveWhiteSpace<T> extends `${infer A}${infer Rest}`
  ? CreateIdentifier<Rest, Acc>
  : Acc;
```

This way, the recursive call is standing on its own again, and the result is the second parameter. When we are done with recursive calls, the recursion-breaking branch, we return the accumulator, as it is our finished result:

```
type Identifier = CreateIdentifier<"Hello Wor!ld!">; // "helloWorld"
```

There might be more clever ways to produce identifiers from any string, but note that the same thing can hit you deep down in any elaborate conditional type where you use recursion. The accumulator technique is a good way to mitigate problems like this.

6.6 Using Template Literals as Discriminants

Problem

You model requests to a backend as a state machine, going from *pending* to either *error* or *success*. Those states should work for different backend requests, but the underlying types should be the same.

Solution

Use string template literals as discriminants for a discriminated union.

Discussion

The way you fetch data from a backend always follows the same structure. You do a request, and it's pending to be either fulfilled and return some data—success—or rejected and return with an error. For example, to log in a user, all possible states can look like this:

```
type UserRequest =
  | {
      state: "USER_PENDING";
    }
  | {
      state: "USER_ERROR";
      message: string;
    }
  | {
      state: "USER_SUCCESS";
      data: User;
    };
```

When we fetch a user's order, we have the same states available. The only difference is in the success payload and in the names of each state, which are tailored to the type of request:

```
type OrderRequest =
  | {
      state: "ORDER_PENDING";
    }
  | {
      state: "ORDER_ERROR";
      message: string;
    }
  | {
      state: "ORDER_SUCCESS";
      data: Order;
    };
```

When we deal with a global state handling mechanism, such as Redux (*https:// redux.js.org*), we want to differentiate by using identifiers like this. We still want to narrow it to the respective state types!

TypeScript allows you to create discriminated union types where the discriminant is a string template literal type. So we can sum up all possible backend requests using the same pattern:

```
type Pending = {
  state: `${Uppercase<string>}_PENDING`;
};

type Err = {
  state: `${Uppercase<string>}_ERROR`;
  message: string;
```

```
};

type Success = {
  state: `${Uppercase<string>}_SUCCESS`;
  data: any;
};

type BackendRequest = Pending | Err | Success;
```

This already gives us an edge. We know that the state property of each union type member needs to start with an uppercase string, followed by an underscore and the respective state as a string. And we can narrow it to the subtypes just as we are used to:

```
function execute(req: BackendRequest) {
  switch (req.state) {
    case "USER_PENDING":
      // req: Pending
      console.log("Login pending...");
      break;
    case "USER_ERROR":
      // req: Err
      throw new Error(`Login failed: ${req.message}`);
    case "USER_SUCCESS":
      // req: Success
      login(req.data);
      break;
    case "ORDER_PENDING":
      // req: Pending
      console.log("Fetching orders pending");
      break;
    case "ORDER_ERROR":
      // req: Err
      throw new Error(`Fetching orders failed: ${req.message}`);
    case "ORDER_SUCCESS":
      // req: Success
      displayOrder(req.data);
      break;
  }
}
```

Having the entire set of strings as the first part of the discriminant might be a bit too much. We can subset to a variety of known requests and use string manipulation types to get the right subtypes:

```
type RequestConstants = "user" | "order";

type Pending = {
  state: `${Uppercase<RequestConstants>}_PENDING`;
};

type Err = {
```

```
  state: `${Uppercase<RequestConstants>}_ERROR`;
  message: string;
};

type Success = {
  state: `${Uppercase<RequestConstants>}_SUCCESS`;
  data: any;
};
```

That's how to get rid of typos! Even better, let's say we store all data in a global state object of type Data. We can derive all possible BackendRequest types from here. By using keyof Data, we get the string keys that make up the BackendRequest state:

```
type Data = {
  user: User | null;
  order: Order | null;
};

type RequestConstants = keyof Data;

type Pending = {
  state: `${Uppercase<RequestConstants>}_PENDING`;
};

type Err = {
  state: `${Uppercase<RequestConstants>}_ERROR`;
  message: string;
};
```

This already works well for Pending and Err, but in the Success case we want to have the actual data type associated with "user" or "order".

A first option would be to use index access to get the correct types for the data property from Data:

```
type Success = {
  state: `${Uppercase<RequestConstants>}_SUCCESS`;
  data: NonNullable<Data[RequestConstants]>;
};
```

 NonNullable<T> gets rid of null and undefined in a union type. With the compiler flag strictNullChecks on, both null and undefined are excluded from all types. This means you need to manually add them if you have nullish states and manually exclude them when you want to make sure that they don't.

But this would mean that `data` can be both `User` or `Order` for all backend requests, and more if we add new ones. To avoid breaking the connection between the identifier and its associated data type, we map through all `RequestConstants`, create state objects, and then use index access of `RequestConstants` again to produce a union type:

```
type Success = {
  [K in RequestConstants]: {
    state: `${Uppercase<K>}_SUCCESS`;
    data: NonNullable<Data[K]>;
  };
}[RequestConstants];
```

`Success` is now equal to the manually created union type:

```
type Success = {
    state: "USER_SUCCESS";
    data: User;
} | {
    state: "ORDER_SUCCESS";
    data: Order;
};
```

CHAPTER 7

Variadic Tuple Types

Tuple types are arrays with a fixed length and where every type of each element is defined. Tuples are heavily used in libraries like React as it's easy to destructure and name elements, but outside of React they also have gained recognition as a nice alternative to objects.

A *variadic tuple type* is a tuple type that has the same properties—defined length and the type of each element is known—but where the *exact shape* is yet to be defined. They basically tell the type system that there will be some elements, but we don't know yet which ones they will be. They are generic and meant to be substituted with real types.

What sounds like a fairly boring feature is much more exciting when we understand that tuple types can also be used to describe function signatures, as tuples can be spread out to function calls as arguments. This means we can use variadic tuple types to get the most information out of functions and function calls, and functions that accept functions as parameters.

This chapter provides a lot of use cases on how we can use variadic tuple types to describe several scenarios where we use functions as parameters and need to get the most information from them. Without variadic tuple types, these scenarios would be hard to develop or outright impossible. After reading through, you will see variadic tuple types as a key feature for functional programming patterns.

7.1 Typing a concat Function

Problem

You have a concat function that takes two arrays and concatenates them. You want to have exact types, but using function overloads is too cumbersome.

Solution

Use variadic tuple types.

Discussion

concat is a lovely helper function that takes two arrays and combines them. It uses array spreading and is short, nice, and readable:

```
function concat(arr1, arr2) {
  return [...arr1, ...arr2];
}
```

Creating types for this function can be hard, especially if you have certain expectations from your types. Passing in two arrays is easy, but what should the return type look like? Are you happy with a single array type in return, or do you want to know the types of each element in this array?

Let's go for the latter: we want tuples so we know the type of each element we pass to this function. To correctly type a function like this so that it takes all possible edge cases into account, we would end up in a sea of overloads:

```
// 7 overloads for an empty second array
function concat(arr1: [], arr2: []): [];
function concat<A>(arr1: [A], arr2: []): [A];
function concat<A, B>(arr1: [A, B], arr2: []): [A, B];
function concat<A, B, C>(arr1: [A, B, C], arr2: []): [A, B, C];
function concat<A, B, C, D>(arr1: [A, B, C, D], arr2: []): [A, B, C, D];
function concat<A, B, C, D, E>(
  arr1: [A, B, C, D, E],
  arr2: []
): [A, B, C, D, E];
function concat<A, B, C, D, E, F>(
  arr1: [A, B, C, D, E, F],
  arr2: []
): [A, B, C, D, E, F];
// 7 more for arr2 having one element
function concat<A2>(arr1: [], arr2: [A2]): [A2];
function concat<A1, A2>(arr1: [A1], arr2: [A2]): [A1, A2];
function concat<A1, B1, A2>(arr1: [A1, B1], arr2: [A2]): [A1, B1, A2];
function concat<A1, B1, C1, A2>(
  arr1: [A1, B1, C1],
  arr2: [A2]
): [A1, B1, C1, A2];
function concat<A1, B1, C1, D1, A2>(
  arr1: [A1, B1, C1, D1],
  arr2: [A2]
): [A1, B1, C1, D1, A2];
function concat<A1, B1, C1, D1, E1, A2>(
  arr1: [A1, B1, C1, D1, E1],
  arr2: [A2]
```

```
): [A1, B1, C1, D1, E1, A2];
function concat<A1, B1, C1, D1, E1, F1, A2>(
  arr1: [A1, B1, C1, D1, E1, F1],
  arr2: [A2]
): [A1, B1, C1, D1, E1, F1, A2];
// and so on, and so forth
```

And this only takes into account arrays that have up to six elements. The combinations for typing a function like this with overloads is exhausting. But there is an easier way: variadic tuple types.

A tuple type in TypeScript is an array with the following features:

- The length of the array is defined.
- The type of each element is known (and does not have to be the same).

For example, this is a tuple type:

```
type PersonProps = [string, number];

const [name, age]: PersonProps = ['Stefan', 37];
```

A *variadic* tuple type is a tuple type that has the same properties—defined length and the type of each element is known—but where the *exact shape* is yet to be defined. Since we don't know the type and length yet, we can only use variadic tuple types in generics:

```
type Foo<T extends unknown[]> = [string, ...T, number];

type T1 = Foo<[boolean]>;  // [string, boolean, number]
type T2 = Foo<[number, number]>;  // [string, number, number, number]
type T3 = Foo<[]>;  // [string, number]
```

This is similar to rest elements in functions, but the big difference is that variadic tuple types can happen anywhere in the tuple, and multiple times:

```
type Bar<
  T extends unknown[],
  U extends unknown[]
> = [...T, string, ...U];

type T4 = Bar<[boolean], [number]>;  // [boolean, string, number]
type T5 = Bar<[number, number], [boolean]>;  // [number, number, string, boolean]
type T6 = Bar<[], []>;  // [string]
```

When we apply this to the concat function, we have to introduce two generic parameters, one for each array. Both need to be constrained to arrays. Then, we can create a return type that combines both array types in a newly created tuple type:

```
function concat<T extends unknown[], U extends unknown[]>(
  arr1: T,
  arr2: U
```

```
): [...T, ...U] {
  return [...arr1, ...arr2];
}

// const test: (string | number)[]
const test = concat([1, 2, 3], [6, 7, "a"]);
```

The syntax is beautiful; it's very similar to the actual concatenation in JavaScript. The result is also really good: we get a (`string | number`)[], which is already something we can work with.

But we work with tuple types. If we want to know *exactly* which elements we are concatenating, we have to transform the array types into tuple types, by spreading out the generic array type into a tuple type:

```
function concat<T extends unknown[], U extends unknown[]>(
  arr1: [...T],
  arr2: [...U]
): [...T, ...U] {
  return [...arr1, ...arr2];
}
```

And with that, we also get a tuple type in return:

```
// const test: [number, number, number, number, number, string]
const test = concat([1, 2, 3], [6, 7, "a"]);
```

The good news is that we don't lose anything. If we pass arrays where we don't know each element up front, we still get array types in return:

```
declare const a: string[]
declare const b: number[]

// const test: (string | number)[]
const test = concat(a, b);
```

Being able to describe this behavior in a single type is definitely much more flexible and readable than writing every possible combination in a function overload.

7.2 Typing a promisify Function

Problem

You want to convert callback-style functions to Promises and have them perfectly typed.

Solution

Function arguments are tuple types. Make them generic using variadic tuple types.

Discussion

Before Promises were a thing in JavaScript it was very common to do asynchronous programming using callbacks. Functions would usually take a list of arguments, followed by a callback function that would be executed once the results were there, such as functions to load a file or do a very simplified HTTP request:

```
function loadFile(
  filename: string,
  encoding: string,
  callback: (result: File) => void
) {
  // TODO
}

loadFile("./data.json", "utf-8", (result) => {
  // do something with the file
});

function request(url: URL, callback: (result: JSON) => void) {
  // TODO
}

request("https://typescript-cookbook.com", (result) => {
  // TODO
});
```

Both follow the same pattern: arguments first, a callback with the result last. This works but can be clumsy if you have lots of asynchronous calls that result in callbacks within callbacks, also known as the "the pyramid of doom" (*https://oreil.ly/Ye3Qr*):

```
loadFile("./data.txt", "utf-8", (file) => {
  // pseudo API
  file.readText((url) => {
    request(url, (data) => {
      // do something with data
    })
  })
})
```

Promises take care of that. Not only do they find a way to chain asynchronous calls instead of nesting them, they also are the gateway for async/await, allowing us to write asynchronous code in a synchronous form:

```
loadFilePromise("./data.txt", "utf-8")
  .then((file) => file.text())
  .then((url) => request(url))
  .then((data) => {
    // do something with data
  });

// with async/await
```

```
const file = await loadFilePromise("./data.txt". "utf-8");
const url = await file.text();
const data = await request(url);
// do something with data.
```

Much nicer! Thankfully, it is possible to convert every function that adheres to the callback pattern to a Promise. We want to create a promisify function to do that for us automatically:

```
function promisify(fn: unknown): Promise<unknown> {
  // To be implemented
}

const loadFilePromise = promisify(loadFile);
const requestPromise = promisify(request);
```

But how do we type this? Variadic tuple types to the rescue!

Every function head can be described as a tuple type. For example:

```
declare function hello(name: string, msg: string): void;
```

is the same as:

```
declare function hello(...args: [string, string]): void;
```

And we can be very flexible in defining it:

```
declare function h(a: string, b: string, c: string): void;
// equal to
declare function h(a: string, b: string, ...r: [string]): void;
// equal to
declare function h(a: string, ...r: [string, string]): void;
// equal to
declare function h(...r: [string, string, string]): void;
```

This is also known as a *rest element*, something we have in JavaScript that allows you to define functions with an almost limitless argument list, where the last element, the rest element, sucks all excess arguments in.

For example, this generic tuple function takes an argument list of any type and creates a tuple out of it:

```
function tuple<T extends any[]>(...args: T): T {
    return args;
}

const numbers: number[] = getArrayOfNumbers();
const t1 = tuple("foo", 1, true);  // [string, number, boolean]
const t2 = tuple("bar", ...numbers);  // [string, ...number[]]
```

The thing is, rest elements always have to be last. In JavaScript, it's not possible to define an almost endless argument list somewhere in between. With variadic tuple types, however, we can do this in TypeScript!

Let's look again at the `loadFile` and `request` functions again. If we described the parameters of both functions as tuples, they would look like this:

```
function loadFile(...args: [string, string, (result: File) => void]) {
  // TODO
}

function request2(...args: [URL, (result: JSON) => void]) {
  // TODO
}
```

Let's look for similarities. Both end with a callback with a varying result type. We can align the types for both callbacks by substituting the variations with a generic one. Later, in usage, we substitute generics for actual types. So `JSON` and `File` become the generic type parameter `Res`.

Now for the parameters *before* `Res`. They are arguably totally different, but even they have something in common: they are elements within a tuple. This calls for a variadic tuple. We know they will have a concrete length and concrete types, but right now we just take a placeholder for them. Let's call them `Args`.

So a function type describing both function signatures could look like this:

```
type Fn<Args extends unknown[], Res> = (
  ...args: [...Args, (result: Res) => void]
) => void;
```

Take your new type for a spin:

```
type LoadFileFn = Fn<[string, string], File>;
type RequestFn = Fn<[URL], JSON>;
```

This is exactly what we need for the `promisify` function. We are able to extract all relevant parameters—the ones before the callback and the result type—and bring them into a new order.

Let's start by inlining the newly created function type directly into the function signature of `promisify`:

```
function promisify<Args extends unknown[], Res>(
  fn: (...args: [...Args, (result: Res) => void]) => void
): (...args: Args) => Promise<Res> {
  // soon
}
```

`promisify` now reads:

- There are two generic type parameters: `Args`, which needs to be an array (or tuple), and `Res`.
- The parameter of `promisify` is a function where the first arguments are the elements of `Args` and the last argument is a function with a parameter of type `Res`.
- `promisify` returns a function that takes `Args` for parameters and returns a Promise of `Res`.

If you try out the new typings for `promisify`, you can see that we get exactly the type we want.

But it gets even better. If you look at the function signature, it's absolutely clear which arguments we expect, even if they are variadic and will be substituted with real types. We can use the same types for the implementation of `promisify`:

```
function promisify<Args extends unknown[], Res>(
  fn: (...args: [...Args, (result: Res) => void]) => void
): (...args: Args) => Promise<Res> {
  return function (...args: Args) { ❶
    return new Promise((resolve) => { ❷
      function callback(res: Res) { ❸
        resolve(res);
      }
      fn.call(null, ...[...args, callback]); ❹
    });
  };
}
```

So what does it do?

❶ We return a function that accepts all parameters except for the callback.

❷ This function returns a newly created `Promise`.

❸ Since we don't have a callback yet, we need to construct it. What does it do? It calls the `resolve` function from the `Promise`, producing a result.

❹ What has been split needs to be brought back together! We add the callback to the arguments and call the original function.

And that's it. A working `promisify` function for functions that adhere to the callback pattern. Perfectly typed. And we even keep the parameter names.

7.3 Typing a curry Function

Problem

You write a curry function. *Currying* is a technique that converts a function that takes several arguments into a sequence of functions that each takes a single argument.

You want to provide excellent types.

Solution

Combine conditional types with variadic tuple types, always shaving off the first parameter.

Discussion

Currying is a very well-known technique in functional programming. Currying converts a function that takes several arguments into a sequence of functions that each takes a single argument.

The underlying concept is called "partial application of function arguments." We use it to maximize the reuse of functions. The "Hello, World!" of currying implements an add function that can partially apply the second argument later:

```
function add(a: number, b: number) {
  return a + b;
}
```

```
const curriedAdd = curry(add); // convert: (a: number) => (b: number) => number
const add5 = curriedAdd(5); // apply first argument. (b: number) => number
const result1 = add5(2); // second argument. Result: 7
const result2 = add5(3); // second argument. Result: 8
```

What feels arbitrary at first is useful when you work with long argument lists. The following generalized function either adds or removes classes to an HTMLElement.

We can prepare everything except for the final event:

```
function applyClass(
  this: HTMLElement, // for TypeScript only
  method: "remove" | "add",
  className: string,
  event: Event
) {
  if (this === event.target) {
    this.classList[method](className);
  }
}
```

```
const applyClassCurried = curry(applyClass); // convert
```

```
const removeToggle = applyClassCurried("remove")("hidden");

document.querySelector(".toggle")?.addEventListener("click", removeToggle);
```

This way, we can reuse `removeToggle` for several events on several elements. We can also use `applyClass` for many other situations.

Currying is a fundamental concept of the programming language Haskell and gives a nod to the mathematician Haskell Brooks Curry, the namesake for both the programming language and the technique. In Haskell, every operation is curried, and programmers make good use of it.

JavaScript borrows heavily from functional programming languages, and it is possible to implement partial application with its built-in functionality of binding:

```
function add(a: number, b: number, c: number) {
  return a + b + c;
}

// Partial application
const partialAdd5And3 = add.bind(this, 5, 3);
const result = partialAdd5And3(2); // third argument
```

Since functions are first-class citizens in JavaScript, we can create a `curry` function that takes a function as an argument and collects all arguments before executing it:

```
function curry(fn) {
  let curried = (...args) => {
    // if you haven't collected enough arguments
    if (fn.length !== args.length) {
      // partially apply arguments and
      // return the collector function
      return curried.bind(null, ...args);
    }
    // otherwise call all functions
    return fn(...args);
  };
  return curried;
}
```

The trick is that every function stores the number of defined arguments in its `length` property. That's how we can recursively collect all necessary arguments before applying them to the function passed.

So what's missing? Types! Let's create a type that works for a currying pattern where every sequenced function can take exactly one argument. We do this by creating a conditional type that does the inverse of what the `curried` function inside the `curry` function does: removing arguments.

So let's create a `Curried<F>` type. The first thing is to check if the type is indeed a function:

```
type Curried<F> = F extends (...args: infer A) => infer R
  ? /* to be done */
  : never; // not a function, this should not happen
```

We also infer the arguments as A and the return type as R. Next step, we shave off the first parameter as F, and store all remaining parameters in L (for *last*):

```
type Curried<F> = F extends (...args: infer A) => infer R
  ? A extends [infer F, ...infer L]
    ? /* to be done */
    : () => R
  : never;
```

Should there be no arguments, we return a function that takes no arguments. Last check: we check if the remaining parameters are empty. This means we reached the end of removing arguments from the argument list:

```
type Curried<F> = F extends (...args: infer A) => infer R
  ? A extends [infer F, ...infer L]
    ? L extends []
      ? (a: F) => R
      : (a: F) => Curried<(...args: L) => R>
    : () => R
  : never;
```

Should some parameters remain, we call the Curried type again, but with the remaining parameters. This way, we shave off a parameter step by step, and if you take a good look, you can see that the process is almost identical to what we do in the curried function. Where we deconstruct parameters in Curried<F>, we collect them again in curried(fn).

With the type done, let's add it to curry:

```
function curry<F extends Function>(fn: F): Curried<F> {
  let curried: Function = (...args: any) => {
    if (fn.length !== args.length) {
      return curried.bind(null, ...args);
    }
    return fn(...args);
  };
  return curried as Curried<F>;
}
```

We need a few assertions and some any because of the flexible nature of the type. But with as and any as keywords, we mark which portions are considered unsafe types.

And that's it! We can get curried away!

7.4 Typing a Flexible curry Function

Problem

The curry function from Recipe 7.3 allows for an arbitrary number of arguments to be passed, but your typings allow you to take only one argument at a time.

Solution

Extend your typings to create function overloads for all possible tuple combinations.

Discussion

In Recipe 7.3 we ended up with function types that allow us to apply function arguments one at a time:

```
function addThree(a: number, b: number, c: number) {
  return a + b + c;
}

const adder = curried(addThree);
const add7 = adder(5)(2);
const result = add7(2);
```

However, the curry function itself can take an arbitrary list of arguments:

```
function addThree(a: number, b: number, c: number) {
  return a + b + c;
}

const adder = curried(addThree);
const add7 = adder(5, 2); // this is the difference
const result = add7(2);
```

This allows us to work on the same use cases but with a lot fewer function invocations. So let's adapt our types to take advantage of the full curry experience.

 This example illustrates really well how the type system works as just a thin layer on top of JavaScript. By adding assertions and any at the right positions, we effectively define how curry should work, whereas the function itself is much more flexible. Be aware that when you define complex types on top of complex functionality, you might cheat your way to the goal, and it's in your hands how the types work in the end. Test accordingly.

Our goal is to create a type that can produce all possible function signatures for every partial application. For the addThree function, all possible types would look like this:

```
type Adder = (a: number) => (b: number) => (c: number) => number;
type Adder = (a: number) => (b: number, c: number) => number;
type Adder = (a: number, b: number) => (c: number) => number;
type Adder = (a: number, b: number, c: number) => number;
```

See also Figure 7-1 for a visualization of all possible call graphs.

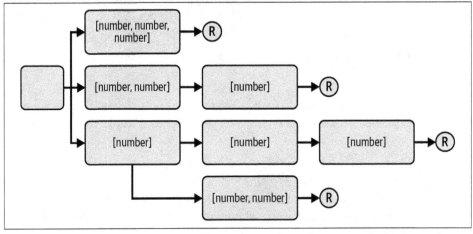

Figure 7-1. A graph showing all possible function call combinations of addThree when curried; there are three branches to start, with a possible fourth branch

The first thing we do is to slightly adapt the way we call the Curried helper type. In the original type, we do the inference of function arguments and return types *in* the helper type. Now we need to carry along the return value over multiple type invocations, so we extract the return type and arguments directly in the curry function:

```
function curry<A extends any[], R extends any>(
  fn: (...args: A) => R
): Curried<A, R> {
  // see before, we're not changing the implementation
}
```

Next, we redefine the Curried type. It now features two generic type parameters: A for arguments, R for the return type. As a first step, we check if the arguments contain tuple elements. We extract the first element F and all remaining elements L. If there are no elements left, we return the return type R:

```
type Curried<A extends any[], R extends any> = A extends [infer F, ...infer L]
  ? // to be done
  : R;
```

It's not possible to extract multiple tuples via the rest operator. That's why we still need to shave off the first element and collect the remaining elements in L. But that's OK; we need at least *one* parameter to effectively do partial application.

When we are in the true branch, we create the function definitions. In the previous example, we returned a function that returns a recursive call; now we need to provide all possible partial applications.

Since function arguments are nothing but tuple types (see Recipe 7.2), arguments of function overloads can be described as a union of tuple types. A type Overloads takes a tuple of function arguments and creates all partial applications:

```
type Overloads<A extends any[]> = A extends [infer A, ...infer L]
  ? [A] | [A, ...Overloads<L>] | []
  : [];
```

If we pass a tuple, we get a union starting from the empty tuple and then growing to one argument, then to two arguments, etc., and up to a tuple that includes all arguments:

```
// type Overloaded = [] | [string, number, string] | [string] | [string, number]
type Overloaded = Overloads<[string, number, string]>;
```

Now that we can define all overloads, we take the remaining arguments of the original functions' argument list and create all possible function calls that also include the first argument:

```
type Curried<A extends any[], R extends any> = A extends [infer F, ...infer L]
  ? <K extends Overloads<L>>(
      arg: F,
      ...args: K
    ) => /* to be done */
  : R;
```

Applied to the addThree example from before, this part would create the first argument F as number and then combine it with [], [number], and [number, number].

Now for the return type. This is again a recursive call to Curried, just like in Recipe 7.2. Remember, we chain functions in a sequence. We pass in the same return type—we need to get there eventually—but also need to pass all remaining arguments that we haven't spread out in the function overloads. So if we call addThree only with number, the two remaining numbers need to be arguments of the next iteration of Curried. This is how we create a tree of possible invocations.

To get to the possible combinations, we need to remove the arguments we already described in the function signature from the remaining arguments. A helper type Remove<T, U> goes through both tuples and shaves off one element each, until one of the two tuples runs out of elements:

```
type Remove<T extends any[], U extends any[]> = U extends [infer _, ...infer UL]
  ? T extends [infer _, ...infer TL]
    ? Remove<TL, UL>
    : never
  : T;
```

Wiring that up to `Curried`, and we get the final result:

```
type Curried<A extends any[], R extends any> = A extends [infer F, ...infer L]
  ? <K extends Overloads<L>>(
      arg: F,
      ...args: K
    ) => Curried<Remove<L, K>, R>
  : R;
```

`Curried<A, R>` now produces the same call graph as described in Figure 7-1 but is flexible for all possible functions that we pass in `curry`. Proper type safety for maximum flexibility (shout-out to GitHub user Akira Matsuzaki who provided the missing piece in their Type Challenges solution).

7.5 Typing the Simplest curry function

Problem

The `curry` functions and their typings are impressive but come with a lot of caveats. Are there any simpler solutions?

Solution

Create a `curry` function with only a single sequential step. TypeScript can figure out the proper types on its own.

Discussion

In the last piece of the `curry` trilogy, I want you to sit back and think a bit about what we saw in Recipes 7.3 and 7.4. We created very complex types that work almost like the actual implementation through TypeScript's metaprogramming features. And while the results are impressive, there are some caveats we have to think about:

- The way the types are implemented for both Recipes 7.3 and 7.4 is a bit different, but the results vary a lot! Still, the `curry` function underneath stays the same. The only way this works is by using `any` in arguments and type assertions for the return type. What this means is that we effectively disable type-checking by forcing TypeScript to adhere to our view of the world. It's great that TypeScript can do that, and at times it's also necessary (such as the creation of new objects), but it can backfire, especially when both implementation and types get very complex.

Tests for both types and implementation are a must. We talk about testing types in Recipe 12.4.

- You lose information. Especially when currying, keeping argument names is essential to know which arguments already have applied. The solutions in the earlier recipes couldn't keep argument names but defaulted to a generic-sounding a or args. If your argument types are, for example, all strings, you can't say which string you are currently writing.

- While the result in Recipe 7.4 gives you proper type-checking, autocomplete is limited because of the nature of the type. You know only that a second argument is needed the moment you type it. One of TypeScript's main features is giving you the right tooling and information to make you more productive. The flexible Curried type reduces your productivity to guesswork again.

Again, while those types are impressive, there is no denying that they come with some huge trade-offs. This raises the question: should we even go for it? I think it really depends on what you try to achieve.

In the case of currying and partial application, there are two camps. The first camp loves functional programming patterns and tries to leverage JavaScript's functional capabilities to the max. They want to reuse partial applications as much as possible and need advanced currying functionalities. The other camp sees the benefit of functional programming patterns in certain situations—for example, waiting for the final parameter to give the same function to multiple events. They often are happy with applying as much as possible, but then provide the rest in a second step.

We have dealt with only the first camp until now. If you're in the second camp, you most likely only need a currying function that applies a few parameters partially, so you can pass in the rest in a second step: no sequence of parameters of one argument, and no flexible application of as many arguments as you like. An ideal interface would look like this:

```
function applyClass(
  this: HTMLElement, // for TypeScript only
  method: "remove" | "add",
  className: string,
  event: Event
) {
  if (this === event.target) {
    this.classList[method](className);
  }
}

const removeToggle = curry(applyClass, "remove", "hidden");

document.querySelector("button")?.addEventListener("click", removeToggle);
```

curry is a function that takes another function f as an argument and then a sequence t of parameters of f. It returns a function that takes the remaining parameters u of f, which calls f with all possible parameters. The function could look like this in JavaScript:

```
function curry(f, ...t) {
  return (...u) => f(...t, ...u);
}
```

Thanks to the rest and spread operator, curry becomes a one-liner. Now let's type this! We will have to use generics, as we deal with parameters that we don't know yet. There's the return type R, as well as both parts of the function's arguments, T and U. The latter are variadic tuple types and need to be defined as such.

With a generic type parameter T and U comprising the arguments of f, a type for f looks like this:

```
type Fn<T extends any[], U extends any[]> =
    (...args: [...T, ...U]) => any;
```

Function arguments can be described as tuples, and here we say those function arguments should be split into two parts. Let's inline this type to curry and use another generic type parameter for the return type R:

```
function curry<T extends any[], U extends any[], R>(
  f: (...args: [...T, ...U]) => R,
  ...t: T
) {
  return (...u: U) => f(...t, ...u);
}
```

And that's all the types we need: simple, straightforward, and the types look very similar to the actual implementation. With a few variadic tuple types, TypeScript gives us:

- 100% type safety. TypeScript directly infers the generic types from your usage, and they are correct. No laboriously crafted types through conditional types and recursion.

- We get autocomplete for all possible solutions. The moment you add a , to announce the next step of your arguments, TypeScript will adapt types and give you a hint about what to expect.

- We don't lose any information. Since we don't construct new types, TypeScript keeps the labels from the original type, and we know which arguments to expect.

Yes, curry is not as flexible as the original version, but for a lot of use cases, this might be the right choice. It's all about the trade-offs we accept for our use case.

 If you work with tuples a lot, you can name the elements of your tuple types: type Person = [name: string, age: number];. Those labels are just annotations and are removed after transpilation.

Ultimately, the curry function and its many different implementations stand for the many ways you can use TypeScript to solve a particular problem. You can go all out with the type system and use it for very complex and elaborate types, or you can reduce the scope a bit and let the compiler do the work for you. Your choice depends on your goals and what you try to achieve.

7.6 Creating an Enum from a Tuple

Problem

You like how enums make it easy to select valid values, but after reading Recipe 3.12 you don't want to deal with all their caveats.

Solution

Create your enums from a tuple. Use conditional types, variadic tuple types, and the "length" property to type the data structure.

Discussion

In Recipe 3.12 we discussed all possible caveats when using number and string enums. We ended up with a pattern that is much closer to the type system but gives you the same developer experience as regular enums:

```
const Direction = {
  Up: 0,
  Down: 1,
  Left: 2,
  Right: 3,
} as const;

// Get to the const values of Direction
type Direction = (typeof Direction)[keyof typeof Direction];

// (typeof Direction)[keyof typeof Direction] yields 0 | 1 | 2 | 3
function move(direction: Direction) {
  // tbd
}
```

```
move(30); // This breaks!

move(0); //This works!

move(Direction.Left); // This also works!
```

It's a very straightforward pattern with no surprises, but it can result in a lot of work for you if you are dealing with lots of entries, especially if you want to have string enums:

```
const Commands = {
  Shift: "shift",
  Xargs: "xargs",
  Tail: "tail",
  Head: "head",
  Uniq: "uniq",
  Cut: "cut",
  Awk: "awk",
  Sed: "sed",
  Grep: "grep",
  Echo: "echo",
} as const;
```

There is duplication, which may result in typos, which may lead to undefined behavior. A helper function that creates an enum like this for you helps deal with redundancy and duplication. Let's say you have a collection of items like this:

```
const commandItems = [
  "echo",
  "grep",
  "sed",
  "awk",
  "cut",
  "uniq",
  "head",
  "tail",
  "xargs",
  "shift",
] as const;
```

A helper function `createEnum` iterates through every item, creating an object with capitalized keys that point either to a string value or to a number value, depending on your input parameters:

```
function capitalize(x: string): string {
  return x.charAt(0).toUpperCase() + x.slice(1);
}

// Typings to be done
function createEnum(arr, numeric) {
  let obj = {};
  for (let [i, el] of arr.entries()) {
```

```
    obj[capitalize(el)] = numeric ? i : el;
  }
  return obj;
}

const Command = createEnum(commandItems); // string enum
const CommandN = createEnum(commandItems, true); // number enum
```

Let's create types for this! We need to take care of two things:

- Create an object from a tuple. The keys are capitalized.
- Set the values of each property key to either a string value or a number value. The number values should start at 0 and increase by one with each step.

To create object keys, we need a union type we can map out. To get all object keys, we need to convert our tuple to a union type. A helper type `TupleToUnion` takes a string tuple and converts it to a union type. Why only string tuples? Because we need object keys, and string keys are the easiest to use.

`TupleToUnion<T>` is a recursive type. Like we did in other lessons, we are shaving off single elements—this time at the end of the tuple—and then calling the type again with the remaining elements. We put each call in a union, effectively getting a union type of tuple elements:

```
type TupleToUnion<T extends readonly string[]> = T extends readonly [
  ...infer Rest extends string[],
  infer Key extends string
]
  ? Key | TupleToUnion<Rest>
  : never;
```

With a map type and a string manipulation type, we can create the string enum version of `Enum<T>`:

```
type Enum<T extends readonly string[], N extends boolean = false> = Readonly<
  {
    [K in TupleToUnion<T> as Capitalize<K>]: K
  }
>;
```

For the number enum version, we need to get a numerical representation of each value. If we think about it, we have already stored it somewhere in our original data. Let's look at how `TupleToUnion` deals with a four-element tuple:

```
// The type we want to convert to a union type
type Direction = ["up", "down", "left", "right"];

// Calling the helper type
type DirectionUnion = TupleToUnion<Direction>;

// Extracting the last, recursively calling TupleToUnion with the Rest
```

```
type DirectionUnion = "right" | TupleToUnion<["up", "down", "left"]>;

// Extracting the last, recursively calling TupleToUnion with the Rest
type DirectionUnion = "right" | "left" | TupleToUnion<["up", "down"]>;

// Extracting the last, recursively calling TupleToUnion with the Rest
type DirectionUnion = "right" | "left" | "down" | TupleToUnion<["up"]>;

// Extracting the last, recursively calling TupleToUnion with an empty tuple
type DirectionUnion = "right" | "left" | "down" | "up" | TupleToUnion<[]>;

// The conditional type goes into the else branch, adding never to the union
type DirectionUnion = "right" | "left" | "down" | "up" | never;

// never in a union is swallowed
type DirectionUnion = "right" | "left" | "down" | "up";
```

If you look closely, you can see that the length of the tuple is decreasing with each call. First, it's three elements, then two, then one, and ultimately there are no elements left. Tuples are defined by the length of the array and the type at each position in the array. TypeScript stores the length as a number for tuples, accessible via the "length" property:

```
type DirectionLength = Direction["length"]; // 4
```

So with each recursive call, we can get the length of the remaining elements and use this as a value for the enum. Instead of just returning the enum keys, we return an object with the key and its possible number value:

```
type TupleToUnion<T extends readonly string[]> = T extends readonly [
  ...infer Rest extends string[],
  infer Key extends string
]
  ? { key: Key; val: Rest["length"] } | TupleToUnion<Rest>
  : never;
```

We use this newly created object to decide whether we want to have number values or string values in our enum:

```
type Enum<T extends readonly string[], N extends boolean = false> = Readonly<
  {
    [K in TupleToUnion<T> as Capitalize<K["key"]>]: N extends true
      ? K["val"]
      : K["key"];
  }
>;
```

And that's it! We wire up our new Enum<T, N> type to the createEnum function:

```
type Values<T> = T[keyof T];

function createEnum<T extends readonly string[], B extends boolean>(
```

```
    arr: T,
    numeric?: B
) {
  let obj: any = {};
  for (let [i, el] of arr.entries()) {
    obj[capitalize(el)] = numeric ? i : el;
  }
  return obj as Enum<T, B>;
}

const Command = createEnum(commandItems, false);
type Command = Values<typeof Command>;
```

Being able to access the length of a tuple within the type system is one of the hidden gems in TypeScript. This allows for many things, as shown in this example, but also fun stuff like implementing calculators in the type system. As with all advanced features in TypeScript, use them wisely.

7.7 Splitting All Elements of a Function Signature

Problem

You know how to grab argument types and return types from functions within a function, but you want to use the same types outside as well.

Solution

Use the built-in Parameters<F> and ReturnType<F> helper types.

Discussion

In this chapter, we have dealt with helper functions and how they can grab information from functions that are arguments. For example, this defer function takes a function and all its arguments and returns another function that will execute it. With some generic types, we can capture everything we need:

```
function defer<Par extends unknown[], Ret>(
  fn: (...par: Par) => Ret,
  ...args: Par
): () => Ret {
  return () => fn(...args);
}

const log = defer(console.log, "Hello, world!");
log();
```

This works great if we pass functions as arguments because we can easily pick the details and reuse them. But certain scenarios need a function's arguments and its return type outside of a generic function. Thankfully, we can leverage some built-in TypeScript helper types. With `Parameters<F>` we get a function's arguments as a tuple; with `ReturnType<F>` we get the return type of a function. So the `defer` function from before could be written like:

```
type Fn = (...args: any[]) => any;

function defer<F extends Fn>(
  fn: F,
  ...args: Parameters<F>
): () => ReturnType<F> {
  return () => fn(...args);
}
```

Both `Parameters<F>` and `ReturnType<F>` are conditional types that rely on function/tuple types and are very similar. In `Parameters<F>` we infer the arguments, and in `ReturnType<F>` we infer the return type:

```
type Parameters<F extends (...args: any) => any> =
  F extends (...args: infer P) => any ? P : never;

type ReturnType<F extends (...args: any) => any> =
  F extends (...args: any) => infer R ? R : any;
```

We can use those helper types, for example, to prepare function arguments outside of functions. Take this `search` function:

```
type Result = {
  page: URL;
  title: string;
  description: string;
};

function search(query: string, tags: string[]): Promise<Result[]> {
  throw "to be done";
}
```

With `Parameters<typeof search>` we get an idea of which parameters to expect. We define them outside of the function call and spread them as arguments when calling:

```
const searchParams: Parameters<typeof search> = [
  "Variadic tuple tpyes",
  ["TypeScript", "JavaScript"],
];

search(...searchParams);
const deferredSearch = defer(search, ...searchParams);
```

Both helpers come in handy when you generate new types as well; see Recipe 4.8 for an example.

CHAPTER 8

Helper Types

One of TypeScript's strengths is the ability to derive types from other types. This allows you to define relationships between types, where updates in one type trickle through to all derived types automatically. This reduces maintenance and ultimately results in more robust type setups.

When creating derived types, we usually apply the same type modifications but in different combinations. TypeScript already has a set of built-in utility types (*https:// oreil.ly/inM2y*), some of which we've already seen in this book. But sometimes they are not enough. Some situations require you either to apply known techniques differently or to dig deep into the inner workings of the type system to produce the desired result. You might need your own set of helper types.

This chapter introduces you to the concept of helper types and shows you some use cases where a custom helper type expands your ability to derive types from others tremendously. Each type is designed to work in different situations, and each type should teach you a new aspect of the type system. Of course, the list of types you see here is by no means complete, but they give you a good entry point and enough resources to branch out.

In the end, TypeScript's type system can be seen as its own functional metaprogramming language, where you combine small, single-purpose helper types with bigger helper types to make type derivates as easy as applying a single type to your existing models.

8.1 Setting Specific Properties Optional

Problem

You want to derive types where you set specific properties optional.

Solution

Create a custom helper type `SetOptional` that intersects two object types: one that maps over all selected properties using the optional mapped type modifier and one that maps over all remaining properties.

Discussion

All your models in your TypeScript project are set and defined, and you want to refer to them throughout your code:

```
type Person = {
  name: string;
  age: number;
  profession: string;
};
```

One situation that occurs pretty often is that you need something that looks like `Person` but does not require all properties to be set; some of them can be *optional*. This will make your API more open to other structures and types that are of similar shape but lack one or two fields. You don't want to maintain different types (see Recipe 12.1) but rather derive them from the original model, which is still in use.

TypeScript has a built-in helper type called `Partial<T>` that modifies all properties to be optional:

```
type Partial<T> = { [P in keyof T]?: T[P]; };
```

It's a *mapped type* that maps out over all keys and uses the *optional mapped type modifier* to set each property to optional. The first step in making a `SetOptional` type is to reduce the set of keys that can be set as optional:

```
type SelectPartial<T, K extends keyof T> = {
  [P in K]?: T[P]
};
```

 The *optional mapped type modifier* applies the symbol for an optional property—the question mark—to a set of properties. You learned about mapped type modifiers in Recipe 4.5.

In `SelectPartial<T, K extends keyof T>`, we don't map over all keys, just a subset of keys provided. With the `extends keyof T` generic constraint, we make sure that we pass only valid property keys. If we apply `SelectPartial` to `Person` to select `"age"`, we end up with a type where we see *only* the `age` property, which is set to optional:

```
type Age = SelectPartial<Person, "age">;

// type Age = { age?: number | undefined };
```

The first half is done: everything we want to set as optional is optional. But the rest of the properties are missing. Let's get them back to the object type.

The easiest way of extending an existing object type with more properties is to create an intersection type with another object type. So in our case, we take what we've written in `SelectPartial` and intersect it with a type that includes all remaining keys.

We can get all remaining keys by using the `Exclude` helper type. `Exclude<T, U>` is a *conditional type* that compares two sets. If elements from set T are in U, they will be removed using `never`; otherwise, they stay in the type:

```
type Exclude<T, U> = T extends U ? never : T;
```

This works in contrast to `Extract<T, U>` which we described in Recipe 5.3. `Exclude<T, U>` is a *distributive conditional type* (see Recipe 5.2) and distributes the conditional type over every element of a union:

```
// This example shows how TypeScript evaluates a
// helper type step by step.

type ExcludeAge = Exclude<"name" | "age", "age">;

// 1. Distribute
type ExcludeAge =
  "name" extends "age" ? never : "name" |
  "age" extends "age" ? never : "age";

// 2. Evaluate
type ExcludeAge = "name" | never;

// 3. Remove unnecessary `never`
type ExcludeAge = "name";
```

This is exactly what we want! In `SetOptional`, we create one type that *picks* all selected keys and makes them optional, then we *exclude* the same keys from the bigger set of all of the object's keys:

```
type SetOptional<T, K extends keyof T> = {
  [P in K]?: T[P];
} &
  {
    [P in Exclude<keyof T, K>]: T[P];
  };
```

The intersection of both types is the new object type, which we can use with any model we like:

```
type OptionalAge = SetOptional<Person, "age">;

/*
type OptionalAge = {
  name: string;
  age?: number | undefined;
  profession: string;
};
*/
```

If we want to make more than one key optional, we need to provide a union type with all desired property keys:

```
type OptionalAgeAndProf = SetOptional<Person, "age" | "profession">;
```

TypeScript not only allows you to define types like this yourself but also has a set of built-in helper types that you can easily combine for similar effect. We could write the same type `SetOptional` solely based on helper types:

```
type SetOptional<T, K extends keyof T> = Partial<Pick<T, K>> & Omit<T, K>;
```

- `Pick<T, K>` selects keys K from object T.
- `Omit<T, K>` selects everything but K from object T (using `Exclude` under the hood).
- And we already learned what `Partial<T>` does.

Depending on how you like to read types, this combination of helper types can be easier to read and understand, especially since the built-in types are much better known among developers.

There is only one problem: if you hover over your newly generated types, TypeScript will show you how the type is made, not what the actual properties are. With the Remap helper type from Recipe 8.3, we can make our types more readable and usable:

```
type SetOptional<T, K extends keyof T> = Remap<
  Partial<Pick<T, K>> & Omit<T, K>
>;
```

If you think about your type arguments as a function interface, you might want to think about your type parameters as well. One optimization you could do is to set the second argument—the selected object keys—to a default value:

```
type SetOptional<T, K extends keyof T = keyof T> = Remap<
  Partial<Pick<T, K>> & Omit<T, K>
>;
```

With `K extends keyof T = keyof T`, we can make sure that we set all property keys as optional, and only select specific ones if we need them. Our helper type just became a little bit more flexible.

In the same vein, you can start creating types for other situations, like `SetRequired`, where you want to make sure that some keys are definitely required:

```
type SetRequired<T, K extends keyof T = keyof T> = Remap<
  Required<Pick<T, K>> & Omit<T, K>
>;
```

Or `OnlyRequired`, where all keys you provide are required, but the rest are optional:

```
type OnlyRequired<T, K extends keyof T = keyof T> = Remap<
  Required<Pick<T, K>> & Partial<Omit<T, K>>
>;
```

The best thing: you end up with an arsenal of helper types that can be used throughout multiple projects.

8.2 Modifying Nested Objects

Problem

Object helper types like `Partial`, `Required`, and `Readonly` modify only the first level of an object and won't touch nested object properties.

Solution

Create recursive helper types that do the same operation on nested objects.

Discussion

Say that your application has different settings that can be configured by users. To make it easy for you to extend settings over time, you store only the difference between a set of defaults and the settings your user configured:

```
type Settings = {
  mode: "light" | "dark";
  playbackSpeed: number;
  subtitles: {
    active: boolean;
    color: string;
  };
};

const defaults: Settings = {
  mode: "dark",
  playbackSpeed: 1.0,
  subtitles: {
    active: false,
    color: "white",
  },
};
```

The function `applySettings` takes both the defaults and the settings from your users. You defined them as `Partial<Settings>`, since the user needs to provide only *some* keys; the rest will be taken from the default settings:

```
function applySettings(
  defaultSettings: Settings,
  userSettings: Partial<Settings>
): Settings {
  return { ...defaultSettings, ...userSettings };
}
```

This works really well if you need to set certain properties on the first level:

```
let settings = applySettings(defaults, { mode: "light" });
```

But this causes problems if you want to modify specific properties deeper down in your object, like setting `subtitles` to `active`:

```
let settings = applySettings(defaults, { subtitles: { active: true } });
//                                            ^
// Property 'color' is missing in type '{ active: true; }'
// but required in type '{ active: boolean; color: string; }'.(2741)
```

TypeScript complains that for `subtitles` you need to provide the entire object. This is because `Partial<T>`—like its siblings `Required<T>` and `Readonly<T>`—modifies only the first level of an object. Nested objects will be treated as simple values.

To change this, we need to create a new type called `DeepPartial<T>`, which recursively goes through every property and applies the *optional mapped type modifier* for each level:

```
type DeepPartial<T> = {
  [K in keyof T]?: DeepPartial<T[K]>;
};
```

The first draft already works well, thanks to TypeScript stopping recursion at primitive values, but it has the potential to result in unreadable output. A simple condition that checks that we go deep only if we are dealing with an object makes our type much more robust and the result more readable:

```
type DeepPartial<T> = T extends object
  ? {
      [K in keyof T]?: DeepPartial<T[K]>;
    }
  : T;
```

For example, `DeepPartial<Settings>` results in the following output:

```
type DeepPartialSettings = {
  mode?: "light" | "dark" | undefined;
  playbackSpeed?: number | undefined;
  subtitles?: {
    active?: boolean | undefined;
```

```
      color?: string | undefined;
    } | undefined;
};
```

This is exactly what we've been aiming for. If we use `DeepPartial<T>` in `apply`
`Settings`, we see that the actual usage of `applySettings` works, but TypeScript greets
us with another error:

```
function applySettings(
  defaultSettings: Settings,
  userSettings: DeepPartial<Settings>
): Settings {
  return { ...defaultSettings, ...userSettings };
//            ^
// Type '{ mode: "light" | "dark"; playbackSpeed: number;
//    subtitles: { active?: boolean | undefined;
//    color?: string | undefined; }; }' is not assignable to type 'Settings'.
}
```

Here, TypeScript complains that it can't merge the two objects into something that
results in `Settings`, as some of the `DeepPartial` set elements might not be assignable
to `Settings`. And this is true! Object merge using destructuring also works only on
the first level, just like `Partial<T>` has defined for us. This means that if we called
`applySettings` like before, we would get a totally different type than for `settings`:

```
let settings = applySettings(defaults, { subtitles: { active: true } });

// results in

let settings = {
  mode: "dark",
  playbackSpeed: 1,
  subtitles: {
    active: true
  }
};
```

`color` is all gone! This is one situation where TypeScript's type might be unintuitive at
first: why do object modification types go only one level deep? Because JavaScript
goes only one level deep! But ultimately, they point out bugs you wouldn't have
caught otherwise.

To circumvent this situation, you need to apply your settings recursively. This can be
nasty to implement yourself, so we resort to `lodash` and its `merge` function for
this functionality:

```
import { merge } from "lodash";

function applySettings(
  defaultSettings: Settings,
  userSettings: DeepPartial<Settings>
```

```
): Settings {
  return merge(defaultSettings, userSettings)
}
```

merge defines its interface to produce an intersection of two objects:

```
function merge<TObject, TSource>(
  object: TObject, source: TSource
): TObject & TSource {
  // ...
}
```

Again, exactly what we are looking for. An intersection of Settings and Deep Partial<Settings> also produces an intersection of both, which is—due to the nature of the types—Settings again.

So we end up with expressive types that tell us exactly what to expect, correct results for the output, and another helper type for our arsenal. You can create DeepReadonly and DeepRequired similarly.

8.3 Remapping Types

Problem

Constructing types gives you flexible, self-maintaining types, but the editor hints leave a lot to be desired.

Solution

Use the Remap<T> and DeepRemap<T> helper types to improve editor hints.

Discussion

When you use TypeScript's type system to construct new types, by using helper types, complex conditional types, or even simple intersections, you might end up with editor hints that are hard to decipher.

Let's look at OnlyRequired from Recipe 8.1. The type uses four helper types and one intersection to construct a new type in which all keys provided as the second type parameter are set to required, while all others are set to optional:

```
type OnlyRequired<T, K extends keyof T = keyof T> =
  Required<Pick<T, K>> & Partial<Omit<T, K>>;
```

This way of writing types gives you a good idea of what's happening. You can read the functionality based on how helper types are composed with one another. However, when you are actually using the types on your models, you might want to know more than the actual construction of the type:

```
type Person = {
  name: string;
  age: number;
  profession: string;
};

type NameRequired = OnlyRequired<Person, "name">;
```

If you hover over `NameRequired`, you see that TypeScript gives you information on how the type was constructed based on the parameters you provide, but the editor hint won't show you the result, the final type being constructed with those helper types. You can see the editor's feedback in Figure 8-1.

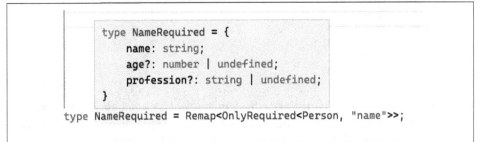

```
type NameRequired = Required<Pick<Person, "name">> &
Partial<Omit<Person, "name">>
type NameRequired = OnlyRequired<Person, "name">;
```

Figure 8-1. Editor hints on complex types expand very shallowly; without knowing the types underneath and their functionality, it becomes hard to understand the result

To make the final result look like an actual type and to spell out all the properties, we have to use a simple yet effective type called `Remap`:

```
type Remap<T> = {
  [K in keyof T]: T[K];
};
```

`Remap<T>` is just an object type that goes through every property and maps it to the value defined. No modifications, no filters, just putting out what's being put in. TypeScript will print out every property of mapped types, so instead of seeing the construction, you see the actual type, as shown in Figure 8-2.

```
type NameRequired = {
  name: string;
  age?: number | undefined;
  profession?: string | undefined;
}
type NameRequired = Remap<OnlyRequired<Person, "name">>;
```

Figure 8-2. With Remap<T>, the presentation of NameRequired becomes much more readable

Beautiful! This has become a staple in TypeScript utility type libraries. Some call it Debug; others call it Simplify. Remap is just another name for the same tool and the same effect: getting an idea of what your result will look like.

Like other mapped types Partial<T>, Readonly<T>, and Required<T>, Remap<T> also works on the first level only. A nested type like Settings that includes the Subtitles type will be remapped to the same output, and the editor feedback will be the same:

```
type Subtitles = {
  active: boolean;
  color: string;
};

type Settings = {
  mode: "light" | "dark";
  playbackSpeed: number;
  subtitles: Subtitles;
};
```

But also, as shown in Recipe 8.2, we can create a recursive variation that remaps *all* nested object types:

```
type DeepRemap<T> = T extends object
  ? {
      [K in keyof T]: DeepRemap<T[K]>;
    }
  : T;
```

Applying DeepRemap<T> to Settings will also expand Subtitles:

```
type SettingsRemapped = DeepRemap<Settings>;

// results in

type SettingsRemapped = {
    mode: "light" | "dark";
    playbackSpeed: number;
    subtitles: {
        active: boolean;
        color: string;
    };
};
```

Using Remap is mostly a matter of taste. Sometimes you want to know about the implementation, and sometimes the terse view of nested types is more readable than the expanded versions. But in other scenarios, you actually care about the result itself. In those cases, having a Remap<T> helper type handy and available is definitely helpful.

8.4 Getting All Required Keys

Problem

You want to create a type that extracts all *required* properties from an object.

Solution

Create a mapped helper type `GetRequired<T>` that filters keys based on a subtype check against its required counterpart.

Discussion

Optional properties have a tremendous effect on type compatibility. A simple type modifier, the question mark, widens the original type significantly. They allow us to define fields that might be there, but they can be used only if we do additional checks.

This means we can make our functions and interfaces compatible with types that lack certain properties entirely:

```
type Person = {
  name: string;
  age?: number;
};

function printPerson(person: Person): void {
  // ...
}


type Student = {
  name: string;
  semester: number;
};

const student: Student = {
  name: "Stefan",
  semester: 37,
};

printPerson(student); // all good!
```

We see that `age` is defined in `Person` but not at all defined in `Student`. Since it's optional, it doesn't keep us from using `printPerson` with objects of type `Student`. The set of compatible values is wider, as we can use objects of types that drop `age` entirely.

TypeScript solves that by attaching `undefined` to properties that are optional. This is the truest representation of "it might be there."

This fact is important if we want to check if property keys are required or not. Let's start by doing the most basic check. We have an object and want to check if all keys are required. We use the helper type `Required<T>`, which modifies all properties to be required. The simplest check is to see if an object type—for example, `Name`—is a subset of its `Required<T>` counterpart:

```
type Name = {
  name: string;
};

type Test = Name extends Required<Name> ? true : false;
// type Test = true
```

Here, `Test` results in `true`, because if we change all properties to `required` using `Required<T>`, we still get the same type. However, things change if we introduce an optional property:

```
type Person = {
  name: string;
  age?: number;
};

type Test = Person extends Required<Person> ? true : false;
// type Test = false
```

Here, `Test` results in `false`, because type `Person` with the optional property `age` accepts a much broader set of values than `Required<Person>`, where `age` needs to be set. Contrary to this check, if we swap `Person` and `Required<Person>`, we can see that the narrower type `Required<Person>` is in fact a subset of `Person`:

```
type Test = Required<Person> extends Person ? true : false;
// type Test = true
```

What we've checked so far is if the entire object has the required keys. But what we actually want is to get an object that includes only property keys that are set to required. This means we need to do this check with each property key. The need to iterate the same check over a set of keys is a good indicator for a mapped type.

Our next step is to create a mapped type that does the subset check for each property, to see if the resulting values include `undefined`:

```
type RequiredPerson = {
  [K in keyof Person]: Person[K] extends Required<Person[K]> ? true : false;
};

/*
type RequiredPerson = {
    name: true;
    age?: true | undefined;
}
*/
```

This is a good guess but gives us results that don't work. Each property resolves to true, meaning that the subset checks only for the value types *without* undefined. This is because `Required<T>` works on objects, not on primitive types. Something that gets us more robust results is checking if `Person[K]` includes any *nullable* values. `NonNullable<T>` removes undefined and null:

```
type RequiredPerson = {
  [K in keyof Person]: Person[K] extends NonNullable<Person[K]> ? true : false;
};

/*
type RequiredPerson = {
    name: true;
    age?: false | undefined;
}
*/
```

That's better, but still not where we want it to be. undefined is back again, as it's being added by the property modifier. Also, the property is still in the type, and we want to get rid of it.

What we need to do is reduce the set of possible keys. So instead of checking for the values, we do a conditional check on each property while we are mapping out keys. We check if `Person[K]` is a subset of `Required<Person>[K]`, doing a proper check against the bigger subset. If this is the case, we print out the key K; otherwise, we drop the property using `never` (see Recipe 5.2):

```
type RequiredPerson = {
  [K in keyof Person as Person[K] extends Required<Person>[K]
    ? K
    : never]: Person[K];
};
```

This gives us the results we want. Now we substitute `Person` for a generic type parameter and our helper type `GetRequired<T>` is done:

```
type GetRequired<T> = {
  [K in keyof T as T[K] extends Required<T>[K]
    ? K
    : never]: T[K];
};
```

From here on, we can derive variations like `GetOptional<T>`. However, checking if something is optional is not as easy as checking if some property keys are required, but we can use `GetRequired<T>` and a `keyof` operator to get all the required property keys:

```
type RequiredKeys<T> = keyof GetRequired<T>;
```

After that, we use the `RequiredKeys<T>` to *omit* them from our target object:

```
type GetOptional<T> = Omit<T, RequiredKeys<T>>;
```

Again, a combination of multiple helper types produces derived, self-maintaining types.

8.5 Allowing at Least One Property

Problem

You have a type for which you want to make sure that at least one property is set.

Solution

Create a `Split<T>` helper type that splits an object into a union of one-property objects.

Discussion

Your application stores a set of URLs—for example, for video formats—in an object where each key identifies a different format:

```
type VideoFormatURLs = {
  format360p: URL;
  format480p: URL;
  format720p: URL;
  format1080p: URL;
};
```

You want to create a function `loadVideo` that can load any of those video format URLs but needs to load at least one URL.

If `loadVideo` accepts parameters of type `VideoFormatURLs`, you need to provide *all* video format URLs:

```
function loadVideo(formats: VideoFormatURLs) {
  // tbd
}

loadVideo({
  format360p: new URL("..."),
  format480p: new URL("..."),
  format720p: new URL("..."),
  format1080p: new URL("..."),
});
```

But some videos might not exist, so a subset of all available types is actually what you're looking for. `Partial<VideoFormatURLs>` gives you that:

```
function loadVideo(formats: Partial<VideoFormatURLs>) {
  // tbd
}

loadVideo({
  format480p: new URL("..."),
  format720p: new URL("..."),
});
```

But since all keys are optional, you would also allow the empty object as a valid parameter:

```
loadVideo({});
```

This results in undefined behavior. You want to have at least one URL so you can load that video.

We have to find a type expressing that we expect at least one of the available video formats: a type that allows us to pass all of them and some of them but also prevents us from passing none.

Let's start with the "only one" cases. Instead of finding one type, let's create a union type that combines all situations where there's only one property set:

```
type AvailableVideoFormats =
  | {
      format360p: URL;
    }
  | {
      format480p: URL;
    }
  | {
      format720p: URL;
    }
  | {
      format1080p: URL;
    };
```

This allows us to pass in objects that only have one property set. Next, let's add the situations where we have two properties set:

```
type AvailableVideoFormats =
  | {
      format360p: URL;
    }
  | {
      format480p: URL;
    }
  | {
      format720p: URL;
```

```
    }
  | {
      format1080p: URL;
    };
```

Wait! That's the same type! But that's the way union types work. If they aren't discriminated (see Recipe 3.2), union types will allow for values that are located at all intersections of the original set, as shown in Figure 8-3.

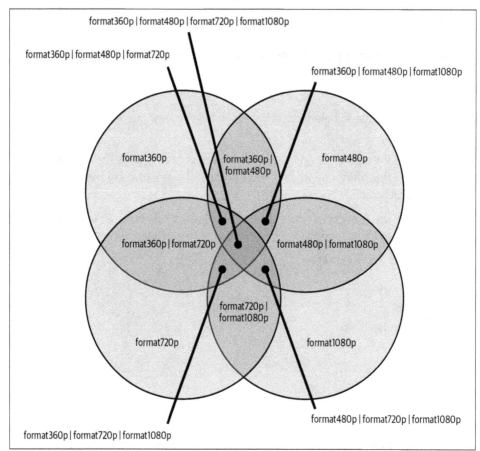

Figure 8-3. The union type AvailableVideoFormats

Each union member defines a set of possible values. The intersections describe the values where both types overlap. All possible combinations can be expressed with this union.

So now that we know the type, it would be fantastic to derive it from the original type. We want to split an object type into a union of types where each member contains exactly one property.

One way to get a union type related to VideoFormatURLs is to use the keyof operator:

```
type AvailableVideoFormats = keyof VideoFormatURLs;
```

This yields "format360p" | "format480p" | "format720p" | "format1080p", a union of the keys. We can use the keyof operator to index access the original type:

```
type AvailableVideoFormats = VideoFormatURLs[keyof VideoFormatURLs];
```

This yields URL, which is just one type, but in reality it is a union of the types of values. Now we only need to find a way to get proper values that represent an actual object type and are related to each property key.

Read this phrase again: "related to each property key." This calls for a mapped type! We can map through all VideoFormatURLs to get the property key to the righthand side of the object:

```
type AvailableVideoFormats = {
  [K in keyof VideoFormatURLs]: K;
};

/* yields
type AvailableVideoFormats = {
  format360p: "format360p";
  format480p: "format480p";
  format720p: "format720p";
  format1080p: "format1080p";
}; */
```

With that, we can index access the mapped type and get value types for each element. But we're not only setting the key to the righthand side but also creating another object type that takes this string as a property key and maps it to the respective value type:

```
type AvailableVideoFormats = {
  [K in keyof VideoFormatURLs]: {
    [P in K]: VideoFormatURLs[P]
  };
};

/* yields
type AvailableVideoFormats = {
  format360p: {
    format360p: URL;
  };
  format480p: {
    format480p: URL;
  };
  format720p: {
    format720p: URL;
  };
  format1080p: {
```

```
    format1080p: URL;
  };
};
```

Now we can use index access again to grep each value type from the righthand side into a union:

```
type AvailableVideoFormats = {
  [K in keyof VideoFormatURLs]: {
    [P in K]: VideoFormatURLs[P]
  };
}[keyof VideoFormatURLs];

/* yields
type AvailableVideoFormats =
  | {
      format360p: URL;
    }
  | {
      format480p: URL;
    }
  | {
      format720p: URL;
    }
  | {
      format1080p: URL;
    };
*/
```

And that's what we've been looking for! As a next step, we take the concrete types and substitute them with generics, resulting in the Split<T> helper type:

```
type Split<T> = {
  [K in keyof T]: {
    [P in K]: T[P];
  };
}[keyof T];
```

Another helper type in our arsenal. Using it with loadVideo gives us exactly the behavior we have been aiming for:

```
function loadVideo(formats: Split<VideoFormatURLs>) {
  // tbd
}

loadVideo({});
//        ^
// Argument of type '{}' is not assignable to parameter
// of type 'Split<VideoFormatURLs>'

loadVideo({
  format480p: new URL("..."),
}); // all good
```

Split<T> is a nice way to see how basic type system functionality can change the behavior of your interfaces significantly, and how some simple typing techniques like mapped types, index access types, and property keys can be used to get a tiny yet powerful helper type.

8.6 Allowing Exactly One and All or None

Problem

Next to requiring *at least one* like in Recipe 8.5, you also want to provide scenarios where users provide *exactly one* or *all or none*.

Solution

Create ExactlyOne<T> and AllOrNone<T, K>. Both rely on the *optional never* technique in combination with a derivate of Split<T>.

Discussion

With Split<T> from Recipe 8.5 we create a nice helper type that makes it possible to describe the scenario where we want *at least one* parameter provided. This is something that Partial<T> can't provide for us, but regular union types can.

Starting from this idea we, might also run into scenarios where we want our users to provide *exactly one*, making sure they don't add too many options.

One technique that can be used here is optional never, which we learned in Recipe 3.8. Next to all the properties you want to allow, you set all the properties you don't want to allow to optional and their value to never. This means the moment you write the property name, TypeScript wants you to set its value to something that is compatible with never, which you can't, as the never has no values.

A union type where we put all property names in an *exclusive or* relation is the key. We get a union type with each property already with Split<T>:

```
type Split<T> = {
  [K in keyof T]: {
    [P in K]: T[P];
  };
}[keyof T];
```

All we need to do is to intersect each element with the remaining keys and set them to optional never:

```
type ExactlyOne<T> = {
  [K in keyof T]: {
    [P in K]: T[P];
  } &
```

```
    {
        [P in Exclude<keyof T, K>]?: never; // optional never
    };
}[keyof T];
```

With that, the resulting type is more extensive but tells us exactly which properties to exclude:

```
type ExactlyOneVideoFormat = ({
    format360p: URL;
} & {
    format480p?: never;
    format720p?: never;
    format1080p?: never;
}) | ({
    format480p: URL;
} & {
    format360p?: never;
    format720p?: never;
    format1080p?: never;
}) | ({
    format720p: URL;
} & {
    format320p?: never;
    format480p?: never;
    format1080p?: never;
}) | ({
    format1080p: URL;
} & {
    format320p?: never;
    format480p?: never;
    format720p?: never;
});
```

And it works as expected:

```
function loadVideo(formats: ExactlyOne<VideoFormatURLs>) {
    // tbd
}

loadVideo({
    format360p: new URL("..."),
}); // works

loadVideo({
    format360p: new URL("..."),
    format1080p: new URL("..."),
});
// ^
// Argument of type '{ format360p: URL; format1080p: URL; }'
// is not assignable to parameter of type 'ExactlyOne<VideoFormatURLs>'.
```

ExactlyOne<T> is so much like Split<T> that we could think of extending Split<T> with the functionality to include the optional never pattern:

```
type Split<T, OptionalNever extends boolean = false> = {
  [K in keyof T]: {
    [P in K]: T[P];
  } &
    (OptionalNever extends false
      ? {}
      : {
          [P in Exclude<keyof T, K>]?: never;
        });
}[keyof T];

type ExactlyOne<T> = Split<T, true>;
```

We add a new generic type parameter OptionalNever, which we default to false. We then intersect the part where we create new objects with a conditional type that checks if the parameter OptionalNever is actually false. If so, we intersect with the empty object (leaving the original object intact); otherwise, we add the optional never part to the object. ExactlyOne<T> is refactored to Split<T, true>, where we activate the OptionalNever flag.

Another scenario very similar to Split<T> or ExactlyOne<T> is to provide all arguments or no arguments. Think of splitting video formats into standard definition (SD: 360p and 480p) and high definition (HD: 720p and 1080p). In your app, you want to make sure that if your users provide SD formats, they should provide all possible formats. It's OK to have a single HD format.

This is also where the optional never technique comes in. We define a type that *requires* all selected keys or sets them to never if only one is provided:

```
type AllOrNone<T, Keys extends keyof T> = (
  | {
      [K in Keys]-?: T[K]; // all available
    }
  | {
      [K in Keys]?: never; // or none
    }
);
```

If you want to make sure that you provide also *all* HD formats, add the rest to it via an intersection:

```
type AllOrNone<T, Keys extends keyof T> = (
  | {
      [K in Keys]-?: T[K];
    }
  | {
      [K in Keys]?: never;
    }
```

```
) & {
  [K in Exclude<keyof T, Keys>]: T[K] // the rest, as it was defined
}
```

Or if HD formats are totally optional, add them via a `Partial<T>`:

```
type AllOrNone<T, Keys extends keyof T> = (
  | {
      [K in Keys]-?: T[K];
    }
  | {
      [K in Keys]?: never;
    }
) & Partial<Omit<T, Keys>>; // the rest, but optional
```

But then you run into the same problem as in Recipe 8.5, where you can provide values that don't include any formats at all. Intersecting the *all or none* variation with `Split<T>` is the solution we are aiming for:

```
type AllOrNone<T, Keys extends keyof T> = (
  | {
      [K in Keys]-?: T[K];
    }
  | {
      [K in Keys]?: never;
    }
) & Split<T>;
```

And it works as intended:

```
function loadVideo(
  formats: AllOrNone<VideoFormatURLs, "format360p" | "format480p">
) {
  // TBD
}

loadVideo({
  format360p: new URL("..."),
  format480p: new URL("..."),
}); // OK

loadVideo({
  format360p: new URL("..."),
  format480p: new URL("..."),
  format1080p: new URL("..."),
}); // OK

loadVideo({
  format1080p: new URL("..."),
}); // OK

loadVideo({
  format360p: new URL("..."),
  format1080p: new URL("..."),
```

```
});
// ^ Argument of type '{ format360p: URL; format1080p: URL; }' is
// not assignable to parameter of type
// '({ format360p: URL; format480p: URL; } & ... (abbreviated)
```

If we look closely at what `AllOrNone` does, we can easily rewrite it with built-in helper types:

```
type AllOrNone<T, Keys extends keyof T> = (
  | Required<Pick<T, Keys>>
  | Partial<Record<Keys, never>>
) &
  Split<T>;
```

This is arguably more readable but also more to the point of metaprogramming in the type system. You have a set of helper types, and you can combine them to create new helper types: almost like a functional programming language, but on sets of values, in the type system.

8.7 Converting Union to Intersection Types

Problem

Your model is defined as a union type of several variants. To derive other types from it, you first need to convert the union type to an intersection type.

Solution

Create a `UnionToIntersection<T>` helper type that uses contravariant positions.

Discussion

In Recipe 8.5 we discussed how we can split a model type into a union of its variants. Depending on how your application works, you may want to define the model as a union type of several variants right from the beginning:

```
type BasicVideoData = {
  // tbd
};

type Format320 = { urls: { format320p: URL } };
type Format480 = { urls: { format480p: URL } };
type Format720 = { urls: { format720p: URL } };
type Format1080 = { urls: { format1080p: URL } };

type Video = BasicVideoData & (Format320 | Format480 | Format720 | Format1080);
```

The type `Video` allows you to define several formats but requires you to define at least one:

```
const video1: Video = {
  // ...
  urls: {
    format320p: new URL("https://..."),
  },
}; // OK

const video2: Video = {
  // ...
  urls: {
    format320p: new URL("https://..."),
    format480p: new URL("https://..."),
  },
}; // OK

const video3: Video = {
  // ...
  urls: {
    format1080p: new URL("https://..."),
  },
}; // OK
```

However, putting them in a union has some side effects—for example, when you need all available keys:

```
type FormatKeys = keyof Video["urls"];
// FormatKeys = never

// This is not what we want here!
function selectFormat(format: FormatKeys): void {
  // tbd.
}
```

You might expect `FormatKeys` to provide a union type of all keys that are nested in `urls`. Index access on a union type, however, tries to find the lowest common denominator. And in this case, there is none. To get a union type of all format keys, you need to have all keys within one type:

```
type Video = BasicVideoData & {
  urls: {
    format320p: URL;
    format480p: URL;
    format720p: URL;
    format1080p: URL;
  };
};

type FormatKeys = keyof Video["urls"];
```

```
// type FormatKeys =
//   "format320p" | "format480p" | "format720p" | "format1080p";
```

A way to create an object like this is to modify the union type to an intersection type.

 In Recipe 8.5, modeling data in a single type was the way to go; in this recipe, we see that modeling data as a union type is more to our liking. In reality, there is no single answer to how you define your models. Use the representation that best fits your application domain and that doesn't get in your way too much. The important thing is to be able to derive other types as you need them. This reduces maintenance and allows you to create more robust types. In Chapter 12 and especially Recipe 12.1 we will look at the principle of "low maintenance types."

Converting a union type to an intersection type is a peculiar task in TypeScript and requires some deep knowledge of the inner workings of the type system. To learn all these concepts, we look at the finished type, and then see what happens under the hood:

```
type UnionToIntersection<T> =
  (T extends any ? (x: T) => any : never) extends
  (x: infer R) => any ? R : never;
```

There is a *lot* to unpack here:

- We have two conditional types. The first one seems to always result in the true branch, so why do we need it?
- The first conditional type wraps the type in a function argument, and the second conditional type unwraps it again. Why is this necessary?
- And how do both conditional types transform a union type to an intersection type?

Let's analyze UnionToIntersection<T> step by step.

In the first conditional within UnionToIntersection<T>, we use the generic type argument as a *naked type*:

```
type UnionToIntersection<T> =
  (T extends any ? (x: T) => any : never) //...
```

This means we check if T is in a subtype condition without wrapping it in some other type:

```
type Naked<T> = T extends ...; // a naked type

type NotNaked<T> = { o: T } extends ...; // a non-naked type
```

Naked types in conditional types have a certain feature. If T is a union, they run the conditional type for each constituent of the union. So with a naked type, a *conditional of union types becomes a union of conditional types*:

```
type WrapNaked<T> =  T extends any ? { o: T } : never;

type Foo = WrapNaked<string | number | boolean>;

// A naked type, so this equals to

type Foo =
  WrapNaked<string> | WrapNaked<number> | WrapNaked<boolean>;

// equals to

type Foo =
  string extends any ? { o: string } : never |
  number extends any ? { o: number } : never |
  boolean extends any ? { o: boolean } : never;

type Foo =
  { o: string } | { o: number } | { o: boolean };
```

As compared to the non-naked version:

```
type WrapNaked<T> = { o: T } extends any ? { o: T } : never;

type Foo = WrapNaked<string | number | boolean>;

// A non-naked type, so this equals to

type Foo =
  { o: string | number | boolean } extends any ?
  { o: string | number | boolean } : never;

type Foo = { o: string | number | boolean };
```

Subtle, but considerably different for complex types!

In our example, we use the naked type and ask if it extends any (which it always does; any is the allow-it-all top type):

```
type UnionToIntersection<T> =
  (T extends any ? (x: T) => any : never) //...
```

Since this condition is always true, we wrap our generic type in a function, where T is the type of the function's parameter. But why are we doing that?

This leads to the second condition:

```
type UnionToIntersection<T> =
  (T extends any ? (x: T) => any : never) extends
  (x: infer R) => any ? R : never
```

As the first condition always yields true, meaning that we wrap our type in a function type, the other condition also always yields true. We are basically checking if the type we just created is a subtype of itself. But instead of passing through T, we infer a new type R, and return the inferred type.

What we do is wrap and unwrap type T via a function type.

Doing this via function arguments brings the new inferred type R in a *contravariant position*.

So what does *contravariance* mean? The opposite of *contravariance* is *covariance*, and what you would expect from normal subtyping:

```
declare let b: string;
declare let c: string | number;

c = b // OK
```

string is a subtype of string | number; all elements of string appear in string | number, so we can assign b to c. c still behaves as we originally intended. This is covariance.

This, on the other hand, won't work:

```
type Fun<X> = (...args: X[]) => void;

declare let f: Fun<string>;
declare let g: Fun<string | number>;

g = f // this cannot be assigned
```

We can't assign f to g, because then we would also be able to call f with a number! We miss part of the contract of g. This is contravariance.

The interesting thing is that contravariance effectively works like an intersection: if f accepts string and g accepts string | number, the type that is accepted by both is (string | number) & string, which is string.

Covariance and Contravariance

Orginate.com (*https://oreil.ly/dX3DM*) says that "variance determines how instances of paramterized types are subtypes or supertypes of one another."

TypeScript uses variance to see if types can be substantiated for another type in an expression. Next to the description in this recipe, Figure 8-4, based on material by Rice University (*https://oreil.ly/ftfP7*), shows how covariance and contravariance play out.

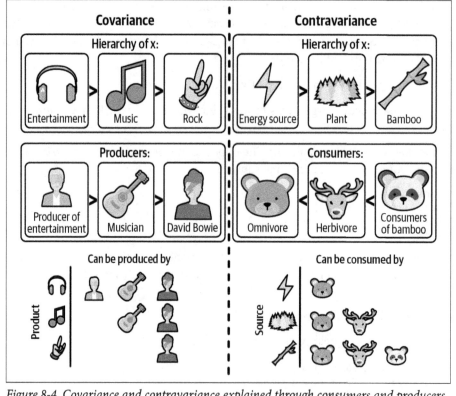

Figure 8-4. Covariance and contravariance explained through consumers and producers

When we put types in contravariant positions within a conditional type, TypeScript creates an *intersection* out of it. Meaning that since we *infer* from a function argument, TypeScript knows that we have to fulfill the complete contract, creating an intersection of all constituents in the union.

Basically, *union to intersection*.

Let's run it through:

```
type UnionToIntersection<T> =
  (T extends any ? (x: T) => any : never) extends
  (x: infer R) => any ? R : never;

type Intersected = UnionToIntersection<Video["urls"]>;

// equals to

type Intersected = UnionToIntersection<
  { format320p: URL } |
  { format480p: URL } |
```

```
    { format720p: URL } |
    { format1080p: URL }
  >;
```

We have a naked type; this means we can do a union of conditionals:

```
type Intersected =
  | UnionToIntersection<{ format320p: URL }>
  | UnionToIntersection<{ format480p: URL }>
  | UnionToIntersection<{ format720p: URL }>
  | UnionToIntersection<{ format1080p: URL }>;
```

Let's expand `UnionToIntersection<T>`:

```
type Intersected =
  | ({ format320p: URL } extends any ?
    (x: { format320p: URL }) => any : never) extends
    (x: infer R) => any ? R : never
  | ({ format480p: URL } extends any ?
    (x: { format480p: URL }) => any : never) extends
    (x: infer R) => any ? R : never
  | ({ format720p: URL } extends any ?
    (x: { format720p: URL }) => any : never) extends
    (x: infer R) => any ? R : never
  | ({ format1080p: URL } extends any ?
    (x: { format1080p: URL }) => any : never) extends
    (x: infer R) => any ? R : never;
```

And evaluate the first conditional:

```
type Intersected =
  | ((x: { format320p: URL }) => any) extends (x: infer R) => any ? R : never
  | ((x: { format480p: URL }) => any) extends (x: infer R) => any ? R : never
  | ((x: { format720p: URL }) => any) extends (x: infer R) => any ? R : never
  | ((x: { format1080p: URL }) => any) extends (x: infer R) => any ? R : never;
```

Let's evaluate conditional two, where we infer R:

```
type Intersected =
  | { format320p: URL } | { format480p: URL }
  | { format720p: URL } | { format1080p: URL };
```

But wait! R is inferred from a contravariant position. We have to make an intersection; otherwise, we lose type compatibility:

```
type Intersected =
  { format320p: URL } & { format480p: URL } &
  { format720p: URL } & { format1080p: URL };
```

And that's what we have been looking for! So, applied to our original example:

```
type FormatKeys = keyof UnionToIntersection<Video["urls"]>;
```

FormatKeys is now `"format320p"` | `"format480p"` | `"format720p"` | `"for`
`mat1080p"`#. Whenever we add another format to the original union, the `FormatKeys`
type updates automatically. Maintain once; use everywhere.

8.8 Using type-fest

Problem

You love your helper types so much that you want to create a utility library for easy
access.

Solution

Chances are *type-fest* already has everything you need.

Discussion

The whole idea of this chapter was to introduce you to a couple of useful helper types
that are not part of standard Typescript but have proven to be highly flexible for
many scenarios: single-purpose generic helper types that can be combined and composed to derive types based on your existing models. You write your models once,
and all other types get updated automatically. This idea of having *low maintenance
types*, by deriving types from others, is unique to TypeScript and appreciated by tons
of developers who create complex applications or libraries.

You might end up using your helper types a lot, so you start out combining them in a
utility library for easy access, but chances are one of the existing libraries already has
everything you need. Using a well-defined set of helper types is nothing new, and
plenty out there give you everything you've seen in this chapter. Sometimes it's exactly
the same but under a different name; other times it's a similar idea but solved differently. The basics are most likely covered by all type libraries, but one library, *type-fest*
(*https://oreil.ly/Cw4Kc*), is not only useful but actively maintained, well documented,
and widely used.

Type-fest has a few aspects that make it stand out. First, it's extensively documented.
Not only does its documentation include the *usage* of a certain helper type, but it also
includes use cases and scenarios that tell you where you might want to use this helper
type. One example is `Integer<T>`, which makes sure that the number you provide
does not have any decimals.

This is a utility type that almost made it into *TypeScript Cookbook*, but I saw that giving you the snippet from *type-fest* tells you everything you need to know about the type:

```
/**
A `number` that is an integer.
You can't pass a `bigint` as they are already guaranteed to be integers.
Use-case: Validating and documenting parameters.

@example
```
import type {Integer} from 'type-fest';
declare function setYear<T extends number>(length: Integer<T>): void;
```

@see NegativeInteger
@see NonNegativeInteger
@category Numeric
*/
// `${bigint}` is a type that matches a valid bigint
// literal without the `n` (ex. 1, 0b1, 0o1, 0x1)
// Because T is a number and not a string we can effectively use
// this to filter out any numbers containing decimal points

export type Integer<T extends number> = `${T}` extends `${bigint}` ? T : never;
```

The rest of the file deals with negative integers, non-negative integers, floating point numbers, and so on. It's a real treasure trove of information if you want to know more about how types are constructed.

Second, *type-fest* deals with edge cases. In Recipe 8.2, we learned about recursive types and defined `DeepPartial<T>`. Its *type-fest* counterpart, `PartialDeep<T>`, is a bit more extensive:

```
export type PartialDeep<T, Opts extends PartialDeepOptions = {}> =
  T extends BuiltIns
  ? T
  : T extends Map<infer KeyType, infer ValueType>
    ? PartialMapDeep<KeyType, ValueType, Opts>
    : T extends Set<infer ItemType>
      ? PartialSetDeep<ItemType, Opts>
      : T extends ReadonlyMap<infer KeyType, infer ValueType>
        ? PartialReadonlyMapDeep<KeyType, ValueType, Opts>
        : T extends ReadonlySet<infer ItemType>
          ? PartialReadonlySetDeep<ItemType, Opts>
          : T extends ((...arguments: any[]) => unknown)
            ? T | undefined
            : T extends object
              ? T extends ReadonlyArray<infer ItemType>
                ? Opts['recurseIntoArrays'] extends true
                  ? ItemType[] extends T
                    ? readonly ItemType[] extends T
                      ? ReadonlyArray<PartialDeep<ItemType | undefined, Opts>>
```

```
                    : Array<PartialDeep<ItemType | undefined, Opts>>
                      : PartialObjectDeep<T, Opts>
                    : T
                  : PartialObjectDeep<T, Opts>
              : unknown;

/**
Same as `PartialDeep`, but accepts only `Map`s and as inputs.
Internal helper for `PartialDeep`.
*/
type PartialMapDeep<KeyType, ValueType, Options extends PartialDeepOptions> =
  {} & Map<PartialDeep<KeyType, Options>, PartialDeep<ValueType, Options>>;

/**
Same as `PartialDeep`, but accepts only `Set`s as inputs.
Internal helper for `PartialDeep`.
*/
type PartialSetDeep<T, Options extends PartialDeepOptions> =
  {} & Set<PartialDeep<T, Options>>;

/**
Same as `PartialDeep`, but accepts only `ReadonlyMap`s as inputs.
Internal helper for `PartialDeep`.
*/
type PartialReadonlyMapDeep<
  KeyType, ValueType,
  Options extends PartialDeepOptions
> = {} & ReadonlyMap<
    PartialDeep<KeyType, Options>,
    PartialDeep<ValueType, Options>
  >;

/**
Same as `PartialDeep`, but accepts only `ReadonlySet`s as inputs.
Internal helper for `PartialDeep`.
*/
type PartialReadonlySetDeep<T, Options extends PartialDeepOptions> =
  {} & ReadonlySet<PartialDeep<T, Options>>;

/**
Same as `PartialDeep`, but accepts only `object`s as inputs.
Internal helper for `PartialDeep`.
*/
type PartialObjectDeep<
  ObjectType extends object,
  Options extends PartialDeepOptions
> = {
  [KeyType in keyof ObjectType]?: PartialDeep<ObjectType[KeyType], Options>
};
```

There is no need to go through the entirety of this implementation, but it should give you an idea about how hardened their implementations for certain utility types are.

`PartialDeep<T>` is extensive and deals with all possible edge cases, but it also comes at a cost of being complex and hard to swallow for the TypeScript type-checker. Depending on your use case, the simpler version from Recipe 8.2 might be the one you're looking for.

Third, they don't add helper types just for the sake of adding them. Their *Readme* file has a list of declined types and the reasoning behind the decline: either the use cases are limited or better alternatives exist. Just like everything, they document their choices really, really well.

Fourth, *type-fest* educates about existing helper types. Helper types have existed in TypeScript forever but barely have been documented in the past. Years ago, my blog (*https://oreil.ly/eRtx9*) attempted to be a resource on built-in helper types, until the official documentation added a chapter on utility types (*https://oreil.ly/K5cXq*). Utility types are not something that you easily pick up just by using TypeScript. You need to understand that they exist and need to read up on them. *type-fest* has an entire section dedicated to built-ins, with examples and use cases.

Last, but not least, it's widely adopted and developed by reliable open source developers. Its creator, Sindre Sorhus (*https://oreil.ly/thSin*), has worked on open source projects for decades and has a track record of fantastic projects. *type-fest* is just another stroke of genius. Chances are a lot of your work relies on his work.

With *type-fest* you get another resource of helper types you can add to your project. Decide for yourself if you want to keep a small set of helper types or if you rely on the implementations by the community.

CHAPTER 9

The Standard Library
and External Type Definitions

TypeScript's lead architect, Anders Hejlsberg, once said that he envisions "TypeScript to be the Switzerland of JavaScript," meaning that it doesn't prefer or work toward compatibility with a single framework but rather tries to cater to all JavaScript frameworks and flavors. In the past, TypeScript worked on a decorator implementation to convince Google not to pursue the JavaScript dialect AtScript (*https://oreil.ly/ZrcKR*) for Angular, which was TypeScript plus decorators. The TypeScript decorator implementation also serves as a template for a respective ECMAScript proposal on decorators (*https://oreil.ly/76JuE*). TypeScript also understands the JSX syntax extension, allowing frameworks like React or Preact to use TypeScript without limitations.

But even if TypeScript tries to cater to all JavaScript developers and makes a huge effort to integrate new and useful features for a plethora of frameworks, there are still things it can't or won't do. Maybe because a certain feature is too niche, or maybe because a decision would have huge implications for too many developers.

This is why TypeScript has been designed to be extensible by default. A lot of TypeScript's features like namespaces, modules, and interfaces allow for declaration merging, which gives you the possibility to add type definitions to your liking.

In this chapter, we look at how TypeScript deals with standard JavaScript functionality like modules, arrays, and objects. We will see some of their limitations, analyze the reasoning behind their limitations, and provide reasonable workarounds. You will see that TypeScript has been designed to be very flexible for various flavors of JavaScript, starting with sensible defaults, and giving you the opportunity to extend when you see fit.

9.1 Iterating over Objects with Object.keys

Problem

When you try to access object properties via iterating over its keys, TypeScript throws red squiggly lines at you, telling you that "'string' can't be used to index type."

Solution

Use a for-in loop instead of Object.keys and lock your type using generic type parameters.

Discussion

A prominent head-scratcher in TypeScript is trying to access an object property via iterating through its keys. This pattern is so common in JavaScript, yet TypeScript seems to keep you from using it at all costs. We use this simple line to iterate over an object's properties:

```
Object.keys(person).map(k => person[k])
```

It leads to TypeScript throwing red squigglies at you and developers flipping tables: "Element implicitly has an 'any' type because expression of type 'string' can't be used to index type 'Person'." In this situation, experienced JavaScript developers feel like TypeScript is working against them. But as with all decisions in TypeScript, there is a good reason why TypeScript behaves like this.

Let's find out why. Take a look at this function:

```
type Person = {
  name: string;
  age: number;
};

function printPerson(p: Person) {
  Object.keys(p).forEach((k) => {
    console.log(k, p[k]);
//                  ^
// Element implicitly has an 'any' type because expression
// of type 'string' can't be used to index type 'Person'.
  });
}
```

All we want is to print a Person's fields by accessing them through its keys. TypeScript won't allow this. Object.keys(p) returns a string[], which is too wide to allow accessing a very defined object shape Person.

But why is that? Isn't it obvious that we only access keys that are available? That's the whole point of using `Object.keys`! It is, but we are also able to pass objects that are subtypes of `Person`, which can have more properties than defined in `Person`:

```
const me = {
  name: "Stefan",
  age: 40,
  website: "https://fettblog.eu",
};

printPerson(me); // All good!
```

`printPerson` still should work correctly. It prints more properties, but it doesn't break. It's still the keys of p, so every property should be accessible. But what if you don't access only p?

Let's assume `Object.keys` gives you `(keyof Person)[]`. You can easily write something like this:

```
function printPerson(p: Person) {
  const you: Person = {
    name: "Reader",
    age: NaN,
  };

  Object.keys(p).forEach((k) => {
    console.log(k, you[k]);
  });
}

const me = {
  name: "Stefan",
  age: 40,
  website: "https://fettblog.eu",
};

printPerson(me);
```

If `Object.keys(p)` returns an array of type `keyof Person[]`, you will be able to access other objects of `Person`, too. This might not add up. In our example, we just print undefined. But what if you try to do something with those values? This will break at runtime.

TypeScript prevents you from scenarios like this. While we might think `Object.keys` is `keyof Person`, in reality, it can be so much more.

One way to mitigate this problem is to use type guards:

```
function isKey<T>(x: T, k: PropertyKey): k is keyof T {
  return k in x;
}
```

```
function printPerson(p: Person) {
  Object.keys(p).forEach((k) => {
    if (isKey(p, k)) console.log(k, p[k]); // All fine!
  });
}
```

But this adds an extra step that frankly shouldn't be there.

There's another way to iterate over objects, using for-in loops:

```
function printPerson(p: Person) {
  for (let k in p) {
    console.log(k, p[k]);
//                  ^
// Element implicitly has an 'any' type because expression
// of type 'string' can't be used to index type 'Person'.
  }
}
```

TypeScript will throw the same error for the same reason because you still can do things like this:

```
function printPerson(p: Person) {
  const you: Person = {
    name: "Reader",
    age: NaN,
  };

  for (let k in p) {
    console.log(k, you[k]);
  }
}

const me = {
  name: "Stefan",
  age: 40,
  website: "https://fettblog.eu",
};

printPerson(me);
```

And it will break at runtime. However, writing it like this gives you a little edge over the Object.keys version. TypeScript can be much more exact in this scenario if you add a generic:

```
function printPerson<T extends Person>(p: T) {
  for (let k in p) {
    console.log(k, p[k]); // This works
  }
}
```

Instead of requiring p to be Person (and thus be compatible with all subtypes of Person), we add a new generic type parameter T that is a subtype of Person. This means all types that have been compatible with this function signature are still compatible, but the moment we use p, we are dealing with an explicit subtype, not the broader supertype Person.

We substitute T for something that is compatible with Person but where TypeScript knows that it's concrete enough to prevent errors.

The preceding code works. k is of type keyof T. That's why we can access p, which is of type T. And this technique still prevents us from accessing types that lack specific properties:

```
function printPerson<T extends Person>(p: T) {
  const you: Person = {
    name: "Reader",
    age: NaN,
  };
  for (let k in p) {
    console.log(k, you[k]);
//                  ^
//  Type 'Extract<keyof T, string>' cannot be used to index type 'Person'
  }
}
```

We can't access a Person with keyof T. They might be different. But since T is a subtype of Person, we still can assign properties, if we know the exact property names:

```
p.age = you.age
```

And that's exactly what we want.

TypeScript being very conservative about its types here is something that might seem odd at first, but it helps you in scenarios you wouldn't think of. I guess this is the part where JavaScript developers usually scream at the compiler and think they're "fighting" it, but maybe TypeScript saved you without you knowing it. For situations where this gets annoying, TypeScript at least gives you ways to work around it.

9.2 Explicitly Highlighting Unsafe Operations with Type Assertions and unknown

Problem

Parsing arbitrary data via JSON operations can go wrong if the data is not correct. TypeScript's defaults don't provide any safeguards for these unsafe operations.

Solution

Explicitly highlight unsafe operations by using type assertions instead of type annotations, and make sure they are enforced by patching the original types with unknown.

Discussion

In Recipe 3.9 we spoke about how to effectively use type assertions. Type assertions are an explicit call to the type system to say that some type should be a different one, and based on some set of guardrails—for example, not saying number is actually string—TypeScript will treat this particular value as the new type.

With TypeScript's rich and extensive type system, sometimes type assertions are inevitable. Sometimes you even want them, as shown in Recipe 3.9 where we use the fetch API to get JSON data from a backend. One way is to call fetch and assign the results to an annotated type:

```
type Person = {
  name: string;
  age: number;
};

const ppl: Person[] = await fetch("/api/people").then((res) => res.json());
```

res.json() results in any,[1] and everything that is any can be changed to any other type through a type annotation. There is no guarantee that the result is actually Person[].

The other way is to use a type assertion instead of a type annotation:

```
const ppl = await fetch("/api/people").then((res) => res.json()) as Person[];
```

For the type system, this is the same thing, but we can easily scan situations where there might be problems. If we don't validate our incoming values against types (with, for example, Zod; see Recipe 12.5), then having a type assertion here is an effective way of highlighting unsafe operations.

Unsafe operations in a type system are situations where we tell the type system that we expect values to be of a certain type, but we don't have any guarantee from the type system itself that this will actually be true. This happens mostly at the borders of our application, where we load data from someplace, deal with user input, or parse data with built-in methods.

Unsafe operations can be highlighted by using certain keywords that indicate an explicit change in the type system. Type assertions (as), type predicates (is), or assertion signatures (asserts) help us find those situations. In some cases, TypeScript even forces us either to comply with its view of types or to explicitly change the rules based on our situations. But not always.

---

1 Back when the API defintiion was created, unknown didn't exist. Also, TypeScript has a strong focus on developer productivity, and with res.json() being a widely used method, this would've broken countless applications.

When we fetch data from some backend, it is just as easy to annotate as it is to write a type assertion. Things like that can be overlooked if we don't force ourselves to use the correct technique.

But we can help TypeScript help us do the right thing. The problem is the call to res.json(), which comes from the Body interface in *lib.dom.d.ts*:

```
interface Body {
  readonly body: ReadableStream<Uint8Array> | null;
  readonly bodyUsed: boolean;
  arrayBuffer(): Promise<ArrayBuffer>;
  blob(): Promise<Blob>;
  formData(): Promise<FormData>;
  json(): Promise<any>;
  text(): Promise<string>;
}
```

The json() call returns a Promise<any>, and any is the loosey-goosey type where TypeScript just ignores any type-check at all. We would need any's cautious brother, unknown. Thanks to declaration merging, we can override the Body type definition and define json() to be a bit more restrictive:

```
interface Body {
  json(): Promise<unknown>;
}
```

The moment we do a type annotation, TypeScript yells at us that we can't assign unknown to Person[]:

```
const ppl: Person[] = await fetch("/api/people").then((res) => res.json());
//        ^
// Type 'unknown' is not assignable to type 'Person[]'.ts(2322)
```

But TypeScript is still happy if we do a type assertion:

```
const ppl = await fetch("/api/people").then((res) => res.json()) as Person[];
```

And with that, we can force TypeScript to highlight unsafe operations.[2]

9.3 Working with defineProperty

Problem

You define properties on the fly using Object.defineProperty, but TypeScript doesn't pick up changes.

---

2 Credit to Dan Vanderkam's *Effective TypeScript* blog (*https://effectivetypescript.com*) for inspiration on this subject.

Solution

Create a wrapper function and use assertion signatures to change the object's type.

Discussion

In JavaScript, you can define object properties on the fly with `Object.define Property`. This is useful if you want your properties to be read-only. Think of a storage object that has a maximum value that shouldn't be overwritten:

```
const storage = {
  currentValue: 0
};

Object.defineProperty(storage, 'maxValue', {
  value: 9001,
  writable: false
});

console.log(storage.maxValue); // 9001

storage.maxValue = 2;

console.log(storage.maxValue); // still 9001
```

`defineProperty` and property descriptors are very complex. They allow you to do everything with properties that usually is reserved for built-in objects. So they're common in larger codebases. TypeScript has a problem with `defineProperty`:

```
const storage = {
  currentValue: 0
};

Object.defineProperty(storage, 'maxValue', {
  value: 9001,
  writable: false
});

console.log(storage.maxValue);
//                  ^
// Property 'maxValue' does not exist on type '{ currentValue: number; }'.
```

If we don't explicitly assert to a new type, we don't get `maxValue` attached to the type of `storage`. However, for simple use cases, we can help ourselves using assertion signatures.

While TypeScript might not feature object changes when using `Object.defineProperty`, there is a chance that the team will add typings or special behavior for cases like this in the future. For example, checking if an object has a certain property using the `in` keyword didn't affect types for years. This changed in 2022 with TypeScript 4.9 (*https://oreil.ly/YpyGG*).

Think of an `assertIsNumber` function where you can make sure some value is of type number. Otherwise, it throws an error. This is similar to the `assert` function in Node.js:

```
function assertIsNumber(val: any) {
  if (typeof val !== "number") {
    throw new AssertionError("Not a number!");
  }
}

function multiply(x, y) {
  assertIsNumber(x);
  assertIsNumber(y);
  // at this point I'm sure x and y are numbers
  // if one assert condition is not true, this position
  // is never reached
  return x * y;
}
```

To comply with behavior like this, we can add an assertion signature that tells Type-Script that we know more about the type after this function:

```
function assertIsNumber(val: any) : asserts val is number
  if (typeof val !== "number") {
    throw new AssertionError("Not a number!");
  }
}
```

This works a lot like type predicates (see Recipe 3.5) but without the control flow of a condition-based structure like `if` or `switch`:

```
function multiply(x, y) {
  assertIsNumber(x);
  assertIsNumber(y);
  // Now also TypeScript knows that both x and y are numbers
  return x * y;
}
```

If you look at it closely, you can see those assertion signatures can *change the type of a parameter or variable on the fly*. This is what `Object.defineProperty` does as well.

The following helper does not aim to be 100% accurate or complete. It might have errors, and it might not tackle every edge case of the `defineProperty` specification.

But it will give us the basic functionality. First, we define a new function called defineProperty that we use as a wrapper function for Object.defineProperty:

```
function defineProperty<
  Obj extends object,
  Key extends PropertyKey,
  PDesc extends PropertyDescriptor>
  (obj: Obj, prop: Key, val: PDesc) {
  Object.defineProperty(obj, prop, val);
}
```

We work with three generics:

- The object we want to modify, of type Obj, which is a subtype of object.
- Type Key, which is a subtype of PropertyKey (built-in): string | number | symbol.
- PDesc, a subtype of PropertyDescriptor (built-in). This allows us to define the property with all its features (writability, enumerability, reconfigurability).

We use generics because TypeScript can narrow them to a very specific unit type. PropertyKey, for example, is all numbers, strings, and symbols. But if we use Key extends PropertyKey, we can pinpoint prop to be, for example, type "maxValue". This is helpful if we want to change the original type by adding more properties.

The Object.defineProperty function either changes the object or throws an error should something go wrong. That's exactly what an assertion function does. Our custom helper defineProperty thus does the same.

Let's add an assertion signature. Once defineProperty successfully executes, our object has another property. We are creating some helper types for that. The signature first:

```
function defineProperty<
  Obj extends object,
  Key extends PropertyKey,
  PDesc extends PropertyDescriptor>
  (obj: Obj, prop: Key, val: PDesc):
    asserts obj is Obj & DefineProperty<Key, PDesc> {
  Object.defineProperty(obj, prop, val);
}
```

obj then is of type Obj (narrowed through a generic) and our newly defined property.

This is the DefineProperty helper type:

```
type DefineProperty<
  Prop extends PropertyKey,
  Desc extends PropertyDescriptor> =
    Desc extends { writable: any, set(val: any): any } ? never :
```

```
Desc extends { writable: any, get(): any } ? never :
Desc extends { writable: false } ? Readonly<InferValue<Prop, Desc>> :
Desc extends { writable: true } ? InferValue<Prop, Desc> :
Readonly<InferValue<Prop, Desc>>;
```

First, we deal with the `writable` property of a `PropertyDescriptor`. It's a set of conditions to define some edge cases and conditions of how the original property descriptors work:

- If we set `writable` and any property accessor (`get`, `set`), we fail. `never` tells us that an error was thrown.

- If we set `writable` to `false`, the property is read-only. We defer to the `Infer Value` helper type.

- If we set `writable` to `true`, the property is not read-only. We defer as well.

- The last default case is the same as `writable: false`, so `Readonly<Infer Value<Prop, Desc>>`. (`Readonly<T>` is built-in.)

This is the `InferValue` helper type, dealing with the set `value` property:

```
type InferValue<Prop extends PropertyKey, Desc> =
  Desc extends { get(): any, value: any } ? never :
  Desc extends { value: infer T } ? Record<Prop, T> :
  Desc extends { get(): infer T } ? Record<Prop, T> : never;
```

Again a set of conditions:

- Do we have a getter and a value set? `Object.defineProperty` throws an error, so `never`.

- If we have set a value, let's infer the type of this value and create an object with our defined property key and the value type.

- Or we infer the type from the return type of a getter.

- Anything else we forget. TypeScript won't let us work with the object as it's becoming `never`.

Lots of helper types, but roughly 20 lines of code to get it right:

```
type InferValue<Prop extends PropertyKey, Desc> =
  Desc extends { get(): any, value: any } ? never :
  Desc extends { value: infer T } ? Record<Prop, T> :
  Desc extends { get(): infer T } ? Record<Prop, T> : never;

type DefineProperty<
  Prop extends PropertyKey,
  Desc extends PropertyDescriptor> =
    Desc extends { writable: any, set(val: any): any } ? never :
    Desc extends { writable: any, get(): any } ? never :
```

```
      Desc extends { writable: false } ? Readonly<InferValue<Prop, Desc>> :
      Desc extends { writable: true } ? InferValue<Prop, Desc> :
      Readonly<InferValue<Prop, Desc>>

function defineProperty<
  Obj extends object,
  Key extends PropertyKey,
  PDesc extends PropertyDescriptor>
  (obj: Obj, prop: Key, val: PDesc):
    asserts  obj is Obj & DefineProperty<Key, PDesc> {
  Object.defineProperty(obj, prop, val)
}
```

Let's see what TypeScript does with our changes:

```
const storage = {
  currentValue: 0
};

defineProperty(storage, 'maxValue', {
  writable: false, value: 9001
});

storage.maxValue; // it's a number
storage.maxValue = 2; // Error! It's read-only

const storageName = 'My Storage';
defineProperty(storage, 'name', {
  get() {
    return storageName
  }
});

storage.name; // it's a string!

// it's not possible to assign a value and a getter
defineProperty(storage, 'broken', {
  get() {
    return storageName
  },
  value: 4000
});

// storage is never because we have a malicious
// property descriptor
storage;
```

While this might not cover everything, there is already a lot done for simple property definitions.

9.4 Expanding Types for Array.prototype.includes

Problem

TypeScript won't be able to look for an element of a broad type like `string` or `number` within a very narrow tuple or array.

Solution

Create generic helper functions with type predicates, where you change the relationship between type parameters.

Discussion

We create an array called `actions`, which contains a set of actions in string format that we want to execute. The resulting type of this `actions` array is `string[]`.

The `execute` function takes any string as an argument. We check if this is a valid action, and if so, do something:

```
// actions: string[]
const actions = ["CREATE", "READ", "UPDATE", "DELETE"];

function execute(action: string) {
  if (actions.includes(action)) {
    // do something with action
  }
}
```

It gets a little trickier if we want to narrow the `string[]` to something more concrete, a subset of all possible strings. By adding *const context* via `as const`, we can narrow `actions` to be of type `readonly ["CREATE", "READ", "UPDATE", "DELETE"]`.

This is handy if we want to do exhaustiveness checking to make sure we have cases for all available actions. However, `actions.includes` does not agree with us:

```
// Adding const context
// actions: readonly ["CREATE", "READ", "UPDATE", "DELETE"]
const actions = ["CREATE", "READ", "UPDATE", "DELETE"] as const;

function execute(action: string) {
  if (actions.includes(action)) {
//                       ^
// Argument of type 'string' is not assignable to parameter of type
// '"CREATE" | "READ" | "UPDATE" | "DELETE"'.(2345)
  }
}
```

Why is that? Let's look at the typings of Array<T> and ReadonlyArray<T> (we work with the latter due to *const context*):

```
interface Array<T> {
  /**
   * Determines whether an array includes a certain element,
   * returning true or false as appropriate.
   * @param searchElement The element to search for.
   * @param fromIndex The position in this array at which
   *   to begin searching for searchElement.
   */
  includes(searchElement: T, fromIndex?: number): boolean;
}

interface ReadonlyArray<T> {
  /**
   * Determines whether an array includes a certain element,
   * returning true or false as appropriate.
   * @param searchElement The element to search for.
   * @param fromIndex The position in this array at which
   *   to begin searching for searchElement.
   */
  includes(searchElement: T, fromIndex?: number): boolean;
}
```

The element we want to search for (searchElement) needs to be of the same type as the array itself! So if we have Array<string> (or string[] or Readonly Array<string>), we can search only for strings. In our case, this would mean that action needs to be of type "CREATE" | "READ" | "UPDATE" | "DELETE".

Suddenly, our program doesn't make a lot of sense anymore. Why do we search for something if the type already tells us that it can be just one of four strings? If we change the type for action to "CREATE" | "READ" | "UPDATE" | "DELETE", actions.includes becomes obsolete. If we don't change it, TypeScript throws an error at us, and rightfully so!

One of the problems is that TypeScript lacks the possibility to check for contravariant types with, for example, upper-bound generics. We can tell if a type should be a *subset* of type T with constructs like extends; we can't check if a type is a *superset* of T. At least not yet!

So what can we do?

Option 1: Redeclare ReadonlyArray

One option that comes to mind is changing how includes in ReadonlyArray should behave. Thanks to declaration merging, we can add our own definitions for Readonly Array that are a bit looser in the arguments and more specific in the result, like this:

```
interface ReadonlyArray<T> {
  includes(searchElement: any, fromIndex?: number): searchElement is T;
}
```

This allows for a broader set of searchElement values to be passed (literally any!), and if the condition is true, we tell TypeScript through a *type predicate* that search Element is T (the subset we are looking for).

Turns out, this works pretty well:

```
const actions = ["CREATE", "READ", "UPDATE", "DELETE"] as const;

function execute(action: string) {
  if(actions.includes(action)) {
    // action: "CREATE" | "READ" | "UPDATE" | "DELETE"
  }
}
```

There's a problem, though. The solution works but takes the assumption of what's correct and what needs to be checked. If you change action to number, TypeScript usually throws an error that you can't search for that kind of type. actions only consists of string, so why even look at number? This is an error you want to catch:

```
// type number has no relation to actions at all
function execute(action: number) {
  if(actions.includes(action)) {
    // do something
  }
}
```

With our change to ReadonlyArray, we lose this check as searchElement is any. While the functionality of action.includes still works as intended, we might not see the right *problem* once we change function signatures along the way.

Also, and more important, we change the behavior of built-in types. This might change your type-checks somewhere else and might cause problems in the long run!

> If you do a *type patch* by changing behavior from the standard library, be sure to do this module scoped, and not globally.

There is another way.

Option 2: A helper with type assertions

As originally stated, one of the problems is that TypeScript lacks the possibility to check if a value belongs to a *superset* of a generic parameter. With a helper function, we can turn this relationship around:

```
function includes<T extends U, U>(coll: ReadonlyArray<T>, el: U): el is T {
  return coll.includes(el as T);
}
```

The `includes` function takes the `ReadonlyArray<T>` as an argument and searches for an element that is of type U. We check through our generic bounds that T extends U, which means that U is a *superset* of T (or T is a *subset* of U). If the method returns `true`, we can say for sure that `el` is of the *narrower* type U.

The only thing that we need to make the implementation work is to do a little type assertion the moment we pass `el` to `Array.prototype.includes`. The original problem is still there! The type assertion `el as T` is OK, though, as we check possible problems already in the function signature.

This means the moment we change, for example, `action` to `number`, we get the right errors throughout our code:

```
function execute(action: number) {
  if(includes(actions, action)) {
//                ^
// Argument of type 'readonly ["CREATE", "READ", "UPDATE", "DELETE"]'
// is not assignable to parameter of type 'readonly number[]'.
  }
}
```

And this is the behavior we want. A nice touch is that TypeScript wants us to change the array, not the element we are looking for. This is due to the relationship between the generic type parameters.

 The same solutions also work if you run into similar troubles with `Array.prototype.indexOf`.

TypeScript aims to get all standard JavaScript functionality correct, but sometimes you have to make trade-offs. This case calls for trade-offs: do you allow for an argument list that's looser than you would expect, or do you throw errors for types where you already should know more?

Type assertions, declaration merging, and other tools help us get around that in situations where the type system can't help us. Not until it becomes better than before, by allowing us to move even further in the type space.

9.5 Filtering Nullish Values

Problem

You want to use the Boolean constructor to filter nullish values from an array, but TypeScript still yields the same types, including null and undefined.

Solution

Overload the filter method from Array using declaration merging.

Discussion

Sometimes you have collections that could include *nullish* values (undefined or null):

```
// const array: (number | null | undefined)[]
const array = [1, 2, 3, undefined, 4, null];
```

To continue working, you want to remove those nullish values from your collection. This is typically done using the filter method of Array, maybe by checking the *truthiness* of a value. null and undefined are *falsy*, so they get filtered out:

```
const filtered = array.filter((val) => !!val);
```

A convenient way of checking the truthiness of a value is by passing it to the Boolean constructor. This is short, on point, and very elegant to read:

```
// const array: (number | null | undefined)[]
const filtered = array.filter(Boolean);
```

But sadly, it doesn't change our type. We still have null and undefined as possible types for the filtered array.

By opening up the Array interface and adding another declaration for filter, we can add this special case as an overload:

```
interface Array<T> {
  filter(predicate: BooleanConstructor): NonNullable<T>[]
}

interface ReadonlyArray<T> {
  filter(predicate: BooleanConstructor): NonNullable<T>[]
}
```

And with that, we get rid of nullish types and have more clarity on the type of our array's contents:

```
// const array: number[]
const filtered = array.filter(Boolean);
```

Neat! What's the caveat? Literal tuples and arrays. `BooleanConstructor` filters not only nullish values but also falsy values. To get the right elements, we not only have to return `NonNullable<T>` but also introduce a type that checks for truthy values:

```
type Truthy<T> = T extends "" | false | 0 | 0n ? never : T;

interface Array<T> {
  filter(predicate: BooleanConstructor): Truthy<NonNullable<T>>[];
}

interface ReadonlyArray<T> {
  filter(predicate: BooleanConstructor): Truthy<NonNullable<T>>[];
}

// as const creates a readonly tuple
const array = [0, 1, 2, 3, ``, -0, 0n, false, undefined, null] as const;

// const filtered: (1 | 2 | 3)[]
const filtered = array.filter(Boolean);

const nullOrOne: Array<0 | 1> = [0, 1, 0, 1];

// const onlyOnes: 1[]
const onlyOnes = nullOrOne.filter(Boolean);
```

 The example includes `0n` which is 0 in the `BigInt` type. This type is available only from ECMAScript 2020 on.

This gives us the right idea of which types to expect, but since `ReadonlyArray<T>` takes the tuple's elements types and not the tuple type itself, we lose information on the order of types within the tuple.

As with all extensions to existing TypeScript types, be aware that this might cause side effects. Scope them locally and use them carefully.

9.6 Extending Modules

Problem

You work with libraries that provide their own view of HTML elements, like Preact or React. But sometimes their type definitions don't include the latest features. You want to patch them.

Solution

Use declaration merging on the module and interface level.

Discussion

JSX is a syntax extension to JavaScript, introducing an XML-like way of describing and nesting components. Basically, everything that can be described as a tree of elements can be expressed in JSX. JSX was introduced by the creators of the popular React framework to make it possible to write and nest components in an HTML-like way within JavaScript, where it is actually transpiled to a series of function calls:

```
<button onClick={() => alert('YES')}>Click me</button>

// Transpiles to:

React.createElement("button", { onClick: () => alert('YES') }, 'Click me');
```

JSX has since been adopted by many frameworks, even if there is little or no connection to React. There's a lot more on JSX in Chapter 10.

React typings for TypeScript come with lots of interfaces for all possible HTML elements. But sometimes your browsers, your frameworks, or your code are a little bit ahead of what's possible.

Let's say you want to use the latest image features in Chrome and load your images lazily. This is a progressive enhancement, so only browsers that understand what's going on know how to interpret this. Other browsers are robust enough not to care:

```
<img src="/awesome.jpg" loading="lazy" alt="What an awesome image" />
```

But your TypeScript JSX code? Errors:

```
function Image({ src, alt }) {
  // Property 'loading' does not exist.
  return <img src={src} alt={alt} loading="lazy" />;
}
```

To prevent this, we can extend the available interfaces with our own properties. This TypeScript feature is called *declaration merging*.

Create an *@types* folder and put a *jsx.d.ts* file in it. Change your TypeScript config so your compiler options allow for extra types:

```
{
  "compilerOptions": {
    ...
    /* Type declaration files to be included in compilation. */
    "types": ["@types/**"],
  },
  ...
}
```

We re-create the exact module and interface structure:

- The module is called 'react'.

- The interface is ImgHTMLAttributes<T> extends HTMLAttributes<T>.

We know that from the original typings. Here, we add the properties we want:

```
import "react";

declare module "react" {
  interface ImgHTMLAttributes<T> extends HTMLAttributes<T> {
    loading?: "lazy" | "eager" | "auto";
  }
}
```

And while we are at it, let's make sure we don't forget alt texts:

```
import "react";

declare module "react" {
  interface ImgHTMLAttributes<T> extends HTMLAttributes<T> {
    loading?: "lazy" | "eager" | "auto";
    alt: string;
  }
}
```

That's much better! TypeScript will take the original definition and merge your declarations. Your autocomplete can give you all available options *and* will error when you forget an alt text.

When working with Preact (*https://preactjs.com*), things are a bit more complicated. The original HTML typings are very generous and not as specific as React's typings. That's why we have to be a bit more explicit when defining images:

```
declare namespace JSX {
  interface IntrinsicElements {
    img: HTMLAttributes & {
      alt: string;
      src: string;
      loading?: "lazy" | "eager" | "auto";
    };
  }
}
```

This makes sure that both alt and src are available and adds a new attribute called loading. The technique is the same, though: declaration merging, which works on the level of namespaces, interfaces, and modules.

9.7 Augmenting Globals

Problem

You use a browser feature like `ResizeObserver` and see that it isn't available in your current TypeScript configuration.

Solution

Augment the global namespace with custom type definitions.

Discussion

TypeScript stores types to all DOM APIs in *lib.dom.d.ts*. This file is autogenerated from Web IDL files. *Web IDL* stands for *Web Interface Definition Language* and is a format the W3C and WHATWG use to define interfaces to web APIs. It came out around 2012 and has been a standard since 2016.

When you read standards at W3C (*https://www.w3.org*)—like on Resize Observer (*https://oreil.ly/XeSUG*)—you can see parts of a definition or the full definition somewhere within the specification. Like this one:

```
enum ResizeObserverBoxOptions {
  "border-box", "content-box", "device-pixel-content-box"
};

dictionary ResizeObserverOptions {
  ResizeObserverBoxOptions box = "content-box";
};

[Exposed=(Window)]
interface ResizeObserver {
  constructor(ResizeObserverCallback callback);
  void observe(Element target, optional ResizeObserverOptions options);
  void unobserve(Element target);
  void disconnect();
};

callback ResizeObserverCallback = void (
  sequence<ResizeObserverEntry> entries,
  ResizeObserver observer
);

[Exposed=Window]
interface ResizeObserverEntry {
  readonly attribute Element target;
  readonly attribute DOMRectReadOnly contentRect;
  readonly attribute FrozenArray<ResizeObserverSize> borderBoxSize;
  readonly attribute FrozenArray<ResizeObserverSize> contentBoxSize;
```

```
    readonly attribute FrozenArray<ResizeObserverSize> devicePixelContentBoxSize;
  };

  interface ResizeObserverSize {
    readonly attribute unrestricted double inlineSize;
    readonly attribute unrestricted double blockSize;
  };

  interface ResizeObservation {
    constructor(Element target);
    readonly attribute Element target;
    readonly attribute ResizeObserverBoxOptions observedBox;
    readonly attribute FrozenArray<ResizeObserverSize> lastReportedSizes;
  };
```

Browsers use this as a guideline to implement respective APIs. TypeScript uses these IDL files to generate *lib.dom.d.ts*. The TypeScript and JavaScript lib generator (*https:// oreil.ly/WLcLB*) project scrapes web standards and extracts IDL information. Then an *IDL to TypeScript* generator parses the IDL file and generates the correct typings.

Pages to scrape are maintained manually. The moment a specification is far enough and supported by all major browsers, people add a new resource and see their change released with an upcoming TypeScript version. So it's just a matter of time until we get `ResizeObserver` in *lib.dom.d.ts*.

If we can't wait, we can add the typings ourselves but only for the project we currently are working with.

Let's assume we generated the types for `ResizeObserver`. We would store the output in a file called *resize-observer.d.ts*. Here are the contents:

```
  type ResizeObserverBoxOptions =
    "border-box" |
    "content-box" |
    "device-pixel-content-box";

  interface ResizeObserverOptions {
    box?: ResizeObserverBoxOptions;
  }

  interface ResizeObservation {
    readonly lastReportedSizes: ReadonlyArray<ResizeObserverSize>;
    readonly observedBox: ResizeObserverBoxOptions;
    readonly target: Element;
  }

  declare var ResizeObservation: {
    prototype: ResizeObservation;
    new(target: Element): ResizeObservation;
  };
```

```
interface ResizeObserver {
  disconnect(): void;
  observe(target: Element, options?: ResizeObserverOptions): void;
  unobserve(target: Element): void;
}

export declare var ResizeObserver: {
  prototype: ResizeObserver;
  new(callback: ResizeObserverCallback): ResizeObserver;
};

interface ResizeObserverEntry {
  readonly borderBoxSize: ReadonlyArray<ResizeObserverSize>;
  readonly contentBoxSize: ReadonlyArray<ResizeObserverSize>;
  readonly contentRect: DOMRectReadOnly;
  readonly devicePixelContentBoxSize: ReadonlyArray<ResizeObserverSize>;
  readonly target: Element;
}

declare var ResizeObserverEntry: {
  prototype: ResizeObserverEntry;
  new(): ResizeObserverEntry;
};

interface ResizeObserverSize {
  readonly blockSize: number;
  readonly inlineSize: number;
}

declare var ResizeObserverSize: {
  prototype: ResizeObserverSize;
  new(): ResizeObserverSize;
};

interface ResizeObserverCallback {
  (entries: ResizeObserverEntry[], observer: ResizeObserver): void;
}
```

We declare a ton of interfaces and some variables that implement our interfaces, like
`declare var ResizeObserver`, which is the object that defines the prototype and
constructor function:

```
declare var ResizeObserver: {
  prototype: ResizeObserver;
  new(callback: ResizeObserverCallback): ResizeObserver;
};
```

This already helps a lot. We can use the (arguably) long type declarations and put
them directly in the file where we need them. `ResizeObserver` is found! We want to
have it available everywhere, though.

Thanks to TypeScript's declaration-merging feature, we can extend *namespaces* and *interfaces* as needed. This time, we're extending the *global namespace*.

The global namespace contains all objects and interfaces that are, well, globally available. Like the window object (and Window interface), as well as everything else that should be part of our JavaScript execution context. We augment the global namespace and add the ResizeObserver object to it:

```
declare global { // opening up the namespace
  var ResizeObserver: { // merging ResizeObserver with it
    prototype: ResizeObserver;
    new(callback: ResizeObserverCallback): ResizeObserver;
  }
}
```

Let's put *resize-observer.d.ts* in a folder called *@types*. Don't forget to add the folder to the sources that TypeScript will parse as well as the list of type declaration folders in *tsconfig.json*:

```
{
  "compilerOptions": {
    //...
    "typeRoots": ["@types", "./node_modules/@types"],
    //...
  },
  "include": ["src", "@types"]
}
```

Since there's a significant possibility that ResizeObserver is not yet available in your target browser, make sure that you make the ResizeObserver object undefined. This urges you to check if the object is available:

```
declare global {
  var ResizeObserver: {
    prototype: ResizeObserver;
    new(callback: ResizeObserverCallback): ResizeObserver;
  } | undefined
}
```

In your application:

```
if (typeof ResizeObserver !== 'undefined') {
  const x = new ResizeObserver((entries) => {});
}
```

This makes working with ResizeObserver as safe as possible!

It might be that TypeScript doesn't pick up your ambient declaration files and the global augmentation. If this happens, make sure that:

- You parse the *@types* folder via the `include` property in *tsconfig.json*.
- Your ambient type declaration files are recognized as such by adding them to `types` or `typeRoots` in the *tsconfig.json* compiler options.
- You add `export {}` at the end of your ambient declaration file so TypeScript recognizes this file as a module.

9.8 Adding Non-JS Modules to the Module Graph

Problem

You use a bundler like Webpack to load files like *.css* or images from JavaScript, but TypeScript does not recognize those files.

Solution

Globally declare modules based on filename extensions.

Discussion

There is a movement in web development to make JavaScript the default entry point of everything and let it handle all relevant assets via `import` statements. What you need for this is a build tool, a bundler, that analyzes your code and creates the right artifacts. A popular tool for this is Webpack (*https://webpack.js.org*), a JavaScript bundler that allows you to bundle *everything*—CSS, Markdown, SVGs, JPEGs, you name it:

```
// like this
import "./Button.css";

// or this
import styles from "./Button.css";
```

Webpack uses a concept called *loaders*, which looks at file endings and activates certain bundling concepts. Importing *.css* files in JavaScript is not native. It's part of Webpack (or whatever bundler you are using). However, we can teach TypeScript to understand files like this.

> There is a proposal in the ECMAScript standards committee to allow imports of files other than JavaScript and assert certain built-in formats for this. This will have an effect on TypeScript eventually. You can read all about it here (*https://oreil.ly/stAm5*).

TypeScript supports *ambient module declarations*, even for a module that is not "physically" there but in the environment or reachable via tooling. One example is Node's main built-in modules, like url, http or path, as described in TypeScript's documentation:

```
declare module "path" {
  export function normalize(p: string): string;
  export function join(...paths: any[]): string;
  export var sep: string;
}
```

This is great for modules where we know the exact name. We can also use the same technique for wildcard patterns. Let's declare a generic ambient module for all our *.css* files:

```
declare module '*.css' {
  // to be done.
}
```

The pattern is ready. This listens to all *.css* files we want to import. What we expect is a list of class names that we can add to our components. Since we don't know which classes are defined in the *.css* files, let's go with an object that accepts every string key and returns a string:

```
declare module '*.css' {
  interface IClassNames {
    [className: string]: string
  }
  const classNames: IClassNames;
  export default classNames;
}
```

That's all we need to make our files compile again. The only downside is that we can't use the exact class names to get autocompletion and similar benefits. A way to solve this is to generate type files automatically. There are packages on NPM (*https://oreil.ly/sDBv0*) that deal with that problem. Feel free to choose one of your liking.

It's a bit easier if we want to import something like MDX into our modules. MDX lets us write Markdown, which parses to regular React (or JSX) components (more on React in Chapter 10).

We expect a functional component (that we can pass props to) that returns a JSX element:

```
declare module '*.mdx' {
  let MDXComponent: (props) => JSX.Element;
  export default MDXComponent;
}
```

And voilà! We can load *.mdx* files in JavaScript and use them as components:

```
import About from '../articles/about.mdx';

function App() {
  return <>
    <About/>
  </>
}
```

If you don't know what to expect, make your life easy. All you need to do is declare the module. Don't provide any types. TypeScript will allow loading but won't give you any type safety:

```
declare module '*.svg';
```

To make ambient modules available to your app, it is recommended to create an *@types* folder somewhere in your project (probably root level). There you can put any amount of *.d.ts* files with your module definitions. Add a referral to your *tsconfig.json*, and TypeScript knows what to do:

```
{
  ...
  "compilerOptions": {
    ...
    "typeRoots": [
      "./node_modules/@types",
      "./@types"
    ],
    ...
  }
}
```

One of TypeScript's main features is to be adaptable to all JavaScript flavors. Some things are built-in, and others need some extra patching from you.

CHAPTER 10

TypeScript and React

React is arguably one of the most popular JavaScript libraries in recent years. Its simple approach to the composition of components has changed the way we write frontend (and, to an extent, backend) applications, allowing you to declaratively write UI code using a JavaScript syntax extension called JSX. Not only was this simple principle easy to pick up and understand, but it also influenced dozens of other libraries.

JSX is undoubtedly a game changer in the JavaScript world, and with TypeScript's goal to cater to all JavaScript developers, JSX found its way into TypeScript. In fact, TypeScript is a full-fledged JSX compiler. If you have no need for additional bundling or extra tooling, TypeScript is all you need to get your React app going. TypeScript is also immensely popular. At the time of writing, the React typings on NPM clocked 20 million downloads per week. The fantastic tooling with VS Code and the excellent types made TypeScript the first choice for React developers around the globe.

While TypeScript's popularity among React developers continues unabated, one circumstance makes the use of TypeScript with React a bit difficult: TypeScript isn't the React team's first choice. While other JSX-based libraries are now mostly written *in* TypeScript and therefore provide excellent types out of the box, the React team works with their own static type-checker called Flow (*https://flow.org*), which is similar to, but ultimately incompatible with, TypeScript. This means the React types millions of developers rely on are made subsequently by a group of community contributors and published on Definitely Typed. While @types/react are considered to be excellent, they are still just the best effort to type a library as complex as React. This inevitably leads to gaps. For the places where those gaps become visible, this chapter will be your guide.

In this chapter, we look at situations where React is supposed to be easy, but Type-Script gives you a hard time by throwing complex error messages. We are going to figure out what those messages mean, how you can work around them, and what solutions help you in the long run. You will also learn about various development patterns and their benefits, and how to use TypeScript's built-in JSX support.

What you won't get is a basic setup guide for React and TypeScript. The ecosystem is so vast and rich, many roads lead to Rome. Pick your framework's documentation pages and look out for TypeScript. Also note that I assume some React experience up front. In this chapter, we deal mostly with typing React.

While there is a strong inclination toward React in this chapter, you will be able to use certain learnings and apply them to other JSX-based frameworks and libraries as well.

10.1 Writing Proxy Components

Problem

You write a lot of standard HTML components, but you don't want to set all necessary properties all the time.

Solution

Create proxy components and apply a few patterns to make them usable for your scenario.

Discussion

Most web applications use buttons. Buttons have a `type` property that defaults to `submit`. This is a sensible default for forms where you perform an action over HTTP, where you POST the contents to a server-side API. But when you just want to have interactive elements on your site, the correct type for buttons is `button`. This is not only an aesthetic choice but also important for accessibility:

```
<button type="button">Click me!</button>
```

When you write React, chances are you rarely submit a form to a server with a `submit` type, but you interact with lots of `button`-type buttons. A good way to deal with situations like these is to write proxy components. They mimic HTML elements but preset a couple of properties:

```
function Button(props) {
  return <button type="button" {...props} />;
}
```

The idea is that `Button` takes the same properties as the HTML `button`, and the attributes are spread out to the HTML element. Spreading attributes to HTML elements is a nice feature where you can make sure that you are able to set all the HTML properties that an element has without knowing up front which you want to set. But how do we type them?

All HTML elements that can be used in JSX are defined through intrinsic elements in the JSX namespace. When you load React, the JSX namespace appears as a global namespace in your file, and you can access all elements via index access. So the correct prop types for `Button` are defined in `JSX.IntrinsicElements`.

An alternative to `JSX.IntrinsicElements` is `React.ElementType`, a generic type within the React package, which also includes class and function components. For proxy components, `JSX.Intrinsic Elements` is sufficient and comes with an extra benefit: your components stay compatible with other React-like frameworks like Preact.

`JSX.IntrinsicElements` is a type within the global `JSX` namespace. Once this namespace is in scope, TypeScript is able to pick up basic elements that are compatible with your JSX-based framework:

```
type ButtonProps = JSX.IntrinsicElements["button"];

function Button(props: ButtonProps) {
  return <button type="button" {...props} />;
}
```

This includes children: we spread them along! As you see, we set a button's type to button. Since props are just JavaScript objects, it's possible to override `type` by setting it as an attribute in props. If two keys with the same name are defined, the last one wins. This may be desired behavior, but you alternatively may want to prevent you and your colleagues from overriding `type`. With the `Omit<T, K>` helper type, you can take all properties from a JSX `button` but drop keys you don't want to override:

```
type ButtonProps = Omit<JSX.IntrinsicElements["button"], "type">;

function Button(props: ButtonProps) {
  return <button type="button" {...props} />;
}

const aButton = <Button type="button">Hi</Button>;
//                      ^
// Type '{ children: string; type: string; }' is not
// assignable to type 'IntrinsicAttributes & ButtonProps'.
// Property 'type' does not exist on type
// 'IntrinsicAttributes & ButtonProps'.(2322)
```

If you need `type` to be `submit`, you can create another proxy component:

```
type SubmitButtonProps = Omit<JSX.IntrinsicElements["button"], "type">;

function SubmitButton(props: SubmitButtonProps) {
  return <button type="submit" {...props} />;
}
```

You can extend this idea of omitting properties if you want to preset even more properties. Perhaps you adhere to a design system and don't want class names to be set arbitrarily:

```
type StyledButton = Omit<
  JSX.IntrinsicElements["button"],
  "type" | "className" | "style"
> & {
  type: "primary" | "secondary";
};

function StyledButton({ type, ...allProps }: StyledButton) {
  return <Button type="button" className={`btn-${type}`} {...allProps}/>;
}
```

This even allows you to reuse the `type` property name.

We dropped some props from the type definition and preset them to sensible defaults. Now we want to make sure our users don't forget to set some props, such as the `alt` attribute of an image or the `src` attribute.

For that, we create a `MakeRequired` helper type that removes the optional flag:

```
type MakeRequired<T, K extends keyof T> = Omit<T, K> & Required<Pick<T, K>>;
```

And build our own props:

```
type ImgProps
  = MakeRequired<
    JSX.IntrinsicElements["img"],
    "alt" | "src"
  >;

export function Img(props: ImgProps) {
  return <img {...props} />;
}

const anImage = <Img />;
//                ^
// Type '{}' is missing the following properties from type
// 'Required<Pick<DetailedHTMLProps<ImgHTMLAttributes<HTMLImageElement>,
//  HTMLImageElement>, "alt" | "src">>': alt, src (2739)
```

With just a few changes to the original intrinsic element's type and a proxy component, we can ensure that our code becomes more robust, more accessible, and less error prone.

10.2 Writing Controlled Components

Problem

Form elements like inputs add another complexity as we need to decide where to manage state: in the browser or in React.

Solution

Write a proxy component that uses discriminated unions and the optional never technique to ensure you won't switch from uncontrolled to controlled at runtime.

Discussion

React differentiates form elements between *controlled components* and *uncontrolled components*. When you use regular form elements like input, textarea, or select, you need to keep in mind that the underlying HTML elements control their own state. Whereas in React, the state of an element is also defined *through* React.

If you set the value attribute, React assumes that the element's value is also controlled by React's state management, which means you are not able to modifiy this value unless you maintain the element's state using useState and the associated setter function.

There are two ways to deal with this. First, you can choose defaultValue as a property instead of value. This will set the value of the input only in the first rendering, and subsequently leaves everything in the hands of the browser:

```
function Input({
  value = "", ...allProps
}: Props) {
  return (
    <input
      defaultValue={value}
      {...allProps}
    />
  );
}
```

Or you manage value interally via React's state management. Usually, it's enough just to intersect the original input element's props with our own type. We drop value from the intrinsic elements and add it as a required string:

```
type ControlledProps =
  Omit<JSX.IntrinsicElements["input"], "value"> & {
    value: string;
  };
```

Then, we wrap the `input` element in a proxy component. It is not best practice to keep state internally in a proxy component; rather, you should manage it from the outside with `useState`. We also forward the `onChange` handler we pass from the original input props:

```
function Input({
  value = "", onChange, ...allProps
}: ControlledProps) {
  return (
    <input
      value={value}
      {...allProps}
      onChange={onChange}
    />
  );
}

function AComponentUsingInput() {
  const [val, setVal] = useState("");
  return <Input
    value={val}
    onChange={(e) => {
      setVal(e.target.value);
    }}
  />
}
```

React raises an interesting warning when dealing with a switch from uncontrolled to controlled at runtime:

> A component is changing an uncontrolled input to be controlled. This is likely caused by the value changing from undefined to a defined value, which should not happen. Decide between using a controlled or uncontrolled input element for the lifetime of the component.

We can prevent this warning by making sure at compile time that we either always provide a defined string `value` or provide a `defaultValue` instead, but not both. This can be solved by using a discriminated union type using the optional never technique (as seen in Recipe 3.8), and using the `OnlyRequired` helper type from Recipe 8.1 to derive possible properties from `JSX.IntrinsicElements["input"]`:

```
import React, { useState } from "react";

// A helper type setting a few properties to be required
type OnlyRequired<T, K extends keyof T = keyof T> = Required<Pick<T, K>> &
  Partial<Omit<T, K>>;
```

```
// Branch 1: Make "value" and "onChange" required, drop `defaultValue`
type ControlledProps = OnlyRequired<
  JSX.IntrinsicElements["input"],
  "value" | "onChange"
> & {
  defaultValue?: never;
};

// Branch 2: Drop `value` and `onChange`, make `defaultValue` required
type UncontrolledProps = Omit<
  JSX.IntrinsicElements["input"],
  "value" | "onChange"
> & {
  defaultValue: string;
  value?: never;
  onChange?: never;
};

type InputProps = ControlledProps | UncontrolledProps;

function Input({ ...allProps }: InputProps) {
  return <input {...allProps} />;
}

function Controlled() {
  const [val, setVal] = useState("");
  return <Input value={val} onChange={(e) => setVal(e.target.value)} />;
}

function Uncontrolled() {
  return <Input defaultValue="Hello" />;
}
```

In all other cases, having an optional `value` or having a `defaultValue` and trying to control values will be prohibited by the type system.

10.3 Typing Custom Hooks

Problem

You want to define custom hooks and get proper types.

Solution

Use tuple types or *const context*.

Discussion

Let's create a custom hook in React and stick to the naming convention as regular React hooks do: returning an array (or tuple) that can be destructured. For example, `useState`:

```
const [state, setState] = useState(0);
```

Why do we even use arrays? Because the array's fields have no name, and you can set names of your own:

```
const [count, setCount] = useState(0);
const [darkMode, setDarkMode] = useState(true);
```

So naturally, if you have a similar pattern, you also want to return an array. A custom toggle hook might look like this:

```
export const useToggle = (initialValue: boolean) => {
  const [value, setValue] = useState(initialValue);
  const toggleValue = () => setValue(!value);
  return [value, toggleValue];
}
```

Nothing out of the ordinary. The only types we have to set are the types of the input parameters. Let's try it:

```
export const Body = () => {
  const [isVisible, toggleVisible] = useToggle(false)
  return (
    <>
      <button onClick={toggleVisible}></button>
    { /* Error. See below */ }
      {isVisible && <div>World</div>}>}
    </>
  )
}
// Error: Type 'boolean | (() => void)' is not assignable to
// type 'MouseEventHandler<HTMLButtonElement> | undefined'.
// Type 'boolean' is not assignable to type
// 'MouseEventHandler<HTMLButtonElement>'.(2322)
```

So why does this fail? The error message might be cryptic, but what we should look out for is the first type, which is declared incompatible: `boolean | (() => void)'`. This comes from returning an array: a list of any length that can hold as many elements as virtually possible. From the return value in `useToggle`, TypeScript infers an array type. Since the type of `value` is `boolean` (great!) and the type of `toggleValue` is `(() => void)` (a function expected to return nothing), TypeScript tells us that both types are possible in this array.

This is what breaks the compatibility with onClick. onClick expects a function. That's fine, but toggleValue (or toggleVisible) is a function. According to Type-Script, however, it can also be a Boolean! TypeScript tells you to be explicit, or at least to do type-checks.

But we shouldn't need to do extra type-checks. Our code is very clear. It's the types that are wrong. Because we're not dealing with an array, let's go for a different name: tuple. While an array is a list of values that can be of any length, we know exactly how many values we get in a tuple. Usually, we also know the type of each element in a tuple.

So we shouldn't return an array but a tuple at useToggle. The problem: in JavaScript an array and a tuple are indistinguishable. In TypeScript's type system, we can distinguish them.

First option: let's be intentional with our return type. Since TypeScript—correctly!—infers an array, we have to tell TypeScript that we are expecting a tuple:

```
// add a return type here
export const useToggle = (initialValue: boolean): [boolean, () => void] => {
  const [value, setValue] = useState(initialValue);
  const toggleValue = () => setValue(!value);
  return [value, toggleValue];
};
```

With [boolean, () => void] as a return type, TypeScript checks that we are returning a tuple in this function. TypeScript does not infer, but rather makes sure that your intended return type is matched by the actual values. And voilà, your code doesn't throw errors anymore.

Second option: use *const context*. With a tuple, we know how many elements we are expecting, and we know the type of these elements. This sounds like a job for freezing the type with a const assertion:

```
export const useToggle = (initialValue: boolean) => {
  const [value, setValue] = useState(initialValue);
  const toggleValue = () => setValue(!value);
  // here, we freeze the array to a tuple
  return [value, toggleValue] as const;
}
```

The return type is now readonly [boolean, () => void], because as const makes sure that your values are constant and not changeable. This type is a little bit different semantically, but in reality you wouldn't be able to change the values you return outside of useToggle. So being readonly would be slightly more correct.

10.4 Typing Generic forwardRef Components

Problem

You use `forwardRef` for your components, but you need them to be generic.

Solution

There are several solutions to this problem.

Discussion

If you are creating component libraries and design systems in React, you might already have fowarded `ref`s to the DOM elements inside your components.

This is especially useful if you wrap basic components or leaves in *proxy components* (see Recipe 10.1), but want to use the `ref` property just like you're used to:

```
const Button = React.forwardRef((props, ref) => (
  <button type="button" {...props} ref={ref}>
    {props.children}
  </button>
));

// Usage: You can use your proxy just like you use
// a regular button!
const reference = React.createRef();
<Button className="primary" ref={reference}>Hello</Button>
```

Providing types for `React.forwardRef` is usually pretty straightforward. The types shipped by `@types/react` have generic type variables that you can set upon calling `React.forwardRef`. In that case, explicitly annotating your types is the way to go:

```
type ButtonProps = JSX.IntrinsicElements["button"];

const Button = React.forwardRef<HTMLButtonElement, ButtonProps>(
  (props, ref) => (
    <button type="button" {...props} ref={ref}>
      {props.children}
    </button>
  )
);

// Usage
const reference = React.createRef<HTMLButtonElement>();
<Button className="primary" ref={reference}>Hello</Button>
```

So far, so good. But things get a bit hairy if you have a component that accepts generic properties. The following component produces a list of list items, where you can select each row with a button element:

```
type ClickableListProps<T> = {
  items: T[];
  onSelect: (item: T) => void;
};

function ClickableList<T>(props: ClickableListProps<T>) {
  return (
    <ul>
      {props.items.map((item, idx) => (
        <li>
          <button key={idx} onClick={() => props.onSelect(item)}>
            Choose
          </button>
          {item}
        </li>
      ))}
    </ul>
  );
}

// Usage
const items = [1, 2, 3, 4];
<ClickableList items={items}
  onSelect={(item) => {
    // item is of type number
    console.log(item);
  } } />
```

You want the extra type safety so you can work with a type-safe item in your on Select callback. Say you want to create a ref to the inner ul element: how do you proceed? Let's change the ClickableList component to an inner function component that takes a ForwardRef and use it as an argument in the React.forwardRef function:

```
// The original component extended with a `ref`
function ClickableListInner<T>(
  props: ClickableListProps<T>,
  ref: React.ForwardedRef<HTMLULIstElement>
) {
  return (
    <ul ref={ref}>
      {props.items.map((item, i) => (
        <li key={i}>
          <button onClick={(el) => props.onSelect(item)}>Select</button>
          {item}
        </li>
      ))}
```

```
      </ul>
  );
}

// As an argument in `React.forwardRef`
const ClickableList = React.forwardRef(ClickableListInner)
```

This compiles but has one downside: we can't assign a generic type variable for ClickableListProps. It becomes unknown by default. This is good compared to any but also slightly annoying. When we use ClickableList, we know which items to pass along, and we want to have them typed accordingly! So how can we achieve this? The answer is tricky ... and you have a couple of options.

The first option is to do a type assertion that restores the original function signature:

```
const ClickableList = React.forwardRef(ClickableListInner) as <T>(
  props: ClickableListProps<T> & { ref?: React.ForwardedRef<HTMLULListElement> }
) => ReturnType<typeof ClickableListInner>;
```

Type assertions work great if you happen to have only a few situations where you need generic forwardRef components, but they might be too clumsy when you work with lots of them. Also, you introduce an unsafe operator for something that should be default behavior.

The second option is to create custom references with wrapper components. While ref is a reserved word for React components, you can use your own custom props to mimic a similar behavior. This works just as well:

```
type ClickableListProps<T> = {
  items: T[];
  onSelect: (item: T) => void;
  mRef?: React.Ref<HTMLULListElement> | null;
};

export function ClickableList<T>(
  props: ClickableListProps<T>
) {
  return (
    <ul ref={props.mRef}>
      {props.items.map((item, i) => (
        <li key={i}>
          <button onClick={(el) => props.onSelect(item)}>Select</button>
          {item}
        </li>
      ))}
    </ul>
  );
}
```

You introduce a new API, however. For the record, there is also the possibility of using a wrapper component that allows you to use forwardRef inside an *inner* component and expose a custom ref property to the outside:

```
function ClickableListInner<T>(
  props: ClickableListProps<T>,
  ref: React.ForwardedRef<HTMLULListElement>
) {
  return (
    <ul ref={ref}>
      {props.items.map((item, i) => (
        <li key={i}>
          <button onClick={(el) => props.onSelect(item)}>Select</button>
          {item}
        </li>
      ))}
    </ul>
  );
}

const ClickableListWithRef = forwardRef(ClickableListInner);

type ClickableListWithRefProps<T> = ClickableListProps<T> & {
  mRef?: React.Ref<HTMLULListElement>;
};

export function ClickableList<T>({
  mRef,
  ...props
}: ClickableListWithRefProps<T>) {
  return <ClickableListWithRef ref={mRef} {...props} />;
}
```

Both are valid solutions if the only thing you want to achieve is passing that ref. If you want to have a consistent API, you might look for something else.

The third and final option is to augment forwardRef with your own type definitions. TypeScript has a feature called *higher-order function type inference* (*https://oreil.ly/rVsq9*) that allows propagating free type parameters to the outer function.

This sounds a lot like what we want with forwardRef to begin with, but it doesn't work with our current typings. The reason is that higher-order function type inference works only on plain function types. The function declarations inside forwardRef also add properties for defaultProps and so on. These are relics from the class component days, things you might not want to use anyway.

So without the additional properties, it should be possible to use higher-order function type inference!

We are using TypeScript, so we have the ability to redeclare and redefine global `module`, `namespace`, and `interface` declarations on our own. Declaration merging is a powerful tool, and we're going to use it:

```
// Redecalare forwardRef
declare module "react" {
  function forwardRef<T, P = {}>(
    render: (props: P, ref: React.Ref<T>) => React.ReactElement | null
  ): (props: P & React.RefAttributes<T>) => React.ReactElement | null;
}


// Just write your components like you're used to!

type ClickableListProps<T> = {
  items: T[];
  onSelect: (item: T) => void;
};
function ClickableListInner<T>(
  props: ClickableListProps<T>,
  ref: React.ForwardedRef<HTMLULListElement>
) {
  return (
    <ul ref={ref}>
      {props.items.map((item, i) => (
        <li key={i}>
          <button onClick={(el) => props.onSelect(item)}>Select</button>
          {item}
        </li>
      ))}
    </ul>
  );
}

export const ClickableList = React.forwardRef(ClickableListInner);
```

The nice thing about this solution is that you write regular JavaScript again and work exclusively on a type level. Also, redeclarations are module scoped: no interference with any `forwardRef` calls from other modules!

10.5 Providing Types for the Context API

Problem

You want to use the context API for globals in your app, but you don't know the best way to deal with type definitions.

Solution

Either set default properties for context and let the type be inferred or create a partial of your context's properties and instantiate the generic type parameter explicitly. If you don't want to provide default values, but want to make sure that all properties are provided, create a helper function.

Discussion

React's context API allows you to share data on a global level. To use it, you need two things:

Providers
> Providers pass data to a subtree.

Consumers
> Consumers are components that *consume* the passed data inside render props.

With React's typings, you can use context without doing anything else most of the time. Everything is done using type inference and generics.

First, we create a context. Here, we want to store global application settings, like a theme and the app's language, along with the global state. When creating a React context, we want to pass default properties:

```
import React from "react";

const AppContext = React.createContext({
  authenticated: true,
  lang: "en",
  theme: "dark",
});
```

And with that, everything you need to do in terms of types is done for you. We have three properties: `authenticated`, `lang`, and `theme`; they are of types `boolean` and `string`. React's typings take this information to provide you with the correct types when you use them.

Next, a component high up in your component tree needs to provide context—for example, the application's root component. This provider trickles down the values you've set to every consumer below:

```
function App() {
  return (
    <AppContext.Provider
      value={{
        authenticated: true,
        lang: "de",
        theme: "light",
      }}
```

```
    >
      <Header />
    </AppContext.Provider>
  );
}
```

Now, every component inside this tree can consume this context. You already get type errors when you forget a property or use the wrong type:

```
function App() {
// Property 'theme' is missing in type '{ lang: string; }' but required
// in type '{ lang: string; theme: string; authenticated: boolean }'.(2741)
  return (
    <AppContext.Provider
      value={{
        lang: "de",
      }}
    >
      <Header />
    </AppContext.Provider>
  );
}
```

Now, let's consume our global state. Consuming context can be done via render props. You can destructure your render props as deep as you like, to get only the props you want to deal with:

```
function Header() {
  return (
    <AppContext.Consumer>
      {(({ authenticated }) => {
        if (authenticated) {
          return <h1>Logged in!</h1>;
        }
        return <h1>You need to sign in</h1>;
      }}
    </AppContext.Consumer>
  );
}
```

Another way of using context is via the respective useContext hook:

```
function Header() {
  const { authenticated } = useContext(AppContext);
  if (authenticated) {
    return <h1>Logged in!</h1>;
  }
  return <h1>You need to sign in</h1>;
}
```

Because we defined our properties earlier with the right types, authenticated is of type boolean at this point. Again, we didn't have to do anything to get this extra type safety.

The whole previous example works best if we have default properties and values. Sometimes you don't have default values or you need to be more flexible in which properties you want to set.

Instead of inferring everything from default values, we annotate the generic type parameter explicitly, not with the full type, but with a `Partial`.

We create a type for the context's props:

```
type ContextProps = {
  authenticated: boolean;
  lang: string;
  theme: string;
};
```

And initialize the new context:

```
const AppContext = React.createContext<Partial<ContextProps>>({});
```

Changing the semantics of the context's default properties has some side effects on your components as well. Now you don't need to provide every value; an empty context object can do the same! All your properties are optional:

```
function App() {
  return (
    <AppContext.Provider
      value={{
        authenticated: true,
      }}
    >
      <Header />
    </AppContext.Provider>
  );
}
```

This also means you need to check for every property if it's defined. This doesn't change the code where you rely on `boolean` values, but every other property needs to have another `undefined` check:

```
function Header() {
  const { authenticated, lang } = useContext(AppContext);
  if (authenticated && lang) {
    return <>
      <h1>Logged in!</h1>
      <p>Your language setting is set to {lang}</p>
    </> ;
  }
  return <h1>You need to sign in (or don't you have a language setting?)</h1>;
}
```

If you can't provide default values and want to make sure that all properties are provided by a context provider, you can help yourself with a helper function. Here, we want explicit generic instantiation to supply a type but give the right type guards so that when consuming context, all possibly undefined values are correctly set:

```
function createContext<Props extends {}>() { ❶
  const ctx = React.createContext<Props | undefined>(undefined); ❷
  function useInnerCtx() { ❸
    const c = useContext(ctx);
    if (c === undefined) ❹
      throw new Error("Context must be consumed within a Provider");
    return c; ❺
  }
  return [useInnerCtx, ctx.Provider as React.Provider<Props>] as const; ❻
}
```

What's going on in `createContext`?

❶ We create a function that has no function arguments but generic type parameters. Without the connection to function parameters, we can't instantiate `Props` via inference. This means that for `createContext` to provide proper types, we need to explicitly instantiate it.

❷ We create a context that allows for `Props` or `undefined`. With `undefined` added to the type, we can pass `undefined` as value. No default values!

❸ Inside `createContext`, we create a custom hook. This hook wraps `useContext` using the newly created context `ctx`.

❹ Then we do a type guard where we check if the returned `Props` includes `undefined`. Remember, when calling `createContext`, we instantiate the generic type parameter with `Props | undefined`. This line removes `undefined` from the union type again.

❺ Which means that here, c is `Props`.

❻ We assert that `ctx.Provider` doesn't take `undefined` values. We call `as const` to return `[useInnerContext, ctx.Provider]` as a tuple type.

Use `createContext` similar to `React.createContext`:

```
const [useAppContext, AppContextProvider] = createContext<ContextProps>();
```

When using `AppContextProvider`, we need to provide all values:

```
function App() {
  return (
    <AppContextProvider
```

```
          value={{ lang: "en", theme: "dark", authenticated: true }}
      >
        <Header />
      </AppContextProvider>
  );
}

function Header() {
  // consuming Context doesn't change much
  const { authenticated } = useAppContext();
  if (authenticated) {
    return <h1>Logged in!</h1>;
  }
  return <h1>You need to sign in</h1>;
}
```

Depending on your use case, you have exact types without too much overhead.

10.6 Typing Higher-Order Components

Problem

You are writing *higher-order components* to preset certain properties for other components but don't know how to type them.

Solution

Use the `React.ComponentType<P>` type from `@types/react` to define a component that extends your preset attributes.

Discussion

React is influenced by functional programming, which we see in the way components are designed (via functions), assembled (via composition), and updated (stateless, unidirectional data flow). It didn't take long for functional programming techniques and paradigms to find their way into React development. One such technique is higher-order components, which draw inspiration from *higher-order functions*.

Higher-order functions accept one or more parameters to return a new function. Sometimes those parameters are here to prefill certain other parameters, as we see, for example, in all currying recipes from Chapter 7. Higher-order components are similar: they take one or more components and return themselves another component. Usually, you create them to prefill certain properties where you want to make sure they won't be changed later on.

Think about a general-purpose `Card` component, which takes `title` and `content` as strings:

```
type CardProps = {
  title: string;
  content: string;
};

function Card({ title, content }: CardProps) {
  return (
    <>
      <h2>{title}</h2>
      <div>{content}</div>
    </>
  );
}
```

You use this card to present certain events, like warnings, information bubbles, and error messages. The most basic information card has `"Info"` as its title:

```
<Card title="Info" content="Your task has been processed" />;
```

You could subset the properties of `Card` to allow for only a certain subset of strings for `title`, but on the other hand, you want to be able to reuse `Card` as much as possible. So you create a new component that already sets `title` to `"Info"` and only allows for other properties to be set:

```
const Info = withInjectedProps({ title: "Info" }, Card);

// This should work
<Info content="Your task has been processed" />;

// This should throw an error
<Info content="Your task has been processed" title="Warning" />;
```

In other words, you *inject* a subset of properties and set the remaining ones with the newly created component. A function `withInjectedProps` is easily written:

```
function withInjectedProps(injected, Component) {
  return function (props) {
    const newProps = { ...injected, ...props };
    return <Component {...newProps} />;
  };
}
```

It takes the `injected` props and a `Component` as parameters, returns a new function component that takes the remaining props as parameters, and instantiates the original component with merged properties.

So how do we type `withInjectedProps`? Let's look at the result and see what's inside:

```
function withInjectedProps<T extends {}, U extends T>( ❶
  injected: T,
  Component: React.ComponentType<U> ❷
) {
  return function (props: Omit<U, keyof T>) { ❸
```

```
    const newProps = { ...injected, ...props } as U;  ❹
    return <Component {...newProps} />;
  };
}
```

Here is what's going on:

❶ We need to define two generic type parameters. T is for the props we already inject; it extends from {} to make sure we only pass objects. U is a generic type parameter for all props of Component. U *extends* T, which means that U is a subset of T. This says that U has more properties than T but needs to include what T already has defined.

❷ We define Component to be of type React.ComponentType<U>. This includes class components as well as function components and says that props will be set to U. With the relationship of T and U and the way we defined the parameters of with InjectedProps, we ensure that everything that will be passed for Component defines a subset of properties for Component with injected. If we make a typo, we quickly get the first error message!

❸ The function component that will be returned takes the remaining props. With Omit<U, keyof T> we make sure that we don't allow prefilled attributes to be set again.

❹ Merging T and Omit<U, keyof T> should result in U again, but since generic type parameters can be explicitly instantiated with something different, they might not fit Component again. A type assertion helps ensure that the props are actually what we want.

And that's it! With those new types, we get proper autocomplete and errors:

```
const Info = withInjectedProps({ title: "Info" }, Card);

<Info content="Your task has been processed" />;
<Info content="Your task has been processed" title="Warning" />;
//                                            ^
// Type '{ content: string; title: string; }' is not assignable
// to type 'IntrinsicAttributes & Omit<CardProps, "title">'.
// Property 'title' does not exist on type
// 'IntrinsicAttributes & Omit<CardProps, "title">'.(2322)
```

withInjectedProps is so flexible that we can derive higher-order functions that create higher-order components for various situations, like withTitle, which is here to prefill title attributes of type string:

```
function withTitle<U extends { title: string }>(
  title: string,
  Component: React.ComponentType<U>
) {
  return withInjectedProps({ title }, Component);
}
```

Your functional programming goodness knows no limits.

10.7 Typing Callbacks in React's Synthetic Event System

Problem

You want to get the best possible typings for all browser events in React and use the type system to restrict your callbacks to compatible elements.

Solution

Use the event types of `@types/react` and specialize on components using generic type parameters.

Discussion

Web applications become alive through user interaction. Every user interaction triggers an event. Events are key, and TypeScript's React typings have great support for events, but they require you not to use the native events from *lib.dom.d.ts*. If you do, React throws errors:

```
type WithChildren<T = {}> = T & { children?: React.ReactNode };

type ButtonProps = {
  onClick: (event: MouseEvent) => void;
} & WithChildren;

function Button({ onClick, children }: ButtonProps) {
  return <button onClick={onClick}>{children}</button>;
//                      ^
// Type '(event: MouseEvent) => void' is not assignable to
// type 'MouseEventHandler<HTMLButtonElement>'.
// Types of parameters 'event' and 'event' are incompatible.
// Type 'MouseEvent<HTMLButtonElement, MouseEvent>' is missing the following
// properties from type 'MouseEvent': offsetX, offsetY, x, y,
// and 14 more.(2322)
}
```

React uses its own event system, which we refer to as *synthetic events*. Synthetic events are cross-browser wrappers around the browser's native event, with the same interface as its native counterpart but aligned for compatibility. A change to the type from `@types/react` makes your callbacks compatible again:

```
import React from "react";

type WithChildren<T = {}> = T & { children?: React.ReactNode };

type ButtonProps = {
  onClick: (event: React.MouseEvent) => void;
} & WithChildren;

function Button({ onClick, children }: ButtonProps) {
  return <button onClick={onClick}>{children}</button>;
}
```

The browser's `MouseEvent` and `React.MouseEvent` are different enough for Type-Script's *structural* type system, meaning that there are some missing properties in the synthetic counterparts. You can see in the preceding error message that the original `MouseEvent` has 18 properties more than `React.MouseEvent`, some of them arguably important, like coordinates and offsets, which come in handy if, for example, you want to draw on a canvas.

If you want to access properties from the original event, you can use the `nativeEvent` property:

```
function handleClick(event: React.MouseEvent) {
  console.log(event.nativeEvent.offsetX, event.nativeEvent.offsetY);
}

const btn = <Button onClick={handleClick}>Hello</Button>};
```

Events supported are: `AnimationEvent`, `ChangeEvent`, `ClipboardEvent`, `Composition Event`, `DragEvent`, `FocusEvent`, `FormEvent`, `KeyboardEvent`, `MouseEvent`, `Pointer Event`, `TouchEvent`, `TransitionEvent`, and `WheelEvent`, as well as `SyntheticEvent` for all other events.

So far, we applied the correct types to make sure we don't have any compiler errors. Easy enough. But we're using TypeScript not only to fulfill the ceremony of applying types to keep the compiler from complaining but also to prevent situations that might be problematic.

Let's think about a button again. Or a link (the a element). Those elements are supposed to be clicked; that's their purpose. But in the browser, click events can be received by every element. Nothing keeps you from adding `onClick` to a `div` element, the element that has the least semantic meaning of all elements, and no assistive technology will tell you that a `div` can receive a `MouseEvent` unless you add lots of attributes to it.

Wouldn't it be great if we could keep our colleagues (and ourselves) from using the defined event handlers on the *wrong* elements? `React.MouseEvent` is a generic type that takes compatible elements as its first type. This is set to `Element`, which is the base type for all elements in the browser. But you are able to define a smaller set of compatible elements by subtyping this generic parameter:

```
type WithChildren<T = {}> = T & { children?: React.ReactNode };

// Button maps to an HTMLButtonElement
type ButtonProps = {
  onClick: (event: React.MouseEvent<HTMLButtonElement>) => void;
} & WithChildren;

function Button({ onClick, children }: ButtonProps) {
  return <button onClick={onClick}>{children}</button>;
}

// handleClick accepts events from HTMLButtonElement or HTMLAnchorElement
function handleClick(
  event: React.MouseEvent<HTMLButtonElement | HTMLAnchorElement>
) {
  console.log(event.currentTarget.tagName);
}

let button = <Button onClick={handleClick}>Works</Button>;
let link = <a href="/" onClick={handleClick}>Works</a>;

let broken = <div onClick={handleClick}>Does not work</div>;
//                          ^
// Type '(event: MouseEvent<HTMLButtonElement | HTMLAnchorElement,
// MouseEvent>) => void' is not assignable to type
//'MouseEventHandler<HTMLDivElement>'.
// Types of parameters 'event' and 'event' are incompatible.
// Type 'MouseEvent<HTMLDivElement, MouseEvent>' is not assignable to
// type 'MouseEvent<HTMLButtonElement | HTMLAnchorElement, MouseEvent>'.
// Type 'HTMLDivElement' is not assignable to type #
// 'HTMLButtonElement | HTMLAnchorElement'.
```

Although React's types give you more flexibility in some areas, it lacks features in others. For example, the browser native InputEvent is not supported in @types/react. The synthetic event system is meant to be a cross-browser solution, and some of React's compatible browsers still lack implementation of InputEvent. Until they catch up, it's safe for you to use the base event SyntheticEvent:

```
function onInput(event: React.SyntheticEvent) {
  event.preventDefault();
  // do something
}

const inp = <input type="text" onInput={onInput} />;
```

Now you get at least *some* type safety.

10.8 Typing Polymorphic Components

Problem

You create a proxy component (see Recipe 10.1) that needs to behave as one of many different HTML elements. It's hard to get the right typings.

Solution

Assert forwarded properties as `any` or use the JSX factory `React.createElement` directly.

Discussion

A common pattern in React is to define polymorphic (or `as`) components, which predefine behavior but can act as different elements. Think of a call-to-action button, or CTA, which can be a link to a website or an actual HTML button. If you want to style them similarly, they should behave alike, but depending on the context they should have the right HTML element for the right action.

 Selecting the right element is an important accessibility factor. `a` and `button` elements represent something users can click, but the semantics of `a` are fundamentally different from the semantics of a `button`. `a` is short for anchor and needs to have a reference (`href`) to a destination. A `button` can be clicked, but the action is usually scripted via JavaScript. Both elements can look the same, but they act differently. Not only do they act differently, but they also are announced differently using assistive technologies, like screen readers. Think about your users and select the right element for the right purpose.

The idea is that you have an `as` prop in your component that selects the element type. Depending on the element type of `as`, you can forward properties that fit the element type. Of course, you can combine this pattern with everything that you have seen in Recipe 10.1:

```
<Cta as="a" href="https://typescript-cookbook.com">
  Hey hey
</Cta>

<Cta as="button" type="button" onClick={(e) => { /* do something */ }}>
  My my
</Cta>
```

When throwing TypeScript into the mix, you want to make sure that you get auto-complete for the right props and errors for the wrong properties. If you add an `href` to a `button`, TypeScript should give you the correct squiggly lines:

```
// Type '{ children: string; as: "button"; type: "button"; href: string; }'
// is not assignable to type 'IntrinsicAttributes & { as: "button"; } &
// ClassAttributes<HTMLButtonElement> &
// ButtonHTMLAttributes<HTMLButtonElement> & { ...; }'.
// Property 'href' does not exist on type ... (2322)
//                              v
<Cta as="button" type="button" href="" ref={(el) => el?.id}>
  My my
</Cta>
```

Let's try to type `Cta`. First, we develop the component without types at all. In JavaScript, things don't look too complicated:

```
function Cta({ as: Component, ...props }) {
  return <Component {...props} />;
}
```

We extract the `as` prop and rename it as `Component`. This is a destructuring mechanism from JavaScript that is syntactically similar to a TypeScript annotation but works on destructured properties and not on the object itself (where you'd need a type annotation). We rename it to an uppercase component so we can instantiate it via JSX. The remaining props will be collected in `...props` and spread out when creating the component. Note that you can also spread out children with `...props`, a nice little side effect of JSX.

When we want to type `Cta`, we create a `CtaProps` type that works on either `"a"` elements or `"button"` elements and takes the remaining props from `JSX.Intrinsic Elements`, similar to what we've seen in Recipe 10.1:

```
type CtaElements = "a" | "button";

type CtaProps<T extends CtaElements> = {
  as: T;
} & JSX.IntrinsicElements[T];
```

When we wire up our types to `Cta`, we see that the function signature works very well with just a few extra annotations. But when instantiating the component, we get quite an elaborate error that tells us how much is going wrong:

```
function Cta<T extends CtaElements>({
  as: Component,
  ...props
}: CtaProps<T>) {
  return <Component {...props} />;
//          ^
// Type 'Omit<CtaProps<T>, "as" | "children"> & { children: ReactNode; }'
// is not assignable to type 'IntrinsicAttributes &
```

```
// LibraryManagedAttributes<T, ClassAttributes<HTMLAnchorElement> &
// AnchorHTMLAttributes<HTMLAnchorElement> & ClassAttributes<...> &
// ButtonHTMLAttributes<...>>'.
// Type 'Omit<CtaProps<T>, "as" | "children"> & { children: ReactNode; }' is not
// assignable to type
//   'LibraryManagedAttributes<T, ClassAttributes<HTMLAnchorElement>
// & AnchorHTMLAttributes<HTMLAnchorElement> & ClassAttributes<...>
// & ButtonHTMLAttributes<...>>'.(2322)
}
```

So where does this message come from? For TypeScript to work correctly with JSX, we need to resort to type definitions in a global namespace called JSX. If this namespace is in scope, TypeScript knows which elements that aren't components can be instantiated and which attributes they can accept. These are the JSX.Intrinsic Elements we use in this example and in Recipe 10.1.

One type that also needs to be defined is LibraryManagedAttributes. This type is used to provide attributes that are defined either by the framework itself (like key) or via means like defaultProps:

```
export interface Props {
  name: string;
}

function Greet({ name }: Props) {
  return <div>Hello {name.toUpperCase()}!</div>;
}
// Goes into LibraryManagedAttributes
Greet.defaultProps = { name: "world" };

// Type-checks! No type assertions needed!
let el = <Greet key={1} />;
```

React's typings solve LibraryManagedAttributes by using a conditional type. And as we see in Recipe 12.7, conditional types won't be expanded with all possible variants of a union type when being evaluated. This means that TypeScript won't be able to check that your typings fit the components because it won't be able to evaluate LibraryManagedAttributes.

One workaround for this is to assert props to any:

```
function Cta<T extends CtaElements>({
  as: Component,
  ...props
}: CtaProps<T>) {
  return <Component {...(props as any)} />;
}
```

That works, but it is a sign of an *unsafe* operation that shouldn't be unsafe. Another way is to not use JSX in this case but use the JSX factory React.createElement.

Every JSX call is syntactic sugar to a JSX factory call:

```
<h1 className="headline">Hello World</h1>

// will be transformed to
React.createElement("h1", { className: "headline" }, ["Hello World"]);
```

If you use nested components, the third parameter of `createElement` will contain nested factory function calls. `React.createElement` is much easier to call than JSX, and TypeScript won't resort to the global JSX namespace when creating new elements. Sounds like a perfect workaround for our needs.

`React.createElement` needs three arguments: the component, the props, and the children. Right now, we've smuggled all child components with `props`, but for `React.createElement` we need to be explicit. This also means that we need to explicitly define `children`.

For that, we create a `WithChildren<T>` helper type. It takes an existing type and adds optional children in the form of `React.ReactNode`:

```
type WithChildren<T = {}> = T & { children?: React.ReactNode };
```

`WithChildren` is highly flexible. We can wrap the type of our props with it:

```
type CtaProps<T extends CtaElements> = WithChildren<{
  as: T;
} & JSX.IntrinsicElements[T]>;
```

Or we can create a union:

```
type CtaProps<T extends CtaElements> = {
  as: T;
} & JSX.IntrinsicElements[T] & WithChildren;
```

Since T is set to {} by default, the type becomes universally usable. This makes it a lot easier for you to attach `children` whenever you need them. As a next step, we destructure `children` out of `props` and pass all arguments into `React.createEle ment`:

```
function Cta<T extends CtaElements>({
  as: Component,
  children,
  ...props
}: CtaProps<T>) {
  return React.createElement(Component, props, children);
}
```

And with that, your polymorphic component accepts the right parameters without any errors.

CHAPTER 11

Classes

When TypeScript was released for the very first time in 2012, the JavaScript ecosystem and the features of the JavaScript language were not comparable to what we have today. TypeScript introduced many features not only in the form of a type system but also syntax, enriching an already existing language with possibilities to abstract parts of your code across modules, namespaces, and types.

One of these features was classes, a staple in object-oriented programming. TypeScript's classes originally drew a lot of influence from C#, which is not surprising if you know the people behind both programming languages.[1] But they are also designed based on concepts from the abandoned ECMAScript 4 proposals.

Over time, JavaScript gained much of the language features pioneered by TypeScript and others; classes, along with private fields, static blocks, and decorators, are now part of the ECMAScript standard and have been shipped to language runtimes in the browser and the server.

This leaves TypeScript in a sweet spot between the innovation it brought to the language in the early days and standards, which is what the TypeScript team sees as a baseline for all upcoming features of the type system. While the original design is close to what JavaScript ended up with, there are some differences worth mentioning.

In this chapter, we look at how classes behave in TypeScript and JavaScript, the possibilities we have to express ourselves, and the differences between the standard and the original design. We look at keywords, types, and generics, and we train an eye to spot what's being added by TypeScript to JavaScript, and what JavaScript brings to the table on its own.

---

1 C# and TypeScript are made by Microsoft, and Anders Hejlsberg has been heavily involved in both programming languages.

11.1 Choosing the Right Visibility Modifier

Problem

There are two flavors in TypeScript for property visibility and access: one through special keyword syntax—public, protected, private—and another one through actual JavaScript syntax, when properties start with a hash character. Which one should you choose?

Solution

Prefer JavaScript-native syntax as it has some implications at runtime that you don't want to miss. If you rely on a complex setup that involves variations of visibility modifiers, stay with the TypeScript ones. They won't go away.

Discussion

TypeScript's classes have been around for quite a while, and while they draw huge inspiration from ECMAScript classes that followed a few years after, the TypeScript team also decided to introduce features that were useful and popular in traditional class-based object-oriented programming at the time.

One of those features is *property visibility modifiers*, also referred to as *access modifiers*. Visibility modifiers are special keywords you can put in front of members—properties and methods—to tell the compiler how they can be seen and accessed from other parts of your software.

 All visibility modifiers, as well as JavaScript private fields, work on methods as well as properties.

The default visibility modifier is public, which can be written explicitly or just omitted:

```
class Person {
  public name; // modifier public is optional
  constructor(name: string) {
    this.name = name;
  }
}

const myName = new Person("Stefan").name; // works
```

Another modifier is protected, limiting visibility to classes and subclasses:

```
class Person {
  protected name;
  constructor(name: string) {
    this.name = name;
  }
  getName() {
    // access works
    return this.name;
  }
}

const myName = new Person("Stefan").name;
//                                   ^
// Property 'name' is private and only accessible within
// class 'Person'.(2341)

class Teacher extends Person {
  constructor(name: string) {
    super(name);
  }

  getFullName() {
    // access works
    return `Professor ${this.name}`;
  }
}
```

protected access can be overwritten in derived classes to be public instead. protected access also prohibits accessing members from class references that are not from the same subclass. So while this works:

```
class Player extends Person {
  constructor(name: string) {
    super(name);
  }

  pair(p: Player) {
    // works
    return `Pairing ${this.name} with ${p.name}`;
  }
}
```

using the base class or a different subclass won't work:

```
class Player extends Person {
  constructor(name: string) {
    super(name);
  }

  pair(p: Person) {
    return `Pairing ${this.name} with ${p.name}`;
    //                                   ^
    // Property 'name' is protected and only accessible through an
```

```
    // instance of class 'Player'. This is an instance of
    // class 'Person'.(2446)
  }
}
```

The last visibility modifier is `private`, which allows access only from within the same class:

```
class Person {
  private name;
  constructor(name: string) {
    this.name = name;
  }
}
```

```
const myName = new Person("Stefan").name;
//                                    ^
// Property 'name' is protected and only accessible within
// class 'Person' and its subclasses.(2445)

class Teacher extends Person {
  constructor(name: string) {
    super(name);
  }

  getFullName() {
    return `Professor ${this.name}`;
    //                        ^
    // Property 'name' is private and only accessible
    // within class 'Person'.(2341)
  }
}
```

Visibility modifiers also can be used in constructors as a shortcut to define properties and initialize them:

```
class Category {
  constructor(
    public title: string,
    public id: number,
    private reference: bigint
  ) {}
}
```

```
// transpiles to

class Category {
  constructor(title, id, reference) {
    this.title = title;
    this.id = id;
    this.reference = reference;
  }
}
```

With all the features described here, it should be noted that TypeScript's visibility modifiers are compile-time annotations that get erased after the compilation step. Often, entire property declarations get removed if they are not initialized via the class description but in the constructor, as we saw in the last example.

They are also valid only during compile-time checks, meaning that a `private` property in TypeScript will be fully accessible in JavaScript afterward; thus, you can bypass the `private` access check by asserting your instances `as any`, or access them directly once your code has been compiled. They are also *enumerable*, which means that their names and values become visible when being serialized via `JSON.stringify` or `Object.getOwnPropertyNames`. In short: the moment they leave the boundaries of the type system they behave like regular JavaScript class members.

Next to visibility modifiers, it's also possible to add `readonly` modifiers to class properties.

Since limited access to properties is a feature that is reasonable not only within a type system, ECMAScript has adopted a similar concept called *private fields* for regular JavaScript classes.

Instead of a visibility modifier, private fields actually introduce new syntax in the form of a pound sign or *hash* in front of the member's name.

Introducing a new syntax for private fields has resulted in heated debate within the community on the pleasance and aesthetics of the pound sign. Some participants even called them abominable. If this addition irritates you as well, it might help to think of the pound sign as a little fence that you put in front of the things you don't want everybody to have access to. Suddenly, the pound sign syntax becomes a lot more pleasant.

The pound sign becomes a part of the property's name, meaning that it also needs to be accessed with the sign in front of it:

```
class Person {
  #name: string;

  constructor(name: string) {
    this.#name = name;
  }

  // we can use getters!
  get name(): string {
```

```
    return this.#name.toUpperCase();
  }
}

const me = new Person("Stefan");
console.log(me.#name);
//              ^
// Property '#name' is not accessible outside
// class 'Person' because it has a private identifier.(18013)

console.log(me.name); // works
```

Private fields are JavaScript through and through; there is nothing the TypeScript compiler will remove, and they retain their functionality—hiding information inside the class—even after the compilation step. The transpiled result, with the latest ECMAScript version as a target, looks almost identical to the TypeScript version, just without type annotations:

```
class Person {
  #name;

  constructor(name) {
    this.#name = name;
  }

  get name() {
    return this.#name.toUpperCase();
  }
}
```

Private fields can't be accessed in runtime code, and they are also not enumerable, meaning that no information of their contents will be leaked in any way.

The problem is now that both private visibility modifiers and private fields exist in TypeScript. Visibility modifiers have been there forever and have more variety combined with protected members. Private fields, on the other hand, are as close to JavaScript as they can get, and with TypeScript's goal to be a "JavaScript syntax for types," they pretty much hit the mark when it comes to the long-term plans of the language. So which one should you choose?

First, no matter which modifier you choose, they both fulfill their goal of telling you at compile time when there's property access where it shouldn't be. This is the first feedback you get informing you that something might be wrong, and this is what we're aiming for when we use TypeScript. So if you need to hide information from the outside, every tool does its job.

But when you look further, it again depends on your setting. If you already set up a project with elaborate visibility rules, you might not be able to migrate them to the native JavaScript version immediately. Also, the lack of protected visibility in

JavaScript might be problematic for your goals. There is no need to change something if what you have already works.

If you run into problems with the runtime visibility showing details you want to hide: if you depend on others using your code as a library and they should not be able to access all the internal information, then private fields are the way to go. They are well-supported in browsers and other language runtimes, and TypeScript comes with polyfills for older platforms.

11.2 Explicitly Defining Method Overrides

Problem

In your class hierarchy, you extend from base classes and override specific methods in subclasses. When you refactor the base class, you might end up carrying around old, unused methods because nothing tells you that the base class has changed.

Solution

Switch on the `noImplicitOverride` flag and use the `override` keyword to signal overrides.

Discussion

You want to draw shapes on a canvas. Your software is able to take a collection of points with x and y coordinates, and based on a specific render function, it will draw either polygons, rectangles, or other elements on an HTML canvas.

You decide to go for a class hierarchy, where the base class `Shape` takes an arbitrary list of `Point` elements and draws lines between them. This class takes care of house-keeping through setters and getters but also implements the `render` function itself:

```
type Point = {
  x: number;
  y: number;
};

class Shape {
  points: Point[];
  fillStyle: string = "white";
  lineWidth: number = 10;

  constructor(points: Point[]) {
    this.points = points;
  }

  set fill(style: string) {
```

```
    this.fillStyle = style;
  }

  set width(width: number) {
    this.lineWidth = width;
  }

  render(ctx: CanvasRenderingContext2D) {
    if (this.points.length) {
      ctx.fillStyle = this.fillStyle;
      ctx.lineWidth = this.lineWidth;
      ctx.beginPath();
      let point = this.points[0];
      ctx.moveTo(point.x, point.y);
      for (let i = 1; i < this.points.length; i++) {
        point = this.points[i];
        ctx.lineTo(point.x, point.y);
      }
      ctx.closePath();
      ctx.stroke();
    }
  }
}
```

To use it, create a 2D context from an HTML canvas element, create a new instance of Shape, and pass the context to the render function:

```
const canvas = document.getElementsByTagName("canvas")[0];
const ctx = canvas?.getContext("2d");

const shape = new Shape([
  { x: 50, y: 140 },
  { x: 150, y: 60 },
  { x: 250, y: 140 },
]);
shape.fill = "red";
shape.width = 20;

shape.render(ctx);
```

Now we want to use the established base class and derive subclasses for specific shapes, like rectangles. We keep the housekeeping methods and specifically override the constructor, as well as the render method:

```
class Rectangle extends Shape {
  constructor(points: Point[]) {
    if (points.length !== 2) {
      throw Error(`Wrong number of points, expected 2, got ${points.length}`);
    }
    super(points);
  }

  render(ctx: CanvasRenderingContext2D) {
```

```
    ctx.fillStyle = this.fillStyle;
    ctx.lineWidth = this.lineWidth;
    let a = this.points[0];
    let b = this.points[1];
    ctx.strokeRect(a.x, a.y, b.x - a.x, b.y - a.y);
  }
}
```

The usage of Rectangle is pretty much the same:

```
const rectangle = new Rectangle([
  {x: 130, y: 190},
  {x: 170, y: 250}
]);
rectangle.render(ctx);
```

As our software evolves, we inevitably change classes, methods, and functions, and somebody in our codebase will rename the render method to draw:

```
class Shape {
  // see above

  draw(ctx: CanvasRenderingContext2D) {
    if (this.points.length) {
      ctx.fillStyle = this.fillStyle;
      ctx.lineWidth = this.lineWidth;
      ctx.beginPath();
      let point = this.points[0];
      ctx.moveTo(point.x, point.y);
      for (let i = 1; i < this.points.length; i++) {
        point = this.points[i];
        ctx.lineTo(point.x, point.y);
      }
      ctx.closePath();
      ctx.stroke();
    }
  }
}
```

This is not a problem per se, but if we are not using the render method of Rectangle anywhere in our code, perhaps because we publish this software as a library and didn't use it in our tests, nothing tells us that the render method in Rectangle still exists, with no connection to the original class whatsoever.

This is why TypeScript allows you to annotate methods you want to override with the override keyword. This is a syntax extension from TypeScript and will be removed the moment TypeScript transpiles your code to JavaScript.

When a method is marked with the `override` keyword, TypeScript will make sure that a method of the same name and signature exists in the base class. If you rename `render` to `draw`, TypeScript will tell you that the method `render` wasn't declared in the base class `Shape`:

```
class Rectangle extends Shape {
  // see above

  override render(ctx: CanvasRenderingContext2D) {
//          ^
// This member cannot have an 'override' modifier because it
// is not declared in the base class 'Shape'.(4113)
    ctx.fillStyle = this.fillStyle;
    ctx.lineWidth = this.lineWidth;
    let a = this.points[0];
    let b = this.points[1];
    ctx.strokeRect(a.x, a.y, b.x - a.x, b.y - a.y);
  }
}
```

This error is a great safeguard to ensure that renames and refactors don't break your existing contracts.

 Even though a `constructor` could be seen as an overridden method, its semantics are different and handled through other rules (for example, making sure that you call `super` when instantiating a subclass).

By switching on the `noImplicitOverrides` flag in your *tsconfig.json*, you can further ensure that you need to mark functions with the `override` keyword. Otherwise, TypeScript will throw another error:

```
class Rectangle extends Shape {
  // see above

  draw(ctx: CanvasRenderingContext2D) {
// ^
// This member must have an 'override' modifier because it
// overrides a member in the base class 'Shape'.(4114)
    ctx.fillStyle = this.fillStyle;
    ctx.lineWidth = this.lineWidth;
    let a = this.points[0];
    let b = this.points[1];
    ctx.strokeRect(a.x, a.y, b.x - a.x, b.y - a.y);
  }
}
```

Techniques like implementing interfaces that define the basic shape of a class already provide a solid baseline to prevent you from running into problems like this. So, it's good to see the `override` keyword and `noImplictOverrides` as additional safeguards when creating class hierarchies.

When your software needs to rely on class hierarchies to work, using `override` together with `noImplicitAny` is a good way to ensure that you don't forget anything. Class hierarchies, like any hierarchies, tend to grow complicated over time, so take any safeguard you can get.

11.3 Describing Constructors and Prototypes

Problem

You want to instantiate subclasses of a specific abstract class dynamically, but TypeScript won't allow you to instantiate abstract classes.

Solution

Describe your classes with the *constructor interface* pattern.

Discussion

If you use class hierarchies with TypeScript, the structural features of TypeScript sometimes get in your way. Look at the following class hierarchy for instance, where we want to filter a set of elements based on different rules:

```
abstract class FilterItem {
  constructor(private property: string) {};
  someFunction() { /* ... */ };
  abstract filter(): void;
}

class AFilter extends FilterItem {
  filter() { /* ... */ }
}


class BFilter extends FilterItem {
  filter() { /* ... */ }
}
```

The `FilterItem` abstract class needs to be implemented by other classes. In this example `AFilter` and `BFilter`, both concretizations of `FilterItem`, serve as a baseline for filters:

```
const some: FilterItem = new AFilter('afilter'); // ok
```

Things get interesting when we are not working with instances right off the bat. Let's say we want to instantiate new filters based on a token we get from an AJAX call. To make it easier for us to select the filter, we store all possible filters in a map:

```
declare const filterMap: Map<string, typeof FilterItem>;

filterMap.set('number', AFilter);
filterMap.set('stuff', BFilter);
```

The map's generics are set to a `string` (for the token from the backend) and everything that complements the type signature of `FilterItem`. We use the `typeof` keyword here to be able to add classes to the map, not objects. We want to instantiate them afterward, after all.

So far everything works as you would expect. The problem occurs when you want to fetch a class from the map and create a new object with it:

```
let obj: FilterItem;
// get the constructor
const ctor = filterMap.get('number');

if(typeof ctor !== 'undefined') {
  obj = new ctor();
//              ^
// cannot create an object of an abstract class
}
```

This is a problem! TypeScript only knows at this point that we get a `FilterItem` back and we can't instantiate `FilterItem`. Abstract classes mix type information (*type namespace*) with an actual implementation (*value namespace*). As a first step, let's just look at the types: what are we expecting to get back from `filterMap`? Let's create an interface (or type alias) that defines how the *shape* of `FilterItem` should look:

```
interface IFilter {
  new(property: string): IFilter;
  someFunction(): void;
  filter(): void;
}

declare const filterMap: Map<string, IFilter>;
```

Note the `new` keyword. This is a way for TypeScript to define the type signature of a constructor function. If we substitute the abstract class for an actual interface, lots of errors start appearing. No matter where you put the `implements IFilter` command, no implementation seems to satisfy our contract:

```
abstract class FilterItem implements IFilter { /* ... */ }
// ^
// Class 'FilterItem' incorrectly implements interface 'IFilter'.
// Type 'FilterItem' provides no match for the signature
// 'new (property: string): IFilter'.

filterMap.set('number', AFilter);
//                      ^
// Argument of type 'typeof AFilter' is not assignable
// to parameter of type 'IFilter'. Type 'typeof AFilter' is missing
// the following properties from type 'IFilter': someFunction, filter
```

What's happening here? It seems like neither the implementation nor the class itself can get all the properties and functions we've defined in our interface declaration. Why?

JavaScript classes are special; they have not just one type we could easily define but two: the type of the static side and the type of the instance side. It might be clearer if we transpile our class to what it was before ES6, a constructor function and a prototype:

```
function AFilter(property) { // this is part of the static side
   this.property = property;  // this is part of the instance side
}

// a function of the instance side
AFilter.prototype.filter = function() {/* ... */}

// not part of our example, but on the static side
Afilter.something = function () { /* ... */ }
```

One type to create the object. One type for the object itself. So let's split it up and create two type declarations for it:

```
interface FilterConstructor {
   new (property: string): IFilter;
}

interface IFilter {
   someFunction(): void;
   filter(): void;
}
```

The first type, FilterConstructor, is the *constructor interface*. Here are all static properties and the constructor function itself. The constructor function returns an instance: IFilter. IFilter contains type information of the instance side. All the functions we declare.

By splitting this up, our subsequent typings also become a lot clearer:

```
declare const filterMap: Map<string, FilterConstructor>;  /* 1 */

filterMap.set('number', AFilter);
filterMap.set('stuff', BFilter);

let obj: IFilter;  /* 2 */
const ctor = filterMap.get('number');
if(typeof ctor !== 'undefined') {
  obj = new ctor('a');
}
```

1. We add instances of type `FilterConstructor` to our map. This means we only can add classes that produce the desired objects.

2. What we want in the end is an instance of `IFilter`. This is what the constructor function returns when being called with `new`.

Our code compiles again, and we get all the autocompletion and tooling we desire. Even better, we are not able to add abstract classes to the map because they don't produce a valid instance:

```
filterMap.set('notworking', FilterItem);
//                             ^
// Cannot assign an abstract constructor type to a
// non-abstract constructor type.
```

The constructor interface pattern is used throughout TypeScript and the standard library. To get an idea, look at the `ObjectContructor` interface from *lib.es5.d.ts*.

11.4 Using Generics in Classes

Problem

TypeScript generics are designed to be inferred a lot, but in classes, this doesn't always work.

Solution

Explicitly annotate generics at instantiation if you can't infer them from your parameters; otherwise, they default to unknown and accept a broad range of values. Use generic constraints and default parameters for extra safety.

Discussion

Classes also allow for generics. Instead of only being able to add generic type parameters to functions, we can also add generic type parameters to classes. While generic

---

type parameters at class methods are valid only in function scope, generic type parameters for classes are valid for the entirety of a class.

Let's create a collection, a simple wrapper around an array with a restricted set of convenience functions. We can add T to the class definition of Collection and reuse this type parameter throughout the entire class:

```
class Collection<T> {
  items: T[];
  constructor() {
    this.items = [];
  }

  add(item: T) {
    this.items.push(item);
  }

  contains(item: T): boolean {
    return this.items.includes(item);
  }
}
```

With that, we are able to explicitly substitute T with a generic type annotation, for example, allowing a collection of only numbers or only strings:

```
const numbers = new Collection<number>();
numbers.add(1);
numbers.add(2);

const strings = new Collection<string>();
strings.add("Hello");
strings.add("World");
```

We as developers are not required to explicitly annotate generic type parameters. TypeScript usually tries to infer generic types from usage. If we *forget* to add a generic type parameter, TypeScript falls back to unknown, allowing us to add everything:

```
const unknowns = new Collection();
unknowns.add(1);
unknowns.add("World");
```

Let's stay at this point for a second. TypeScript is very honest with us. The moment we construct a new instance of Collection, we don't know what the type of our items is. unknown is the most accurate depiction of the collection's state. And it comes with all the downsides: we can add anything, and we need to do type-checks every time we retrieve a value. While TypeScript does the only thing possible at this point, we might want to do better. A concrete type for T is mandatory for Collection to properly work.

Let's see if we can rely on inference. TypeScript's inference on classes works just like it does on functions. If there is a parameter of a certain type, TypeScript will take this type and substitute the generic type parameter. Classes are designed to keep state, and state changes throughout their use. The state also defines our generic type parameter T. To correctly infer T, we need to require a parameter at construction, maybe an initial value:

```
class Collection<T> {
  items: T[];
  constructor(initial: T) {
    this.items = [initial];
  }

  add(item: T) {
    this.items.push(item);
  }

  contains(item: T): boolean {
    return this.items.includes(item);
  }
}

// T is number!
const numbersInf = new Collection(0);
numbersInf.add(1);
```

This works, but it leaves a lot to be desired for our API design. What if we don't have initial values? While other classes might have parameters that can be used for inference, this might not make a lot of sense for a collection of various items.

For Collection, it is absolutely essential to provide a type through annotation. The only way left is to ensure we don't forget to add an annotation. To achieve this, we can make sure of TypeScript's generic default parameters and the bottom type never:

```
class Collection<T = never> {
  items: T[];
  constructor() {
    this.items = [];
  }

  add(item: T) {
    this.items.push(item);
  }

  contains(item: T): boolean {
    return this.items.includes(item);
  }
}
```

We set the generic type parameter T to default to never, which adds some very interesting behavior to our class. T still can be explicitly substituted with every type through annotation, working just as before, but the moment we forget an annotation the type is not unknown, it's never. Meaning that no value is compatible with our collection, resulting in many errors the moment we try to add something:

```
const nevers = new Collection();
nevers.add(1);
//       ^
// Argument of type 'number' is not assignable
// to parameter of type 'never'.(2345)
nevers.add("World");
//       ^
// Argument of type 'string' is not assignable
// to parameter of type 'never'.(2345)
```

This fallback makes the use of our generic classes a lot safer.

11.5 Deciding When to Use Classes or Namespaces

Problem

TypeScript offers a lot of syntax for object-oriented concepts like namespaces, or static and abstract classes. Those features don't exist in JavaScript, so what should you do?

Solution

Stick with namespace declarations for additional type declarations, avoid abstract classes when possible, and prefer ECMAScript modules instead of static classes.

Discussion

One thing we see from people who worked a lot with traditional object-oriented programming languages like Java or C# is their urge to wrap everything inside a class. In Java, you don't have any other options as classes are the only way to structure code. In JavaScript (and thus TypeScript), plenty of other possibilities do what you want without any extra steps. One of those is static classes or classes with static methods:

```
// Environment.ts

export default class Environment {
  private static variableList: string[] = []
  static variables(): string[] { /* ... */ }
  static setVariable(key: string, value: any): void  { /* ... */ }
  static getValue(key: string): unknown  { /* ... */ }
}

// Usage in another file
import * as Environment from "./Environment";

console.log(Environment.variables());
```

While this works and is even—sans type annotations—valid JavaScript, it's way too much ceremony for something that can easily be just plain, boring functions:

```
// Environment.ts
const variableList: string = []

export function variables(): string[] { /* ... */ }
export function setVariable(key: string, value: any): void  { /* ... */ }
export function getValue(key: string): unknown  { /* ... */ }

// Usage in another file
import * as Environment from "./Environment";

console.log(Environment.variables());
```

The interface for your users is exactly the same. You can access module scope variables just the way you would access static properties in a class, but you have them module scoped automatically. You decide what to export and what to make visible, not some TypeScript field modifiers. Also, you don't end up creating an `Environment` instance that doesn't do anything.

Even the implementation becomes easier. Check out the class version of `variables()`:

```
export default class Environment {
  private static variableList: string[] = [];
  static variables(): string[] {
    return this.variableList;
  }
}
```

as opposed to the module version:

```
const variableList: string = []

export function variables(): string[] {
  return variableList;
}
```

No this means less to think about. As an added benefit, your bundlers have an easier time doing tree shaking, so you end up with only the things you actually use:

```
// Only the variables function and variableList
// end up in the bundle
import { variables } from "./Environment";

console.log(variables());
```

That's why a proper module is always preferred to a class with static fields and methods. That's just an added boilerplate with no extra benefit.

As with static classes, people with a Java or C# background cling to namespaces, a feature that TypeScript introduced to organize code long before ECMAScript modules were standardized. They allowed you to split things across files, merging them again with reference markers:

```
// file users/models.ts
namespace Users {
  export interface Person {
    name: string;
    age: number;
  }
}

// file users/controller.ts

/// <reference path="./models.ts" />
namespace Users {
  export function updateUser(p: Person) {
    // do the rest
  }
}
```

Back then, TypeScript even had a bundling feature. It should still work. But as noted, this was before ECMAScript introduced modules. Now with modules, we have a way to organize and structure code that is compatible with the rest of the JavaScript ecosystem. And that's a plus.

So why do we need namespaces? Namespaces are still valid if you want to extend definitions from a third-party dependency, for example, that lives inside node modules. Say you want to extend the global JSX namespace and make sure img elements feature alt texts:

```
declare namespace JSX {
  interface IntrinsicElements {
    "img": HTMLAttributes & {
      alt: string;
      src: string;
      loading?: 'lazy' | 'eager' | 'auto';
    }
  }
}
```

Or you want to write elaborate type definitions in ambient modules. But other than that? There is not much use for it anymore.

Namespaces wrap your definitions into an object, writing something like this:

```
export namespace Users {
  type User = {
    name: string;
    age: number;
  };

  export function createUser(name: string, age: number): User {
```

```
        return { name, age };
    }
}
```

This emits something very elaborate:

```
export var Users;
(function (Users) {
    function createUser(name, age) {
        return {
            name, age
        };
    }
    Users.createUser = createUser;
})(Users || (Users = {}));
```

This not only adds cruft but also keeps your bundlers from tree shaking properly! Using them also becomes a bit wordier:

```
import * as Users from "./users";

Users.Users.createUser("Stefan", "39");
```

Dropping them makes things a lot easier. Stick to what JavaScript offers. Not using namespaces outside of declaration files makes your code clear, simple, and tidy.

Last but not least, there are abstract classes. Abstract classes are a way to structure a more complex class hierarchy where you predefine a behavior but leave the actual implementation of some features to classes that *extend* from your abstract class:

```
abstract class Lifeform {
    age: number;
    constructor(age: number) {
        this.age = age;
    }

    abstract move(): string;
}

class Human extends Lifeform {
    move() {
        return "Walking, mostly...";
    }
}
```

It's for all subclasses of `Lifeform` to implement `move`. This is a concept that exists in basically every class-based programming language. The problem is that JavaScript isn't traditionally class based. For example, an abstract class like the following generates a valid JavaScript class but is not allowed to be instantiated in TypeScript:

```
abstract class Lifeform {
    age: number;
    constructor(age: number) {
```

```
    this.age = age;
  }
}

const lifeform = new Lifeform(20);
//                    ^
// Cannot create an instance of an abstract class.(2511)
```

This can lead to some unwanted situations if you're writing regular JavaScript but rely on TypeScript to provide the information in the form of implicit documentation, such as if a function definition looks like this:

```
declare function moveLifeform(lifeform: Lifeform);
```

- You or your users might read this as an invitation to pass a `Lifeform` object to `moveLifeform`. Internally, it calls `lifeform.move()`.
- `Lifeform` can be instantiated in JavaScript, as it is a valid class.
- The method `move` does not exist in `Lifeform`, thus breaking your application!

This is due to a false sense of security. What you actually want is to put some predefined implementation in the prototype chain and have a contract that tells you what to expect:

```
interface Lifeform {
  move(): string;
}

class BasicLifeForm {
  age: number;
  constructor(age: number) {
    this.age = age;
  }
}

class Human extends BasicLifeForm implements Lifeform {
  move() {
    return "Walking";
  }
}
```

The moment you look up `Lifeform`, you can see the interface and everything it expects, but you seldom run into a situation where you instantiate the wrong class by accident.

With everything said about when *not* to use classes and namespaces, when should you use them? Every time you need multiple instances of the same object, where the internal state is paramount to the functionality of the object.

11.6 Writing Static Classes

Problem

Class-based object-oriented programming taught you to use static classes for certain features, but you wonder how those principles are supported in TypeScript.

Solution

Traditional static classes don't exist in TypeScript, but TypeScript has static modifiers for class members for several purposes.

Discussion

Static classes are classes that can't be instantiated into concrete objects. Their purpose is to contain methods and other members that exist once and are the same when being accessed from various points in your code. Static classes are necessary for programming languages that have only classes as their means of abstraction, like Java or C#. In JavaScript, and subsequently TypeScript, there are many more ways to express ourselves.

In TypeScript, we can't declare classes to be `static`, but we can define `static` members on classes. The behavior is what you'd expect: the method or property is not part of an object but can be accessed from the class itself.

As we saw in Recipe 11.5, classes with only static members are an antipattern in TypeScript. Functions exist; you can keep state per module. A combination of exported functions and module-scoped entries is usually the way to go:

```
// Anti-Pattern
export default class Environment {
  private static variableList: string[] = []
  static variables(): string[] { /* ... */ }
  static setVariable(key: string, value: any): void  { /* ... */ }
  static getValue(key: string): unknown  { /* ... */ }
}

// Better: Module-scoped functions and variables
const variableList: string = []

export function variables(): string[] { /* ... */ }
export function setVariable(key: string, value: any): void  { /* ... */ }
export function getValue(key: string): unknown  { /* ... */ }
```

But there is still a use for `static` parts of a class. We established in Recipe 11.3 that a class consists of static members and dynamic members.

The constructor is part of the static features of a class, and properties and methods are part of the dynamic features of a class. With the static keyword we can add to those static features.

Let's think of a class called Point that describes a point in a two-dimensional space. It has x and y coordinates, and we create a method that calculates the distance between this point and another one:

```
class Point {
  x: number;
  y: number;

  constructor(x: number, y: number) {
    this.x = x;
    this.y = y;
  }

  distanceTo(point: Point): number {
    const dx = this.x - point.x;
    const dy = this.y - point.y;
    return Math.sqrt(dx * dx + dy * dy);
  }
}

const a = new Point(0, 0);
const b = new Point(1, 5);

const distance = a.distanceTo(b);
```

This is good behavior, but the API might feel a bit weird if we choose a starting point and end point, especially since the distance is the same no matter which one is first. A static method on Point gets rid of the order, and we have a nice distance method that takes two arguments:

```
class Point {
  x: number;
  y: number;

  constructor(x: number, y: number) {
    this.x = x;
    this.y = y;
  }

  distanceTo(point: Point): number {
    const dx = this.x - point.x;
    const dy = this.y - point.y;
    return Math.sqrt(dx * dx + dy * dy);
  }

  static distance(p1: Point, p2: Point): number {
    return p1.distanceTo(p2);
```

```
    }
}

const a = new Point(0, 0);
const b = new Point(1, 5);

const distance = Point.distance(a, b);
```

A similar version using the constructor function/prototype pattern that was used pre-ECMAScript classes in JavaScript would look like this:

```
function Point(x, y) {
  this.x = x;
  this.y = y;
}

Point.prototype.distanceTo = function(p) {
  const dx = this.x - p.x;
  const dy = this.y - p.y;
  return Math.sqrt(dx * dx + dy * dy);
}

Point.distance = function(a, b) {
  return a.distanceTo(b);
}
```

As in Recipe 11.3, we can easily see which parts are static and which parts are dynamic. Everything that is in the *prototype* belongs to the dynamic parts. Everything else is *static*.

But classes are not only syntactic sugar to the constructor function/prototype pattern. With the inclusion of private fields, which are absent in regular objects, we can do something that is actually related to classes and their instances.

If we want to, for example, hide the distanceTo method because it might be confusing and we'd prefer our users to use the static method instead, a simple private modifier in front of distanceTo makes it inaccessible from the outside but still keeps it accessible from within static members:

```
class Point {
  x: number;
  y: number;

  constructor(x: number, y: number) {
    this.x = x;
    this.y = y;
  }

  #distanceTo(point: Point): number {
    const dx = this.x - point.x;
    const dy = this.y - point.y;
    return Math.sqrt(dx * dx + dy * dy);
```

```
  }

  static distance(p1: Point, p2: Point): number {
    return p1.#distanceTo(p2);
  }
}
```

The visibility also goes in the other direction. Let's say you have a class that represents a certain Task in your system, and you want to limit the number of existing tasks.

We use a static private field called nextId that we start at 0, and we increase this private field with every constructed instance Task. If we reach 100, we throw an error:

```
class Task {
  static #nextId = 0;
  #id: number;

  constructor() {
    if (Task.#nextId > 99) {
      throw "Max number of tasks reached";
    }
    this.#id = Task.#nextId++;
  }
}
```

If we want to limit the number of instances by a dynamic value from a backend, we can use a static instantiation block that fetches this data and updates the static private fields accordingly:

```
type Config = {
  instances: number;
};

class Task {
  static #nextId = 0;
  static #maxInstances: number;
  #id: number;

  static {
    fetch("/available-slots")
      .then((res) => res.json())
      .then((result: Config) => {
        Task.#maxInstances = result.instances;
      });
  }

  constructor() {
    if (Task.#nextId > Task.#maxInstances) {
      throw "Max number of tasks reached";
    }
    this.#id = Task.#nextId++;
  }
}
```

Other than fields in instances, TypeScript at the time of writing does not check if static fields are instantiated. If we, for example, load the number of available slots from a backend asynchronously, we have a certain time frame during which we can construct instances but have no check if we reached our maximum.

So, even if there is no construct of a static class in TypeScript and static-only classes are considered an antipattern, there might be a good use for static members in many situations.

11.7 Working with Strict Property Initialization

Problem

Classes keep state, but nothing tells you if this state is being initialized.

Solution

Activate strict property initialization by setting `strictPropertyInitialization` to true in your *tsconfig*.

Discussion

Classes can be seen as code templates for creating objects. You define properties and methods, and only through instantiation do actual values get assigned. TypeScript classes take basic JavaScript classes and enhance them with more syntax to define types. For example, TypeScript allows you to define the properties of the instance in a type- or interface-like manner:

```
type State = "active" | "inactive";

class Account {
  id: number;
  userName: string;
  state: State;
  orders: number[];
}
```

However, this notation only defines the shape: it doesn't set any concrete values, yet. When being transpiled to regular JavaScript, all those properties are erased; they exist only in the *type namespace*.

This notation is arguably very readable and gives the developer a good idea of what properties to expect. But there is no guarantee that these properties actually exist. If we don't initialize them, everything is either missing or `undefined`.

TypeScript has safeguards for this. With the `strictPropertyInitialization` flag set to `true` in your *tsconfig.json*, TypeScript will make sure that all properties you'd expect are actually initialized when creating a new object from your class.

 `strictPropertyInitialization` is part of TypeScript's `strict` mode. If you set `strict` to `true` in your *tsconfig*—which you should—you also activate strict property initialization.

Once this is activated, TypeScript will greet you with many red squiggly lines:

```
class Account {
  id: number;
// ^ Property 'id' has no initializer and is
// not definitely assigned in the constructor.(2564)
  userName: string;
// ^ Property 'userName' has no initializer and is
// not definitely assigned in the constructor.(2564)
  state: State;
// ^ Property 'state' has no initializer and is
// not definitely assigned in the constructor.(2564)
  orders: number[];
// ^ Property 'orders' has no initializer and is
// not definitely assigned in the constructor.(2564)
}
```

Beautiful! Now it's up to us to make sure that every property will receive a value. There are multiple ways to do this. If we look at the `Account` example, we can define some constraints or rules, if our application's domain allows us to do so:

- `id` and `userName` need to be set; they control the communication to our backend and are necessary for display.

- `state` also needs to be set, but it has a default value of `active`. Usually, accounts in our software are active, unless they are set intentionally to `inactive`.

- `orders` is an array that contains order IDs, but what if we haven't ordered anything? An empty array works just as well, or maybe we set `orders` to not be defined yet.

Given those constraints, we already can rule out two errors. We set `state` to be `active` by default, and we make `orders` optional. There's also the possibility to set `orders` to be of type `number[] | undefined`, which is the same thing as optional:

```
class Account {
  id: number; // still errors
  userName: string; // still errors
  state: State = "active"; // ok
  orders?: number[]; // ok
}
```

The other two properties still throw errors. By adding a constructor and initializing these properties, we rule out the other errors as well:

```
class Account {
  id: number;
  userName: string;
  state: State = "active";
  orders?: number[];

  constructor(userName: string, id: number) {
    this.userName = userName;
    this.id = id;
  }
}
```

That's it, a proper TypeScript class! TypeScript also allows for a constructor shorthand, where you can turn constructor parameters into class properties with the same name and value by adding a visibility modifier like public, private, or protected. It's a convenient feature that gets rid of a lot of boilerplate code. It's important that you don't define the same property in the class shape:

```
class Account {
  state: State = "active";
  orders?: number[];

  constructor(public userName: string, public id: number) {}
}
```

If you look at the class right now, you see that we rely only on TypeScript features. The transpiled class, the JavaScript equivalent, looks a lot different:

```
class Account {
  constructor(userName, id) {
    this.userName = userName;
    this.id = id;
    this.state = "active";
  }
}
```

Everything is in the constructor, because the constructor defines an instance.

While TypeScript shortcuts and syntax for classes seem nice, be careful how much you buy into them. TypeScript switched gears in recent years to be mostly a syntax extension for types on top of regular JavaScript, but their class features that have existed for many years now are still available and add different semantics to your code than you'd expect. If you lean toward your code being "JavaScript with types," be careful when you venture into the depths of TypeScript class features.

Strict property initialization also understands complex scenarios, like setting the property within a function that is being called via the constructor. It also understands that an async class might leave your class with a potentially uninitialized state.

Let's say you just want to initialize your class via an id property and fetch the user Name from a backend. If you do the async call within your constructor and set user Name after the fetch call is complete, you still get strict property initialization errors:

```
type User = {
  id: number;
  userName: string;
};

class Account {
  userName: string;
// ^ Property 'userName' has no initializer and is
// not definitely assigned in the constructor.(2564)
  state: State = "active";
  orders?: number[];

  constructor(public id: number) {
    fetch(`/api/getName?id=${id}`)
      .then((res) => res.json())
      .then((data: User) => (this.userName = data.userName ?? "not-found"));
  }
}
```

And it's true! Nothing tells you that the fetch call will be successful, and even if you catch errors and make sure that the property will be initialized with a fallback value, there is a certain amount of time when your object has an uninitialized userName state.

You can do a few things to get around this. One nice pattern is having a static factory function that works asynchronously, where you get the data first and then call a constructor that expects both properties:

```
class Account {
  state: State = "active";
  orders?: number[];
```

```
  constructor(public id: number, public userName: string) {}

  static async create(id: number) {
    const user: User = await fetch(`/api/getName?id=${id}`).then((res) =>
      res.json()
    );
    return new Account(id, user.userName);
  }
}
```

This allows both objects to be instantiated in a non-async context if you have access to both properties, or within an async context if you have only id available. We switch responsibilities and remove async from the constructor entirely.

Another technique is to simply ignore the uninitialized state. What if the state of user Name is totally irrelevant to your application, and you want to access it only when needed? Use the *definite assignment assertion* (an exclamation mark) to tell TypeScript you will treat this property as initialized:

```
class Account {
  userName!: string;
  state: State = "active";
  orders?: number[];

  constructor(public id: number) {
    fetch(`/api/getName?id=${id}`)
      .then((res) => res.json())
      .then((data: User) => (this.userName = data.userName));
  }
}
```

The responsibility is now in your hands, and with the exclamation mark you have TypeScript-specific syntax you can qualify as unsafe operation, runtime errors included.

11.8 Working with this Types in Classes

Problem

You extend from base classes to reuse functionality, and your methods have signatures that refer to an instance of the same class. You want to make sure that no other subclasses are getting mixed in your interfaces, but you don't want to override methods just to change the type.

Solution

Use this as type instead of the actual class type.

Discussion

In this example, we want to model a bulletin board software's different user roles using classes. We start with a general User class that is identified by its user ID and has the ability to open threads:

```
class User {
  #id: number;
  static #nextThreadId: number;

  constructor(id: number) {
    this.#id = id;
  }

  equals(user: User): boolean {
    return this.#id === user.#id;
  }

  async openThread(title: string, content: string): Promise<number> {
    const threadId = User.#nextThreadId++;
    await fetch("/createThread", {
      method: "POST",
      body: JSON.stringify({
        content,
        title,
        threadId,
      }),
    });
    return threadId;
  }
}
```

This class also contains an equals method. Somewhere in our codebase, we need to make sure that two references to users are the same, and since we identify users by their ID, we can easily compare numbers.

User is the base class of all users, so if we add roles with more privileges, we can easily inherit from the base User class. For example, Admin has the ability to close threads, and it stores a set of other privileges that we might use in other methods.

 There is much debate in the programming community if inheritance is a technique better to ignore since its benefits hardly outweigh its pitfalls. Nevertheless, some parts of JavaScript rely on inheritance, such as Web Components.

Since we inherit from User, we don't need to write another openThread method, and we can reuse the same equals method since all administrators are also users:

```
class Admin extends User {
  #privileges: string[];
  constructor(id: number, privileges: string[] = []) {
    super(id);
    this.#privileges = privileges;
  }

  async closeThread(threadId: number) {
    await fetch("/closeThread", {
      method: "POST",
      body: "" + threadId,
    });
  }
}
```

After setting up our classes, we can create new objects of type User and Admin by instantiating the right classes. We can also call the equals method to compare if two users might be the same:

```
const user = new User(1);
const admin = new Admin(2);

console.log(user.equals(admin));
console.log(admin.equals(user));
```

One thing is bothersome, though: the direction of comparison. Of course, comparing two numbers is commutative; it shouldn't matter if we compare a user to an admin, but if we think about the surrounding classes and subtypes, there is some room for improvement:

- It's OK to check if a user equals an admin, because it might gain privileges.

- It's doubtful if we want an admin to equal a user, because the broader supertype has less information.

- If we have another subclass of Moderator adjacent to Admin, we definitely don't want to be able to compare them as they don't share properties outside the base class.

Still, in the way equals is developed now, all comparisons would work. We can work around this by changing the type of what we want to compare. We annotated the input parameter with User first, but in reality we want to compare *with another instance of the same type*. There is a type for that, and it is called this:

```
class User {
  // ...

  equals(user: this): boolean {
    return this.#id === user.#id;
  }
}
```

This is different from the erasable `this` parameter we know from functions, which we learned about in Recipe 2.7, as the `this` parameter type allows us to set a concrete type for the `this` global variable within the scope of a function. The `this` type is a reference to the class where the method is located. And it changes depending on the implementation. So if we annotate a `user` with `this` in `User`, it becomes an `Admin` in the class that inherits from `User`, or a `Moderator`, and so on. With that, `admin.equals` expects another `Admin` class to be compared to; otherwise, we get an error:

```
console.log(admin.equals(user));
//                       ^
// Argument of type 'User' is not assignable to parameter of type 'Admin'.
```

The other way around still works. Since `Admin` contains all properties from `User` (it's a subclass, after all), we can easily compare `user.equals(admin)`.

`this` types can also be used as return types. Take a look at this `OptionBuilder`, which implements the *builder pattern*:

```
class OptionBuilder<T = string | number | boolean> {
  #options: Map<string, T> = new Map();
  constructor() {}

  add(name: string, value: T): OptionBuilder<T> {
    this.#options.set(name, value);
    return this;
  }

  has(name: string) {
    return this.#options.has(name);
  }

  build() {
    return Object.fromEntries(this.#options);
  }
}
```

It's a soft wrapper around a `Map`, which allows us to set key/value pairs. It has a chainable interface, which means that after each `add` call, we get the current instance back, allowing us to do add call after add call. Note that we annotated the return type with `OptionBuilder<T>`:

```
const options = new OptionBuilder()
  .add("deflate", true)
  .add("compressionFactor", 10)
  .build();
```

We are now creating a `StringOptionBuilder` that inherits from `OptionBuilder` and sets the type of possible elements to `string`. We also add a `safeAdd` method with checks if a certain value is already set before it is written, so we don't override previous settings:

```
class StringOptionBuilder extends OptionBuilder<string> {
  safeAdd(name: string, value: string) {
    if (!this.has(name)) {
      this.add(name, value);
    }
    return this;
  }
}
```

When we start using the new builder, we see that we can't reasonably use safeAdd if we have an add as the first step:

```
const languages = new StringOptionBuilder()
  .add("en", "English")
  .safeAdd("de", "Deutsch")
// ^
// Property 'safeAdd' does not exist on type 'OptionBuilder<string>'.(2339)
  .safeAdd("de", "German")
  .build();
```

TypeScript tells us that safeAdd does not exist on type OptionBuilder<string>. Where has this function gone? The problem is that add has a very broad annotation. Of course StringOptionBuilder is a subtype of OptionBuilder<string>, but with the annotation, we lose the information on the narrower type. The solution? Use this as return type:

```
class OptionBuilder<T = string | number | boolean> {
  // ...

  add(name: string, value: T): this {
    this.#options.set(name, value);
    return this;
  }
}
```

The same effect happens as with the previous example. In OptionBuilder<T>, this becomes OptionBuilder<T>. In StringBuilder, this becomes StringBuilder. If you return this and leave out the return type annotation, this becomes the *inferred* return type. So using this explicitly depends on your preference (see Recipe 2.1).

11.9 Writing Decorators

Problem

You want to log the execution of your methods for your telemetry, but adding manual logs to every method is cumbersome.

Solution

Write a class method decorator called `log` to annotate your methods.

Discussion

The *decorator* design pattern has been described in the renowned book *Design Patterns: Elements of Reusable Object-Oriented Software* by Erich Gamma et al. (Addison-Wesley) and describes a technique that can *decorate* classes and methods to dynamically add or overwrite certain behavior.

What began as a naturally emerging design pattern in object-oriented programming has become so popular that programming languages that feature object-oriented aspects have added decorators as a language feature with a special syntax. You can see forms of it in Java (called *annotations*) or C# (called *attributes*) and in JavaScript.

The ECMAScript proposal for decorators has been in proposal hell for quite a while but reached stage 3 (ready for implementation) in 2022. And with all features reaching stage 3, TypeScript is one of the first tools to pick up the new specification.

 Decorators have existed in TypeScript for a long time under the `experimentalDecorators` compiler flag. With TypeScript 5.0, the native ECMAScript decorator proposal is fully implemented and available without a flag. The actual ECMAScript implementation differs fundamentally from the original design, and if you developed decorators prior to TypeScript 5.0, they won't work with the new specification. Note that a switched-on `experimentalDecorators` flag turns off the ECMAScript native decorators. Also, in regard to types, *lib.decorators.d.ts* contains all type information for the ECMAScript native decorators, while types in *lib.decorators.legacy.d.ts* contain old type information. Make sure your settings are correct and that you don't consume types from the wrong definition file.

Decorators allow us to decorate almost anything in a class. For this example, we want to start with a method decorator that allows us to log the execution of method calls.

Decorators are described as functions with a *value* and a *context*, both depending on the type of class element you want to decorate. Those decorator functions return another function that will be executed before your own method (or before field initialization, or before an accessor call, etc.).

A simple `log` decorator for methods could look like this:

```
function log(value: Function, context: ClassMethodDecoratorContext) {
  return function (this: any, ...args: any[]) {
    console.log(`calling ${context.name.toString()}`);
```

```
      return value.call(this, ...args);
    };
}

class Toggler {
  #toggled = false;

  @log
  toggle() {
    this.#toggled = !this.#toggled;
  }
}

const toggler = new Toggler();
toggler.toggle();
```

The `log` function follows a `ClassMethodDecorator` type defined in the original decorator proposal (*https://oreil.ly/76JuE*):

```
type ClassMethodDecorator = (value: Function, context: {
  kind: "method";
  name: string | symbol;
  access: { get(): unknown };
  static: boolean;
  private: boolean;
  addInitializer(initializer: () => void): void;
}) => Function | void;
```

Many decorator context types are available. *lib.decorator.d.ts* defines the following decorators:

```
type ClassMemberDecoratorContext =
    | ClassMethodDecoratorContext
    | ClassGetterDecoratorContext
    | ClassSetterDecoratorContext
    | ClassFieldDecoratorContext
    | ClassAccessorDecoratorContext
    ;

/**
 * The decorator context types provided to any decorator.
 */
type DecoratorContext =
    | ClassDecoratorContext
    | ClassMemberDecoratorContext
    ;
```

You can read from the names exactly which part of a class they target.

Note that we haven't written detailed types yet. We resort to a lot of any, mostly because the types can get very complex. If we want to add types for all parameters, we need to resort to a lot of generics:

```
function log<This, Args extends any[], Return>(
  value: (this: This, ...args: Args) => Return,
  context: ClassMethodDecoratorContext
): (this: This, ...args: Args) => Return {
  return function (this: This, ...args: Args) {
    console.log(`calling ${context.name.toString()}`);
    return value.call(this, ...args);
  };
}
```

The generic type parameters are necessary to describe the method we are passing in. We want to catch the following types:

- `This` is a generic type parameter for the `this` parameter type (see Recipe 2.7). We need to set `this` as decorators are run in the context of an object instance.

- Then we have the method's arguments as `Args`. As we learned in Recipe 2.4, a method or function's arguments can be described as a tuple.

- Last, but not least, the `Return` type parameter. The method needs to return a value of a certain type, and we want to specify this.

With all three, we are able to describe the input method as well as the output method in the most generic way, for all classes. We can use generic constraints to make sure that our decorator works only in certain cases, but for `log`, we want to be able to log every method call.

> At the time of writing, ECMAScript decorators in TypeScript are fairly new. Types get better over time, so the type information you get may already be much better.

We also want to log our class fields and their initial value before the `constructor` method is called:

```
class Toggler {
  @logField #toggled = false;

  @log
  toggle() {
    this.#toggled = !this.#toggled;
  }
}
```

For that, we create another decorator called `logField`, which works on a `ClassField DecoratorContext`. The decorator proposal (*https://oreil.ly/76JuE*) describes the decorator for class fields as follows:

```
type ClassFieldDecorator = (value: undefined, context: {
  kind: "field";
  name: string | symbol;
  access: { get(): unknown, set(value: unknown): void };
  static: boolean;
  private: boolean;
}) => (initialValue: unknown) => unknown | void;
```

Note that the *value* is undefined. The initial value is being passed to the replacement method:

```
type FieldDecoratorFn = (val: any) => any;

function logField<Val>(
  value: undefined,
  context: ClassFieldDecoratorContext
): FieldDecoratorFn {
  return function (initialValue: Val): Val {
    console.log(`Initializing ${context.name.toString()} to ${initialValue}`);
    return initialValue;
  };
}
```

There's one thing that feels off. Why would we need different decorators for different kinds of members? Shouldn't our log decorator be capable of handling it all? Our decorator is called in a specific *decorator context*, and we can identify the right context via the kind property (a pattern we saw in Recipe 3.2). So there's nothing easier than writing a log function that does different decorator calls depending on the context, right?

Well, yes and no. Of course, having a wrapper function that branches correctly is the way to go, but the type definitions, as we've seen, are pretty complex. Finding *one* function signature that can handle them all is close to impossible without defaulting to any everywhere. And remember: we need the right function signature typings; otherwise, the decorators won't work with class members.

Multiple different function signatures just scream *function overloads*. So instead of finding one function signature for all possible decorators, we create overloads for *field decorators*, *method decorators*, and so on. Here, we can type them just as we would type the single decorators. The function signature for the implementation takes any for value and brings all required decorator context types in a union, so we can do proper discrimination checks afterward:

```
function log<This, Args extends any[], Return>(
  value: (this: This, ...args: Args) => Return,
  context: ClassMethodDecoratorContext
): (this: This, ...args: Args) => Return;
function log<Val>(
  value: Val,
  context: ClassFieldDecoratorContext
```

```
): FieldDecoratorFn;
function log(
  value: any,
  context: ClassMethodDecoratorContext | ClassFieldDecoratorContext
) {
  if (context.kind === "method") {
    return logMethod(value, context);
  } else {
    return logField(value, context);
  }
}
```

Instead of fumbling all the actual code into the `if` branches, we'd rather call the original methods. If you don't want to have your `logMethod` or `logField` functions exposed, then you can put them in a module and only export `log`.

 There are a lot of different decorator types, and they all have various fields that differ slightly. The type definitions in *lib.decorators.d.ts* are excellent, but if you need a bit more information, check out the original decorator proposal at TC39 (*https://oreil.ly/76JuE*). Not only does it include extensive information on all types of decorators, but it also contains additional TypeScript typings that complete the picture.

There is one last thing we want to do: adapt `logMethod` to log both *before* and *after* the call. For normal methods, it's as easy as temporarily storing the return value:

```
function log<This, Args extends any[], Return>(
  value: (this: This, ...args: Args) => Return,
  context: ClassMethodDecoratorContext
) {
  return function (this: This, ...args: Args) {
    console.log(`calling ${context.name.toString()}`);
    const val = value.call(this, ...args);
    console.log(`called ${context.name.toString()}: ${val}`);
    return val;
  };
}
```

But for asynchronous methods, things get a little more interesting. Calling an asynchronous method yields a `Promise`. The `Promise` itself might already have been executed, or the execution is deferred to later. This means if we stick with the implementation from before, the *called* log message might appear before the method actually yields a value.

As a workaround, we need to chain the log message as the next step after the `Promise` yields a result. To do so, we need to check if the method is actually a `Promise`. JavaScript Promises are interesting because all they need to be awaited is having a `then` method. This is something we can check in a helper method:

```
function isPromise(val: any): val is Promise<unknown> {
  return (
    typeof val === "object" &&
    val &&
    "then" in val &&
    typeof val.then === "function"
  );
}
```

And with that, we decide whether to log directly or deferred based on if we have a `Promise`:

```
function logMethod<This, Args extends any[], Return>(
  value: (this: This, ...args: Args) => Return,
  context: ClassMethodDecoratorContext
): (this: This, ...args: Args) => Return {
  return function (this: This, ...args: Args) {
    console.log(`calling ${context.name.toString()}`);
    const val = value.call(this, ...args);
    if (isPromise(val)) {
      val.then((p: unknown) => {
        console.log(`called ${context.name.toString()}: ${p}`);
        return p;
      });
    } else {
      console.log(`called ${context.name.toString()}: ${val}`);
    }

    return val;
  };
}
```

Decorators can get very complex but are ultimately a useful tool to make classes in JavaScript and TypeScript more expressive.

CHAPTER 12

Type Development Strategies

All recipes up until now have dealt with specific aspects of the TypeScript programming language and its type system. You have learned about effectively using basic types in Chapters 2 and 3, making your code more reusable through generics in Chapter 4, and crafting advanced types for very delicate situations using conditional types in Chapter 5, string template literal types in Chapter 6, and variadic tuple types in Chapter 7.

We established a collection of helper types in Chapter 8 and worked around standard library limitations in Chapter 9. We learned how to work with JSX as a language extension in Chapter 10 and how and when to use classes in Chapter 11. Every recipe discussed in detail the pros and cons of each approach, giving you better tools to decide correctly for every situation, creating better types, more robust programs, and a stable development flow.

That's a lot! One thing is still missing, though, the final piece that brings everything together: how do we approach new type challenges? Where do we start? What do we need to look out for?

The answers to these questions make up the contents of this chapter. Here you will learn about the concept of *low maintenance types*. We will explore a process on how you can start with simple types first and gradually get more refined and stronger. You will learn about the secret features of the TypeScript playground (*https://www.type scriptlang.org/play*) and how to deal with libraries that make validation easier. You will find guides to help you make hard decisions and learn about workarounds to the most common yet tough-to-beat type errors that will definitely hit you in your TypeScript journey.

If the rest of the book brought you from novice to apprentice, the next recipes will lead you to become an expert. Welcome to the last chapter.

12.1 Writing Low Maintenance Types

Problem

Every time your model changes, you need to touch a dozen types throughout your codebase. That is tedious, and it's also easy to miss something.

Solution

Derive types from others, infer from usage, and create low maintenance types.

Discussion

Throughout this book, we have spent a lot of time creating types from other types. The moment we can derive a type from something that already exists means we spend less time writing and adapting type information and more time fixing bugs and errors in JavaScript.

TypeScript is a layer of metainformation on top of JavaScript. Our goal is still to write JavaScript but make it as robust and easy as possible: tooling helps you stay productive and doesn't get in your way.

That's how I write TypeScript in general: I write regular JavaScript, and where TypeScript needs extra information, I happily add some extra annotations. One condition: I don't want to be bothered maintaining types. I'd rather create types that can update themselves if their dependencies or surroundings change. I call this approach *creating low maintenance types*.

Creating low maintenance types is a three-part process:

1. Model your data or infer from existing models.
2. Define derivates (mapped types, partials, etc.).
3. Define behavior with conditional types.

Let's take a look at this brief and incomplete `copy` function. I want to copy files from one directory to another. To make my life easier, I created a set of default options so I don't have to repeat myself too much:

```
const defaultOptions = {
  from: "./src",
  to: "./dest",
};

function copy(options) {
  // Let's merge default options and options
  const allOptions = { ...defaultOptions, ...options};
```

```
  // todo: Implementation of the rest
}
```

That's a pattern you might see a lot in JavaScript. What you see immediately is that TypeScript misses *some* type information. Especially the `options` argument of the copy function is any at the moment. So let's add a type for that!

I could create types explicitly:

```
type Options = {
  from: string;
  to: string;
};

const defaultOptions: Options = {
  from: "./src",
  to: "./dest",
};

type PartialOptions = {
  from?: string;
  to?: string;
};

function copy(options: PartialOptions) {
  // Let's merge default options and options
  const allOptions = { ...defaultOptions, ...options};

  // todo: Implementation of the rest
}
```

That's a reasonable approach. You think about types, then you assign types, and then you get all the editor feedback and type-checking you are used to. But what if something changes? Let's assume we add another field to `Options`; we would have to adapt our code three times:

```
type Options = {
  from: string;
  to: string;
  overwrite: boolean; // added
};

const defaultOptions: Options = {
  from: "./src",
  to: "./dest",
  overwrite: true, // added
};

type PartialOptions = {
  from?: string;
  to?: string;
```

```
    overwrite?: boolean; // added
  };
```

But why? The information is already there! In `defaultOptions`, we tell TypeScript exactly what we're looking for. Let's optimize:

1. Drop the `PartialOptions` type and use the utility type `Partial<T>` to get the same effect. You might have guessed this one already.

2. Use the `typeof` operator in TypeScript to create a new type on the fly:

```
const defaultOptions = {
  from: "./src",
  to: "./dest",
  overwrite: true,
};

function copy(options: Partial<typeof defaultOptions>) {
  // Let's merge default options and options
  const allOptions = { ...defaultOptions, ...options};

  // todo: Implementation of the rest
}
```

There you go. Just annotate where we need to tell TypeScript what we're looking for:

- If we add new fields, we don't have to maintain anything at all.

- If we rename a field, we get *just* the information we care about: all uses of `copy` where we have to change the options we pass to the function.

- We have one single source of truth: the actual `defaultOptions` object. This is the object that counts because it's the only information we have at runtime.

And our code becomes a little bit more concise. TypeScript becomes less intrusive and more aligned to how we write JavaScript.

Another example is one that has accompanied us from the beginning: the toy shop that started in Recipe 3.1, and has continued in Recipes 4.5 and 5.3. Revisit all three items and think about how we can change only the model to get all other types updated.

12.2 Refining Types Step by Step

Problem

Your API needs elaborate types, using advanced features like generics, conditional types, and string template literal types. You don't know where to start.

Solution

Refine your types step by step. Start with basic primitive and object types, subset, add generics, and then go all-in advanced. The process described in this lesson will help you craft types. It's also a good way to recap everything you've learned.

Discussion

Take a look at the following example:

```
app.get("/api/users/:userID", function (req, res) {
  if (req.method === "POST") {
    res.status(20).send({
      message: "Got you, user " + req.params.userId,
    });
  }
});
```

We have an Express-style server (*https://expressjs.com*) that allows us to define a route (or path) and executes a callback if the URL is requested.

The callback takes two arguments:

The request object
Here we get information on the HTTP method used (*https://oreil.ly/zcoUS*)—for example, GET, POST, PUT, DELETE—and additional parameters that come in. In this example userID should be mapped to a parameter userID that, well, contains the user's identifier!

The response or reply object
Here we want to prepare a proper response from the server to the client. We want to send correct status codes (method status) and send JSON output over the wire.

What we see in this example is heavily simplified, but it gives a good idea of what we are up to. The previous example is also riddled with errors! Take a look:

```
app.get("/api/users/:userID", function (req, res) {
  if (req.method === "POST") { /* Error 1 */
    res.status(20).send({ /* Error 2 */
      message: "Welcome, user " + req.params.userId /* Error 3 */,
    });
  }
});
```

Three lines of implementation code and three errors? What happened?

1. The first error is nuanced. While we tell our app that we want to listen to GET requests (hence app.get), we do something only if the request method is POST. At this particular point in our application, req.method can't be POST. So we would never send any response, which might lead to unexpected timeouts.

2. It's great that we explicitly send a status code! 20 isn't a valid status code, though. Clients might not understand what's happening here.

3. This is the response we want to send back. We access the parsed arguments but have a typo. It's userID, not userId. All our users would be greeted with "Welcome, user undefined!" Something you definitely have seen in the wild!

Solving issues like this is TypeScript's main purpose. TypeScript wants to understand your JavaScript code better than you do. And where TypeScript can't figure out what you mean, you can assist by providing extra type information. The problem is that it's often hard to start adding types. You might have the most puzzling edge cases in your mind but don't know how to get to them.

I want to propose a process that may help you get started and also shows you where there's a good place to stop. You can increase the strengths of your types step by step. It gets better with each refinement, and you can increase type safety over a longer period of time. Let's start!

Step 1: Basic typing

We start with some basic type information. We have an app object that points to a get function. The get function takes a path, which is a string, and a callback:

```
const app = {
  get /* post, put, delete, ... to come! */,
};

function get(path: string, callback: CallbackFn) {
  // to be implemented --> not important right now
}
```

CallbackFn is a function type that returns void and takes two arguments:

- req, which is of type ServerRequest
- reply, which is of type ServerReply

```
type CallbackFn = (req: ServerRequest, reply: ServerReply) => void;
```

ServerRequest is a pretty complex object in most frameworks. We do a simplified version for demonstration purposes. We pass in a method string, for "GET", "POST", "PUT", "DELETE", and so on. It also has a params record. Records are objects that associate a set of keys with a set of properties. For now, we want to allow every `string` key to be mapped to a `string` property. We'll refactor this one later:

```
type ServerRequest = {
  method: string;
  params: Record<string, string>;
};
```

For `ServerReply`, we lay out some functions, knowing that a real `ServerReply` object has many more. A **send** function takes an optional argument `obj` with the data we want to send. We have the possibility to set a status code with the **status** function using a fluent interface:[1]

```
type ServerReply = {
  send: (obj?: any) => void;
  status: (statusCode: number) => ServerReply;
};
```

With some very basic compound types and a simple primitive type for paths, we already added a lot of type safety to our project. We can rule out a couple of errors:

```
app.get("/api/users/:userID", function(req, res) {
  if(req.method === 2) {
//    ^ This condition will always return 'false' since the types
//      'string' and 'number' have no overlap.(2367)

    res.status("200").send()
//              ^
// Argument of type 'string' is not assignable to
// parameter of type 'number'.(2345)
  }
});
```

That's great, but there's still a lot to do. We can still send wrong status codes (any number is possible) and have no clue about the possible HTTP methods (any string is possible). So let's refine our types.

Step 2: Subset primitive types

You can see primitive types as a set of all possible values of that certain category. For example, `string` includes all possible strings that can be expressed in JavaScript, `number` includes all possible numbers with double float precision, and `boolean` includes all possible Boolean values, which are `true` and `false`.

TypeScript allows you to refine those sets to smaller subsets. For example, we can create a type `Methods` that includes all possible strings we can receive for HTTP methods:

---

1 Fluent interfaces allow for chainable operations by returning the instance with every method call.

```
type Methods = "GET" | "POST" | "PUT" | "DELETE";

type ServerRequest = {
  method: Methods;
  params: Record<string, string>;
};
```

Methods is a smaller set of the bigger string set. Methods is also a union type of literal types, the smallest unit of a given set. A literal string. A literal number. There is no ambiguity: it's just "GET". You put them in a union with other literal types, creating a subset of whatever bigger types you have. You can also do a subset with literal types of both string and number, or different compound object types. There are lots of possibilities to combine and put literal types into unions.

This has an immediate effect on our server callback. Suddenly, we can differentiate between those four methods (or more if necessary) and can exhaust all possibilities in code. TypeScript will guide us.

That's one less category of errors. We now know exactly which possible HTTP methods are available. We can do the same for HTTP status codes, by defining a subset of valid numbers that statusCode can take:

```
type StatusCode =
  100 | 101 | 102 | 200 | 201 | 202 | 203 | 204 | 205 |
  206 | 207 | 208 | 226 | 300 | 301 | 302 | 303 | 304 |
  305 | 306 | 307 | 308 | 400 | 401 | 402 | 403 | 404 |
  405 | 406 | 407 | 408 | 409 | 410 | 411 | 412 | 413 |
  414 | 415 | 416 | 417 | 418 | 420 | 422 | 423 | 424 |
  425 | 426 | 428 | 429 | 431 | 444 | 449 | 450 | 451 |
  499 | 500 | 501 | 502 | 503 | 504 | 505 | 506 | 507 |
  508 | 509 | 510 | 511 | 598 | 599;

type ServerReply = {
  send: (obj?: any) => void;
  status: (statusCode: StatusCode) => ServerReply;
};
```

Type StatusCode is again a union type. And with that, we exclude another category of errors. Suddenly, code like that fails:

```
app.get("/api/user/:userID", (req, res) => {
  if(req.method === "POS") {
//      ^ This condition will always return 'false' since
//        the types 'Methods' and '"POS"' have no overlap.(2367)
    res.status(20)
//               ^
// Argument of type '20' is not assignable to parameter of
// type 'StatusCode'.(2345)
  }
})
```

And our software becomes a lot safer. But we can do more!

Step 3: Adding generics

When we define a route with `app.get`, we implicitly know that the only HTTP method possible is `"GET"`. But with our type definitions, we still have to check for all possible parts of the union.

The type for `CallbackFn` is correct, as we could define callback functions for all possible HTTP methods, but if we explicitly call `app.get`, it would be nice to save some extra steps, which are only necessary to comply with typings.

TypeScript generics can help. We want to define `ServerRequest` in a way that we can specify a part of `Methods` instead of the entire set. For that, we use the generic syntax where we can define parameters as we would do with functions:

```
type ServerRequest<Met extends Methods> = {
  method: Met;
  params: Record<string, string>;
};
```

Here is what happens:

- `ServerRequest` becomes a generic type, as indicated by the angle brackets.
- We define a generic parameter called `Met`, which is a subset of type `Methods`.
- We use this generic parameter as a generic variable to define the method.

With that change, we can specify different `ServerRequest` variants without duplicating:

```
type OnlyGET = ServerRequest<"GET">;
type OnlyPOST = ServerRequest<"POST">;
type POSTorPUT = ServerRquest<"POST" | "PUT">;
```

Since we changed the interface of `ServerRequest`, we have to change all our other types that use `ServerRequest`, like `CallbackFn` and the `get` function:

```
type CallbackFn<Met extends Methods> = (
  req: ServerRequest<Met>,
  reply: ServerReply
) => void;

function get(path: string, callback: CallbackFn<"GET">) {
  // to be implemented
}
```

With the `get` function, we pass an actual argument to our generic type. We know that this won't be just a subset of `Methods`; we know exactly which subset we are dealing with.

Now, when we use `app.get`, we only have one possible value for `req.method`:

```
app.get("/api/users/:userID", function (req, res) {
  req.method; // can only be GET
});
```

This ensures we don't assume HTTP methods like `"POST"` or similar are available when we create an `app.get` callback. We know exactly what we are dealing with at this point, so let's reflect that in our types.

We already did a lot to make sure that `request.method` is reasonably typed and represents the actual state of affairs. One nice benefit of subsetting the `Methods` union type is that we can create a general-purpose callback function *outside* of `app.get` that is type safe:

```
const handler: CallbackFn<"PUT" | "POST"> = function(res, req) {
  res.method // can be "POST" or "PUT"
};

const handlerForAllMethods: CallbackFn<Methods> = function(res, req) {
  res.method // can be all methods
};


app.get("/api", handler);
//                    ^
// Argument of type 'CallbackFn<"POST" | "PUT">' is not
// assignable to parameter of type 'CallbackFn<"GET">'.

app.get("/api", handlerForAllMethods); // This works
```

Step 4: Advanced types to type-check

What we haven't touched yet is typing the `params` object. So far, we get a record that allows accessing every `string` key. It's our task now to make that a little more specific!

We do so by adding another generic variable, one for methods and one for the possible keys in our Record:

```
type ServerRequest<Met extends Methods, Par extends string = string> = {
  method: Met;
  params: Record<Par, string>;
};
```

The generic type variable `Par` can be a subset of type `string`, and the default value is every string. With that, we can tell `ServerRequest` which keys we expect:

```
// request.method = "GET"
// request.params = {
//   userID: string
// }
type WithUserID = ServerRequest<"GET", "userID">;
```

Let's add the new argument to our `get` function and the `CallbackFn` type, so we can set the requested parameters:

```
function get<Par extends string = string>(
  path: string,
  callback: CallbackFn<"GET", Par>
) {
  // to be implemented
}

const app = {
  get /* post, put, delete, ... to come! */,
};

type CallbackFn<Met extends Methods, Par extends string> = (
  req: ServerRequest<Met, Par>,
  reply: ServerReply
) => void;
```

If we don't set `Par` explicitly, the type works like we are accustomed to, since `Par` defaults to `string`. If we set it, though, we suddenly have a proper definition for the `req.params` object:

```
app.get<"userID">("/api/users/:userID", function (req, res) {
  req.params.userID; // Works!!
  req.params.anythingElse; // doesn't work!!
});
```

That's great! One little thing can be improved, though. We still can pass *every* string to the `path` argument of `app.get`. Wouldn't it be better if we could reflect `Par` in there as well? We can! This is where *string template literal types* (see Chapter 6) come into play.

Let's create a type called `IncludesRouteParams` to make sure that `Par` is properly included in the Express-style way of adding a colon in front of the parameter name:

```
type IncludesRouteParams<Par extends string> =
  | `${string}/:${Par}`
  | `${string}/:${Par}/${string}`;
```

The generic type `IncludesRouteParams` takes one argument, which is a subset of `string`. It creates a union type of two template literals:

- The first template literal starts with *any* `string`, then includes a / character followed by a : character, followed by the parameter name. This ensures that we catch all cases where the parameter is at the end of the route string.
- The second template literal starts with *any* `string`, followed by the same pattern of /, :, and the parameter name. Then we have another / character, followed by

any string. This branch of the union type makes sure we catch all cases where the parameter is somewhere within a route.

This is how `IncludesRouteParams` with the parameter name `userID` behaves with different test cases:

```
const a: IncludesRouteParams<"userID"> = "/api/user/:userID"; // works
const b: IncludesRouteParams<"userID"> = "/api/user/:userID/orders"; // works
const c: IncludesRouteParams<"userID"> = "/api/user/:userId"; // breaks
const d: IncludesRouteParams<"userID"> = "/api/user"; // breaks
const e: IncludesRouteParams<"userID"> = "/api/user/:userIDAndmore"; // breaks
```

Let's include our new utility type in the `get` function declaration:

```
function get<Par extends string = string>(
  path: IncludesRouteParams<Par>,
  callback: CallbackFn<"GET", Par>
) {
  // to be implemented
}

app.get<"userID">(
  "/api/users/:userID",
  function (req, res) {
    req.params.userID; // Yes!
  }
);
```

Great! We get another safety mechanism to ensure that we don't miss out on adding the parameters to the actual route. That's powerful.

Step 5: Locking literal types

But guess what: I'm still not happy with it. A few issues with that approach become apparent the moment your routes get a little more complex:

- The first issue is that we need to explicitly state our parameters in the generic type parameter. We have to bind `Par` to `"userID"`, even though we would specify it anyway in the `path` argument of the function. This is not JavaScript-y!
- This approach handles only one route parameter. The moment we add a union— for example, `"userID" | "orderId"`—the fail-safe check is satisfied with only *one* of those arguments being available. That's how sets work. It can be one or the other.

There must be a better way. And there is. Otherwise, this recipe would end on a very bitter note.

Let's inverse the order! Instead of defining the route params in a generic type variable, we extract the variables from the `path` passed as the first argument of `app.get`:

```
function get<Path extends string = string>(
  path: Path,
  callback: CallbackFn<"GET", ParseRouteParams<Path>>
) {
  // to be implemented
}
```

We remove the `Par` generic type and add `Path`, which can be a subset of any `string`. When we set `path` to this generic type `Path`, the moment we pass a parameter to `get`, we catch its string literal type. We pass `Path` to a new generic type `ParseRouteParams` that we haven't created yet.

Let's work on `ParseRouteParams`. Here, we switch the order of events again. Instead of passing the requested route params to the generic to make sure the path is all right, we pass the route path and extract the possible route params. For that, we need to create a conditional type.

Step 6: Adding conditional types

Conditional types are syntactically similar to the ternary operator in JavaScript. You check for a condition, and if the condition is met, you return branch A; otherwise, you return branch B. For example:

```
type ParseRouteParams<Route> =
  Route extends `${string}/:${infer P}`
  ? P
  : never;
```

Here, we check if `Route` is a subset of every path that ends with the parameter at the end Express-style (with a preceding `"/:"`). If so, we infer this string, which means we capture its contents into a new variable. If the condition is met, we return the newly extracted string; otherwise, we return `never`, as in: "there are no route parameters."

If we try it, we get something like:

```
type Params = ParseRouteParams<"/api/user/:userID">; // Params is "userID"

type NoParams = ParseRouteParams<"/api/user">; // NoParams is never: no params!
```

That's already much better than we did earlier. Now, we want to catch all other possible parameters. For that, we have to add another condition:

```
type ParseRouteParams<Route> = Route extends `${string}/:${infer P}/${infer R}`
  ? P | ParseRouteParams<`/${R}`>
  : Route extends `${string}/:${infer P}`
  ? P
  : never;
```

Our conditional type now works as follows:

1. In the first condition, we check if there is a route parameter somewhere in between the route. If so, we extract both the route parameter and everything else that comes after. We return the newly found route parameter P in a union where we call the same generic type recursively with the rest R. For example, if we pass the route `"/api/users/:userID/orders/:orderID"` to `ParseRouteParams`, we infer `"userID"` into P and `"orders/:orderID"` into R. We call the same type with R.

2. This is where the second condition comes in. Here we check if there is a type at the end. This is the case for `"orders/:orderID"`. We extract `"orderID"` and return this literal type.

3. If there are no more route parameters left, we return `never`:

```
// Params is "userID"
type Params = ParseRouteParams<"/api/user/:userID">;

// MoreParams is "userID" | "orderID"
type MoreParams = ParseRouteParams<"/api/user/:userID/orders/:orderId">;
```

Let's apply this new type and see what our final usage of **app.get** looks like:

```
app.get("/api/users/:userID/orders/:orderID", function (req, res) {
  req.params.userID; // Works
  req.params.orderID; // Also available
});
```

And that's it! Let's recap. The types we just created for one function **app.get** make sure that we exclude a ton of possible errors:

- We can only pass proper numeric status codes to `res.status()`.
- `req.method` is one of four possible strings, and when we use `app.get`, we know it can only be `"GET"`.
- We can parse route params and make sure we don't have any typos inside our callback parameters.

If we look at the example from the beginning of this recipe, we get the following error messages:

```
app.get("/api/users/:userID", function(req, res) {
  if (req.method === "POST") {
//      ^ This condition will always return 'false' since
//        the types 'Methods' and '"POST"' have no overlap.(2367)
    res.status(20).send({
//              ^
// Argument of type '20' is not assignable to parameter of
// type 'StatusCode'.(2345)
      message: "Welcome, user " + req.params.userId
```

```
    //                                    ^
    //     Property 'userId' does not exist on type
    //     '{ userID: string; }'. Did you mean 'userID'?
      });
    }
});
```

And all that before we actually run our code! Express-style servers are a perfect example of the dynamic nature of JavaScript. Depending on the method you call and the string you pass for the first argument, a lot of behavior changes inside the callback. Take another example and all your types look entirely different.

The great thing about this approach is that every step added more type safety:

1. You can easily stop at basic types and get more out of it than having no types at all.

2. Subsetting helps you get rid of typos by reducing the number of valid values.

3. Generics help you tailor behavior to use case.

4. Advanced types like string template literal types give your app more meaning in a stringly-typed world.

5. Locking in generics allows you to work with literals in JavaScript and treat them as types.

6. Conditional types make your types as flexible as your JavaScript code.

The best thing? Once you added your types, people will just write plain JavaScript and still get all the type information. That's a win for everybody.

12.3 Checking Contracts with satisfies

Problem

You want to work with literal types but need an annotation type-check to make sure you fulfill a contract.

Solution

Use the `satisfies` operator to do annotation-like type-checking while retaining the literal types.

Discussion

Mapped types are great, as they allow for the flexibility in object structures JavaScript is known for. But they have some crucial implications for the type system. Take this example from a generic messaging library, which takes a "channel definition" where multiple channel tokens can be defined:

```
type Messages =
  | "CHANNEL_OPEN"
  | "CHANNEL_CLOSE"
  | "CHANNEL_FAIL"
  | "MESSAGE_CHANNEL_OPEN"
  | "MESSAGE_CHANNEL_CLOSE"
  | "MESSAGE_CHANNEL_FAIL";

type ChannelDefinition = {
  [key: string]: {
    open: Messages;
    close: Messages;
    fail: Messages;
  };
};
```

The keys from this channel definition object are what the user wants them to be. So this is a valid channel definition:

```
const impl: ChannelDefinition = {
  test: {
    open: 'CHANNEL_OPEN',
    close: 'CHANNEL_CLOSE',
    fail: 'CHANNEL_FAIL'
  },
  message: {
    open: 'MESSAGE_CHANNEL_OPEN',
    close: 'MESSAGE_CHANNEL_CLOSE',
    fail: 'MESSAGE_CHANNEL_FAIL'
  }
}
```

We have a problem, however: when we want to access the keys we defined so flexibly. Let's say we have a function that opens a channel. We pass the whole channel definition object, as well as the channel we want to open:

```
function openChannel(
  def: ChannelDefinition,
  channel: keyof ChannelDefinition
) {
  // to be implemented
}
```

So what are the keys of ChannelDefinition? Well, it's every key: [key: string]. So the moment we assign a specific type, TypeScript treats impl as this specific type, ignoring the actual implementation. The contract is fulfilled. Moving on. This allows for wrong keys to be passed:

```
// Passes, even though "massage" is not part of impl
openChannel(impl, "massage");
```

So we are more interested in the actual implementation, not the type we assign to our constant. This means we have to get rid of the `ChannelDefinition` type and make sure we care about the actual type of the object.

First, the `openChannel` function should take any object that is a subtype of `ChannelDefinition` but work with the concrete subtype:

```
function openChannel<
  T extends ChannelDefinition
>(def: T, channel: keyof T) {
  // to be implemented
}
```

TypeScript now works on two levels:

- It checks if T actually extends `ChannelDefinition`. If so, we work with type T.
- All our function parameters are typed with the generic T. This also means we get the *real* keys of T through `keyof T`.

To benefit from that, we have to get rid of the type definition for `impl`. The explicit type definition overrides all actual types. From the moment we explicitly specify the type, TypeScript treats it as `ChannelDefinition`, not the actual underlying subtype. We also have to set *const context*, so we can convert all strings to their unit type (and thus be compliant with `Messages`):

```
const impl = {
  test: {
    open: "CHANNEL_OPEN",
    close: "CHANNEL_CLOSE",
    fail: "CHANNEL_FAIL",
  },
  message: {
    open: "MESSAGE_CHANNEL_OPEN",
    close: "MESSAGE_CHANNEL_CLOSE",
    fail: "MESSAGE_CHANNEL_FAIL",
  },
} as const;
```

Without *const context*, the inferred type of `impl` is:

```
/// typeof impl
{
  test: {
    open: string;
    close: string;
    fail: string;
  };
  message: {
    open: string;
    close: string;
```

```
      fail: string;
    };
  }
```

With *const context*, the actual type of `impl` is now:

```
/// typeof impl
{
  test: {
    readonly open: "CHANNEL_OPEN";
    readonly close: "CHANNEL_CLOSE";
    readonly fail: "CHANNEL_FAIL";
  };
  message: {
    readonly open: "MESSAGE_CHANNEL_OPEN";
    readonly close: "MESSAGE_CHANNEL_CLOSE";
    readonly fail: "MESSAGE_CHANNEL_FAIL";
  };
}
```

Const context allows us to satisfy the contract made by `ChannelDefinition`. Now `openChannel` works correctly:

```
openChannel(impl, "message"); // satisfies contract
openChannel(impl, "massage");
//                   ^
// Argument of type '"massage"' is not assignable to parameter
// of type '"test" | "message"'.(2345)
```

This works but comes with a caveat. The only point where we can check if `impl` is actually a valid subtype of `ChannelDefinition` is when we are using it. Sometimes we want to annotate early to figure out potential breaks in our contract. We want to see if this specific implementation *satisfies* a contract.

Thankfully, there is a keyword for that. We can define objects and do a type-check to see if this implementation satisfies a type, but TypeScript will treat it as a literal type:

```
const impl = {
  test: {
    open: "CHANNEL_OPEN",
    close: "CHANNEL_CLOSE",
    fail: "CHANNEL_FAIL",
  },
  message: {
    open: "MESSAGE_CHANNEL_OPEN",
    close: "MESSAGE_CHANNEL_CLOSE",
    fail: "MESSAGE_CHANNEL_FAIL",
  },
} satisfies ChannelDefinition;

function openChannel<T extends ChannelDefinition>(
  def: T,
  channel: keyof T
```

```
) {
  // to be implemented
}
```

With that, we can make sure that we fulfill contracts but have the same benefits as with *const context*. The only difference is that the fields are not set to `readonly`, but since TypeScript takes the literal type of everything, there is no way to set fields to anything else after a satisfaction type-check:

```
impl.test.close = "CHANEL_CLOSE_MASSAGE";
//                 ^
// Type '"CHANEL_CLOSE_MASSAGE"' is not assignable
// to type '"CHANNEL_CLOSE"'.(2322)
```

With that, we get the best of both worlds: proper type-checks at annotation time as well as the power of narrowed types for specific situations.

12.4 Testing Complex Types

Problem

You have written very elaborate and complex types, and you want to make sure that they behave correctly.

Solution

Some commonly known helper types work like a test framework. Test your types!

Discussion

In dynamically typed programming languages people always circle around the discussion of if you need types when you can have a proper test suite. This is at least what one camp says; the other thinks, why should we test so much when we can have types? The answer is probably somewhere in the middle.

It is true that types can solve a lot of test cases. Is the result a number? Is the result an object with certain properties of certain types? This is something we can easily check via types. Does my function produce correct results? Are the values what I expect them to be? This belongs to tests.

Throughout this book, we learned a lot about very complex types. With conditional types, we opened up the metaprogramming capabilities of TypeScript, where we could craft new types based on certain features of previous types. Powerful, Turing complete, and very advanced. This leads to the question: how do we ensure that those complex types actually do what they should do? Maybe we should *test our types*?

We actually can. There are a few helper types known within the community that can serve as some sort of testing framework. The following types come from the excellent Type Challenges repository (*https://tsch.js.org*), which allows you to test your TypeScript type system skills to an extreme. They include very challenging tasks: some that have relevance to real-world use cases and others that are just for fun.

Their testing library starts with a few types that expect a truthy or a falsy value. They are pretty straightforward. By using generics and literal types, we can check if this one Boolean is true or false:

```
export type Expect<T extends true> = T;
export type ExpectTrue<T extends true> = T;
export type ExpectFalse<T extends false> = T;
export type IsTrue<T extends true> = T;
export type IsFalse<T extends false> = T;
```

They don't do much on their own but are fantastic when being used with `Equal<X, Y>` and `NotEqual<X, Y>`, which return either `true` or `false`:

```
export type Equal<X, Y> =
  (<T>() => T extends X ? 1 : 2) extends
  (<T>() => T extends Y ? 1 : 2) ? true : false;
export type NotEqual<X, Y> = true extends Equal<X, Y> ? false : true;
```

`Equal<X, Y>` is interesting as it creates generic functions and checks them against both types that should be compared with each other. Since there is no resolution on each conditional type, TypeScript compares both conditional types and can see if there is compatibility. It's a step within TypeScript's conditional type logic that is masterfully explained by Alex Chashin on Stack Overflow (*https://oreil.ly/ywWd4*).

The next batch allows us to check if a type is `any`:

```
export type IsAny<T> = 0 extends 1 & T ? true : false;
export type NotAny<T> = true extends IsAny<T> ? false : true;
```

It's a simple conditional type that checks `0` against `1 & T`, which should always narrow down to `1` or `never`, which always yields the `false` branch of the conditional type. Except when we intersect with `any`. An intersection with `any` is always `any`, and `0` is a subset of `any`.

The next batch is reinterpretations of `Remap` and `DeepRemap` we saw in Recipe 8.3, along with `Alike` as a way to compare types that are equal in structure but not construction:

```
export type Debug<T> = { [K in keyof T]: T[K] };
export type MergeInsertions<T> = T extends object
  ? { [K in keyof T]: MergeInsertions<T[K]> }
  : T;

export type Alike<X, Y> = Equal<MergeInsertions<X>, MergeInsertions<Y>>;
```

The `Equal` check before should theoretically be able to understand that `{ x : num ber, y: string }` is equal to `{ x: number } & { y: string }`, but implementation details of the TypeScript type-checker don't see them as equal. That's where `Alike` comes into play.

The last batch of the type challenges testing file does two things:

- It does subset checks with a simple conditional type.
- It checks if a tuple you have constructed can be seen as a valid argument for a function:

```
export type ExpectExtends<VALUE, EXPECTED> = EXPECTED extends VALUE
  ? true
  : false;
export type ExpectValidArgs<
  FUNC extends (...args: any[]) => any,
  ARGS extends any[]
> = ARGS extends Parameters<FUNC> ? true : false;
```

Having a small helper type library like this for type testing and debugging is really helpful when your types get more complex. Add them to your global type definition files (see Recipe 9.7) and use them.

12.5 Validating Data Types at Runtime with Zod

Problem

You rely on data from external sources and can't trust them to be correct.

Solution

Define schemas using a library called *Zod* and use it to validate data from external sources.

Discussion

Congratulations! We're almost at the end. If you have followed along from start to finish, you have been constantly reminded that TypeScript's type system follows a couple of goals. First and foremost, it wants to give you excellent tooling so you can be productive when developing applications. It also wants to cater to all JavaScript frameworks and make sure they are fun and easy to use. It sees itself as an add-on to JavaScript, as a syntax for static types. There are also some non-goals or trade-offs. It prefers productivity over correctness, it allows developers to bend the rules to their needs, and it has no claim of being provably sound.

In Recipe 3.9 we learned that we can influence TypeScript if we think that types should be something different through *type assertions*, and in Recipe 9.2 we learned how we can make *unsafe operations* more robust and easier to spot. Since TypeScript's type system is compile-time only, all our safeguards evaporate once we run JavaScript in our selected runtime.

Usually, compile-time type-checks are good enough. As long as we are within the *inner world* where we write our own types, let TypeScript check that everything is OK, and our code is good to go. In JavaScript applications, however, we also deal with a lot of things beyond our control: user input, for example. APIs from third parties that we need to access and process. Inevitably, we reach a point in our development process where we need to leave the boundaries of our well-typed application and deal with data that we can't trust.

While developing, working with external sources or user input might work well enough, but to make sure that the data we use stays the same when running in production requires extra effort. You may want to validate that your data adheres to a certain scheme.

Thankfully, there are libraries that deal with that kind of task. One library that has gained popularity in recent years is Zod (*https://zod.dev*). Zod is TypeScript-first, which means it makes sure not only that the data you consume is valid and what you expect but also that you get TypeScript types you can use throughout your program. Zod sees itself as the guard between the outer world outside of your control and the inner world where everything is well-typed and also type-checked.

Think of an API that gives you data for the `Person` type we've seen throughout the book. A `Person` has a name and age, a profession that is optional, and also a status: in our system, they can be either active, inactive, or only registered, waiting for confirmation.

The API also packs a couple of `Person` objects in an array contained within a `Result` type. In short, it's an example for a classic response type for HTTP calls:

```
type Person = {
  name: string;
  age: number;
  profession?: string | undefined;
  status: "active" | "inactive" | "registered";
};

type Results = {
  entries: Person[]
};
```

You know how to type models like this. By now, you are fluent in recognizing and applying both syntax and patterns. We want to have the same type, but at runtime for data outside our control, we use Zod. And writing the same type in JavaScript (the value namespace) looks very familiar:

```
import { z } from "zod";

const Person = z.object({
  name: z.string(),
  age: z.number().min(0).max(150),
  profession: z.string().optional(),
  status: z.union([
    z.literal("active"),
    z.literal("inactive"),
    z.literal("registered"),
  ]),
});

const Results = z.object({
  entries: z.array(Person),
});
```

As you see, we are in JavaScript, and we add names to the *value* namespace, not the *type* namespace (see Recipe 2.9), but the tools we get from Zod's fluent interface are very familiar to us TypeScript developers. We define objects, strings, numbers, and arrays. We can also define union types and literals. All the building blocks for defining models are here, and we can also nest types, as we see by defining Person first and reusing it in Results.

The fluent interface also allows us to make certain properties optional. All things that we know from TypeScript. Furthermore, we can set validation rules. We can say that age should be above or equal to 0 and below 100. Things that we can't do reasonably within the type system.

Those objects are not types that we can use like we would use TypeScript types. They are *schemas*, waiting for data they can parse and validate. Since Zod is TypeScript-first, we have helper types that allow us to cross the bridge from the value space to the type space. With z.infer (a type, not a function), we can extract the type we defined through Zod's schema functions:

```
type PersonType = z.infer<typeof Person>;
type ResultType = z.infer<typeof Results>;
```

So, how do we apply Zod's validation techniques? Let's talk about a function called fetchData, which calls an API that gets entries of type ResultType. We just don't know if the values we receive actually adhere to the types we've defined. So, after fetching data as json, we use the Results schema to parse the data we've received. If this process is successful, we get data that is of type ResultType:

```
type ResultType = z.infer<typeof Results>;

async function fetchData(): Promise<ResultType> {
  const data = await fetch("/api/persons").then((res) => res.json());
  return Results.parse(data);
}
```

Note that we already had our first safeguard in how we defined the function interface. Promise<ResultType> is based on what we get from z.infer.

Results.parse(data) is of the inferred type but without a name. The structural type system makes sure that we return the right thing. There might be errors, and we can catch them using the respective Promise.catch methods or try-catch blocks.

Usage with try-catch:

```
fetchData()
  .then((res) => {
    // do something with results
  })
  .catch((e) => {
    // a potential zod error!
  });

// or

try {
  const res = await fetchData();
  // do something with results
} catch (e) {
  // a potential zod error!
}
```

While we can ensure that we continue only if we have correct data, we are not forced to do error checking. If we want to make sure that we look at the parsing result first before we continue with our program, safeParse is the way to go:

```
async function fetchData(): Promise<ResultType> {
  const data = await fetch("/api/persons").then((res) => res.json());
  const results = Results.safeParse(data);
  if (results.success) {
    return results.data;
  } else {
    // Depending on your application, you might want to have a
    // more sophisticated way of error handling than returning
    // an empty result.
    return { entries: [] };
  }
}
```

This already makes Zod a valuable asset if you need to rely on external data. Furthermore, it allows you to adapt to API changes. Let's say that your program can work only with active and inactive states of `Person`; it does not know how to handle `registered`. It's easy to apply a transform where, based on the data you get, you modify the `"registered"` state to be actually `"active"`:

```
const Person = z.object({
  name: z.string(),
  age: z.number().min(0).max(150),
  profession: z.string().optional(),
  status: z
    .union([
      z.literal("active"),
      z.literal("inactive"),
      z.literal("registered"),
    ])
    .transform((val) => {
      if (val === "registered") {
        return "active";
      }
      return val;
    }),
});
```

You then work with two different types: the *input* type represents what the API is giving you, and the *output* type is the data you have after parsing. Thankfully, we can get both types from the respective Zod helper types `z.input` and `z.output`:

```
type PersonTypeIn = z.input<typeof Person>;
/*
type PersonTypeIn = {
  name: string;
  age: number;
  profession?: string | undefined;
  status: "active" | "inactive" | "registered";
};
*/

type PersonTypeOut = z.output<typeof Person>;
/*
type PersonTypeOut = {
  name: string;
  age: number;
  profession?: string | undefined;
  status: "active" | "inactive";
};
*/
```

Zod's typings are clever enough to understand that you removed one of the three literals from `status`. So there are no surprises and you actually deal with the data you've been expecting.

Zod's API is elegant, easy to use, and closely aligned with TypeScript's features. For data at the boundaries that you can't control, where you need to rely on third parties

---

to provide the expected shape of data, Zod is a lifesaver without you having to do too much work. It comes at a cost, though: runtime validation takes time. The bigger the dataset, the longer it takes. Also, at 12KB it's big. Be certain that you need this kind of validation for data at your boundaries.

If the data you request comes from some other team within your company, maybe the person sitting next to you, no library, not even Zod, beats talking with each other and collaborating toward the same goals. Types are a way to guide collaboration, not a means to get rid of it.

12.6 Working Around Index Access Restrictions

Problem

When accessing an object's property using index access, TypeScript complains that the type you want to assign is not assignable to never.

Solution

TypeScript looks for the lowest common denominator of possible values. Use a generic type to lock in specific keys so TypeScript doesn't assume the rule needs to apply for all.

Discussion

Sometimes when writing TypeScript, actions you'd usually do in JavaScript work a little differently and cause some weird and puzzling situations. Sometimes you just want to assign a value to an object property via index access and get an error like "Type 'string | number' is not assignable to type 'never'. Type 'string' is not assignable to type 'never'.(2322)."

This isn't out of the ordinary; it's just where "unexpected intersection types" make you think a little bit more about the type system.

Let's look at this example. We create a function that lets us update from one object anotherPerson to object person via providing a key. Both person and another Person have the same type Person, but TypeScript throws errors:

```
let person = {
  name: "Stefan",
  age: 39,
};

type Person = typeof person;

let anotherPerson: Person = {
  name: "Not Stefan",
```

```
    age: 20,
};

function update(key: keyof Person) {
  person[key] = anotherPerson[key];
//^ Type 'string | number' is not assignable to type 'never'.
//  Type 'string' is not assignable to type 'never'.(2322)
}

update("age");
```

Property assignments via the index access operator are hard for TypeScript to track down. Even if you narrow all possible access keys via keyof Person, the possible values that can be assigned are string or number (for name and age, respectively). While this is fine if you have index access on the righthand side of a statement (reading), it gets a little interesting if you have index access on the lefthand side of a statement (writing).

TypeScript can't guarantee that the value you pass along is actually correct. Look at this function signature:

```
function updateAmbiguous(key: keyof Person, value: Person[keyof Person]) {
  //...
}

updateAmbiguous("age", "Stefan");
```

Nothing prevents me from adding a falsely typed value to every key. Except for TypeScript, which throws an error. But why does TypeScript tell us the type is never?

To allow for *some* assignments TypeScript compromises. Instead of not allowing *any* assignments at all on the righthand side, TypeScript looks for the lowest common denominator of possible values, for example:

```
type Switch = {
  address: number,
  on: 0 | 1
};

declare const switcher: Switch;
declare const key: keyof Switch;
```

Here, both keys are subsets of number. address is the entire set of numbers; on on the other side is either 0 or 1. It's absolutely possible to set 0 or 1 to both fields! And this is what you get with TypeScript as well:

```
switcher[key] = 1; // This works
switcher[key] = 2; // Error
// ^ Type '2' is not assignable to type '0 | 1'.(2322)
```

TypeScript gets to the possible assignable values by doing an *intersection type* of all property types. In the case of the `Switch`, it's `number & (0 | 1)`, which boils down to `0 | 1`. In the case of all `Person` properties, it's `string & number`, which has no overlap; therefore it's `never`. Hah! There's the culprit!

One way to get around this strictness (which is for your own good) is by using generics. Instead of allowing all `keyof Person` values to access, we *bind* a specific subset of `keyof Person` to a generic variable:

```
function update<K extends keyof Person>(key: K) {
  person[key] = anotherPerson[key]; // works
}

update("age");
```

When I `update("age")`, K is bound to the literal type of `"age"`. No ambiguity there!

There is a theoretical loophole since we could instantiate `update` with a much broader generic value:

```
update<"age" | "name">("age");
```

This is something the TypeScript team allows, for now. See also this comment (*https://oreil.ly/0Fetp*) by Anders Hejlsberg. Note that he asks to see use cases for such a scenario, which perfectly details how the TypeScript team works. The original assignment via index access on the righthand side has so much potential for error that they give you enough safeguards until you make it very intentional what you want to do. This is ruling out entire classes of errors without getting too much in the way.

12.7 Deciding Whether to Use Function Overloads or Conditional Types

Problem

With conditional types, you have more possibilities to define function signatures than before. You wonder if you still need function overloads or if they're obsolete.

Solution

Function overloads provide better readability and an easier way to define expectations from your type than conditionals. Use them when the situation requires.

Discussion

With type system features like conditional types or variadic tuple types, one technique to describe a function's interface has faded into the background: function overloads. And for good reason. Both features have been implemented to deal with the shortcomings of regular function overloads.

See this concatenation example directly from the TypeScript 4.0 release notes. This is an array concat function:

```
function concat(arr1, arr2) {
  return [...arr1, ...arr2];
}
```

To correctly type a function like this so it takes all possible edge cases into account, we would end up in a sea of overloads:

```
// 7 overloads for an empty second array
function concat(arr1: [], arr2: []): [];
function concat<A>(arr1: [A], arr2: []): [A];
function concat<A, B>(arr1: [A, B], arr2: []): [A, B];
function concat<A, B, C>(arr1: [A, B, C], arr2: []): [A, B, C];
function concat<A, B, C, D>(arr1: [A, B, C, D], arr2: []): [A, B, C, D];
function concat<A, B, C, D, E>(
  arr1: [A, B, C, D, E],
  arr2: []
): [A, B, C, D, E];
function concat<A, B, C, D, E, F>(
  arr1: [A, B, C, D, E, F],
  arr2: []
): [A, B, C, D, E, F];
// 7 more for arr2 having one element
function concat<A2>(arr1: [], arr2: [A2]): [A2];
function concat<A1, A2>(arr1: [A1], arr2: [A2]): [A1, A2];
function concat<A1, B1, A2>(arr1: [A1, B1], arr2: [A2]): [A1, B1, A2];
function concat<A1, B1, C1, A2>(
  arr1: [A1, B1, C1],
  arr2: [A2]
): [A1, B1, C1, A2];
function concat<A1, B1, C1, D1, A2>(
  arr1: [A1, B1, C1, D1],
  arr2: [A2]
): [A1, B1, C1, D1, A2];
function concat<A1, B1, C1, D1, E1, A2>(
  arr1: [A1, B1, C1, D1, E1],
  arr2: [A2]
): [A1, B1, C1, D1, E1, A2];
function concat<A1, B1, C1, D1, E1, F1, A2>(
  arr1: [A1, B1, C1, D1, E1, F1],
  arr2: [A2]
): [A1, B1, C1, D1, E1, F1, A2];
// and so on, and so forth
```

And this only takes into account arrays that have up to six elements. Variadic tuple types help greatly with these situations:

```
type Arr = readonly any[];

function concat<T extends Arr, U extends Arr>(arr1: T, arr2: U): [...T, ...U] {
  return [...arr1, ...arr2];
}
```

The new function signature requires a lot less effort to parse and is very clear on what types it expects to get as arguments and what it returns. The return value also maps to the return type. No extra assertions: TypeScript can make sure that you are returning the correct value.

It's a similar situation with conditional types. This example is very similar to Recipe 5.1. Think of software that retrieves orders based on customer, article, or order ID. You might want to create something like this:

```
function fetchOrder(customer: Customer): Order[]
function fetchOrder(product: Product): Order[]
function fetchOrder(orderId: number): Order
// the implementation
function fetchOrder(param: any): Order | Order[] {
  //...
}
```

But this is just half the truth. What if you end up with ambiguous types where you don't know exactly if you get *only* a Customer or only a Product? You need to take care of all possible combinations:

```
function fetchOrder(customer: Customer): Order[]
function fetchOrder(product: Product): Order[]
function fetchOrder(orderId: number): Order
function fetchOrder(param: Customer | Product): Order[]
function fetchOrder(param: Customer | number): Order | Order[]
function fetchOrder(param: number | Product): Order | Order[]
// the implementation
function fetchOrder(param: any): Order | Order[] {
  //...
}
```

Add more possibilities, and you end up with more combinations. Here, conditional types can reduce your function signature tremendously:

```
type FetchParams = number | Customer | Product;

type FetchReturn<T> = T extends Customer
  ? Order[]
  : T extends Product
  ? Order[]
  : T extends number
  ? Order
```

```
    : never;

function fetchOrder<T extends FetchParams>(params: T): FetchReturn<T> {
  //...
}
```

Since conditional types distribute a union, `FetchReturn` returns a union of return types.

So there is good reason to use those techniques instead of drowning in too many function overloads. So, to return to the question: do we still need function overloads?

Yes, we do.

Different function shapes

One scenario where function overloads remain handy is if you have different argument lists for your function variants. This means not only the arguments (parameters) themselves can have some variety (this is where conditionals and variadic tuples are fantastic) but also the number and position of arguments.

Imagine a search function that has two different ways of being called:

- Call it with the search query. It returns a `Promise` you can await.
- Call it with the search query and a callback. In this scenario, the function does not return anything.

This *can* be done with conditional types but is very unwieldy:

```
// => (1)
type SearchArguments =
  // Argument list one: a query and a callback
  | [query: string, callback: (results: unknown[]) => void]
  // Argument list two:: just a query
  | [query: string];

// A conditional type picking either void or a Promise depending
// on the input => (2)
type ReturnSearch<T> = T extends [query: string]
  ? Promise<Array<unknown>>
  : void;

// the actual function => (3)
declare function search<T extends SearchArguments>(...args: T): ReturnSearch<T>;

// z is void
const z = search("omikron", (res) => {});

// y is Promise<unknown>
const y = search("omikron");
```

Here's what we did:

1. We defined our argument list using tuple types. Since TypeScript 4.0, we can name tuple fields just like we would objects. We create a union because we have two different variants of our function signature.

2. The `ReturnSearch` type selects the return type based on the argument list variant. If it's just a string, return a `Promise`. Otherwise return `void`.

3. We add our types by constraining a generic variable to `SearchArguments` so that we can correctly select the return type.

That is a lot! And it features a ton of complex features we love to see in TypeScript's feature list: conditional types, generics, generic constraints, tuple types, union types! We get *some* nice autocomplete, but it's nowhere near the clarity of a simple function overload:

```
function search(query: string): Promise<unknown[]>;
function search(query: string, callback: (result: unknown[]) => void): void;
// This is the implementation, it only concerns you
function search(
  query: string,
  callback?: (result: unknown[]) => void
): void | Promise<unknown> {
  // Implement
}
```

We use a union type only for the implementation part. The rest is very explicit and clear. We know our arguments, and we know what to expect in return. No ceremony, just simple types. The best part of function overloads is that the *actual* implementation does not pollute the type space. You can go for a round of any and just not care.

Exact arguments

Another situation where function overloads can make things easier is when you need exact arguments and their mapping. Let's look at a function that applies an event to an event handler. For example, we have a `MouseEvent` and want to call a `MouseEvent Handler` with it. Same for keyboard events and so on. If we use conditionals and union types to map event and handler, we might end up with something like this:

```
// All the possible event handlers
type Handler =
  | MouseEventHandler<HTMLButtonElement>
  | KeyboardEventHandler<HTMLButtonElement>;

// Map Handler to Event
type Ev<T> = T extends MouseEventHandler<infer R>
  ? MouseEvent<R>
  : T extends KeyboardEventHandler<infer R>
  ? KeyboardEvent<R>
```

```
  : never;

// Create a
function apply<T extends Handler>(handler: T, ev: Ev<T>): void {
  handler(ev as any); // We need the assertion here
}
```

At first glance, this looks fine. It might be a bit cumbersome, though, if you think about all the variants you need to keep track of.

But there's a bigger problem. The way TypeScript deals with all possible variants of the event is causing an *unexpected intersection*, as we see in Recipe 12.6. This means that, in the function body, TypeScript can't tell what kind of handler you are passing. Therefore, it also can't tell which kind of event we're getting. So TypeScript says the event can be both: a mouse event and a keyboard event. You need to pass handlers that can deal with both, which is not how we intend our function to work.

The actual error message is "TS 2345: Argument of type *KeyboardEvent<HTMLButton Element> | MouseEvent<HTMLButtonElement, MouseEvent>* is not assignable to parameter of type *MouseEvent<HTMLButtonElement, MouseEvent> & Keyboard Event<HTMLButtonElement>*."

This is why we need an `as` any type assertion to make it possible to actually call the handler with the event.

The function signature works in a lot of scenarios:

```
declare const mouseHandler: MouseEventHandler<HTMLButtonElement>;
declare const mouseEv: MouseEvent<HTMLButtonElement>;
declare const keyboardHandler: KeyboardEventHandler<HTMLButtonElement>;
declare const keyboardEv: KeyboardEvent<HTMLButtonElement>;

apply(mouseHandler, mouseEv); // works
apply(keyboardHandler, keyboardEv); // woirks
apply(mouseHandler, keyboardEv); // breaks like it should!
//                  ^
// Argument of type 'KeyboardEvent<HTMLButtonElement>' is not assignable
// to parameter of type 'MouseEvent<HTMLButtonElement, MouseEvent>'
```

But once there's ambiguity, things don't work out as they should:

```
declare const mouseOrKeyboardHandler:
  MouseEventHandler<HTMLButtonElement> |
  KeyboardEventHandler<HTMLButtonElement>;;

// This is accepted but can cause problems!
apply(mouseOrKeyboardHandler, mouseEv);
```

When `mouseOrKeyboardHandler` is a keyboard handler, we can't reasonably pass a mouse event. Wait: this is exactly what the TS2345 error from before tried to tell us!

We just shifted the problem to another place and made it silent with an `as any` assertion.

Explicit, exact function signatures make *everything* easier. The mapping becomes clearer, the type signatures are easier to understand, and there's no need for conditionals or unions:

```
// Overload 1: MouseEventHandler and MouseEvent
function apply(
  handler: MouseEventHandler<HTMLButtonElement>,
  ev: MouseEvent<HTMLButtonElement>
): void;
// Overload 2: KeyboardEventHandler and KeyboardEvent
function apply(
  handler: KeyboardEventHandler<HTMLButtonElement>,
  ev: KeyboardEvent<HTMLButtonElement>
): void;
// The implementation. Fall back to any. This is not a type!
// TypeScript won't check for this line nor
// will it show in the autocomplete.
// This is just for you to implement your stuff.
function apply(handler: any, ev: any): void {
  handler(ev);
}
```

Function overloads help us with all possible scenarios. We make sure there are no ambiguous types:

```
apply(mouseHandler, mouseEv); // works!
apply(keyboardHandler, keyboardEv); // works!
apply(mouseHandler, keyboardEv); // breaks like it should!
// ^ No overload matches this call.
apply(mouseOrKeyboardHandler, mouseEv); // breaks like it should
// ^ No overload matches this call.
```

For the implementation, we can even use any. Since you can make sure that you won't run into a situation that implies ambiguity, you can rely on the happy-go-lucky type and don't need to bother.

The catch-all function body

Last but not least, there's the combination of conditional types *and* function overloads. Remember the example from Recipe 5.1: we saw that conditional types gave the function body a hard time to map values to the respective generic return types. Moving the conditional type to a function overload and using a very broad function signature for implementation helps both the users of the function as well as the implementers:

```
function createLabel<T extends number | string | StringLabel | NumberLabel>(
  input: T
): GetLabel<T>;
```

```
function createLabel(
  input: number | string | StringLabel | NumberLabel
): NumberLabel | StringLabel {
  if (typeof input === "number") {
    return { id: input };
  } else if (typeof input === "string") {
    return { name: input };
  } else if ("id" in input) {
    return { id: input.id };
  } else {
    return { name: input.name };
  }
}
```

Function overloads are still very useful and, for a lot of scenarios, the way to go. They're easier to read, easier to write, and, in a lot of cases, more exact than what we get with other means.

But it's not either-or. You can happily mix and match conditionals and function overloads if your scenario needs it.

12.8 Naming Generics

Problem

T and U don't tell you anything about generic type parameters.

Solution

Follow a naming pattern.

Discussion

TypeScript's generics are arguably one of the most powerful features of the language. They open a door to TypeScript's own metaprogramming language, which allows for a very flexible and dynamic generation of types. It comes close to being its own functional programming language.

Especially with the arrival of *string literal types* and *recursive conditional types* in the most recent TypeScript versions, we can craft types that do astonishing things. This type from Recipe 12.2 parses Express-style from route information and retrieves an object with all its parameters:

```
type ParseRouteParameters<T> =
  T extends `${string}/:${infer U}/${infer R}` ?
    { [P in U | keyof ParseRouteParameters<`/${R}`>]: string } :
  T extends `${string}/:${infer U}` ?
    { [P in U]: string } : {}
```

```
type X = ParseRouteParameters<"/api/:what/:is/notyou/:happening">
// type X = {
//   what: string,
//   is: string,
//   happening: string,
// }
```

When we define a *generic type*, we also define *generic type parameters*. They can be of a certain type (or more correctly, be a certain subtype):

```
type Foo<T extends string> = ...
```

They can have default values:

```
type Foo<T extends string = "hello"> = ...
```

And when using default values, *order* is important. This is just one of many similarities to regular JavaScript functions! So since we are almost talking functions, why are we using single-letter names for generic type parameters?

Most generic type parameters start with the letter T. Subsequent parameters go along the alphabet (U, V, W) or are abbreviations like K for key. This can lead to highly unreadable types, however. If I look at Extract<T, U>, it is hard to tell if we extract T from U, or the other way around.

Being a bit more elaborate helps:

```
type Extract<From, Union> = ...
```

Now we know that we want to extract *from* the first parameter everything that is assignable to Union. Furthermore, we understand that we want to have a union type.

Types are documentation, and our type parameters can have speaking names, just like you would do with regular functions. Go for a naming scheme, like this one:

- All type parameters start with an uppercase letter, like you would name all other types!
- Only use single letters if the usage is completely clear. For example, ParseRoute Params can have only one argument, the route.
- Don't abbreviate to T (that's way too ... generic!) but to something that clarifies what we are dealing with. For example, ParseRouteParams<R>, where R stands for Route.
- Rarely use single letters; stick to short words or abbreviations: Elem for Element, Route can stand as is.
- Use prefixes to differentiate from built-in types. For example, Element is taken, so use GElement (or stick with Elem).

- Use prefixes to make generic names clearer: `URLObj` is clearer than `Obj`, for instance.

- Same patterns apply to inferred types within a generic type.

Let's look at `ParseRouteParams` again and be more explicit with our names:

```
type ParseRouteParams<Route> =
  Route extends `${string}/:${infer Param}/${infer Rest}` ?
    { [Entry in Param | keyof ParseRouteParameters<`/${Rest}`>]: string } :
  Route extends `${string}/:${infer Param}` ?
    { [Entry in Param]: string } : {}
```

It becomes a lot clearer what each type is meant to be. We also see that we need to iterate over all `Entry`s in `Param`, even if `Param` is just a set of one type.

Arguably, it's a lot more readable than before!

There is one caveat: it's almost impossible to distinguish type parameters from actual types. There's another scheme that has been heavily popularized by Matt Pocock (*https://oreil.ly/Y1i-Q*): using a T prefix:

```
type ParseRouteParameters<TRoute> =
  Route extends `${string}/:${infer TParam}/${infer TRest}` ?
    { [TEntry in TParam | keyof ParseRouteParameters<`/${TRest}`>]: string } :
  Route extends `${string}/:${infer TParam}` ?
    { [TEntry in TParam]: string } : {}
```

This comes close to a Hungarian Notation (*https://oreil.ly/c23gW*) for types.

Whatever variation you use, making sure that generic types are readable to you and your colleagues, and that their parameters speak for themselves, is as important as in other programming languages.

12.9 Prototyping on the TypeScript Playground

Problem

Your project is so big, it's hard for you to properly fix bugs in typings.

Solution

Move your types to the TypeScript playground and develop them in isolation.

Discussion

The TypeScript playground (*https://www.typescriptlang.org/play*) as shown in Figure 12-1 is a web application that has been with TypeScript since its first release, showcasing how TypeScript syntax is compiled to JavaScript. Its capabilities were originally limited and focused on "breaking the ice" for new developers, but in recent years it has become a powerhouse of online development, rich in features and indispensable for TypeScript development. The TypeScript team asks people to submit issues including a re-creation of the bug using the playground. They also test new and upcoming features by allowing the nightly version to be loaded into the application. In short: the TypeScript playground is essential for TypeScript development.

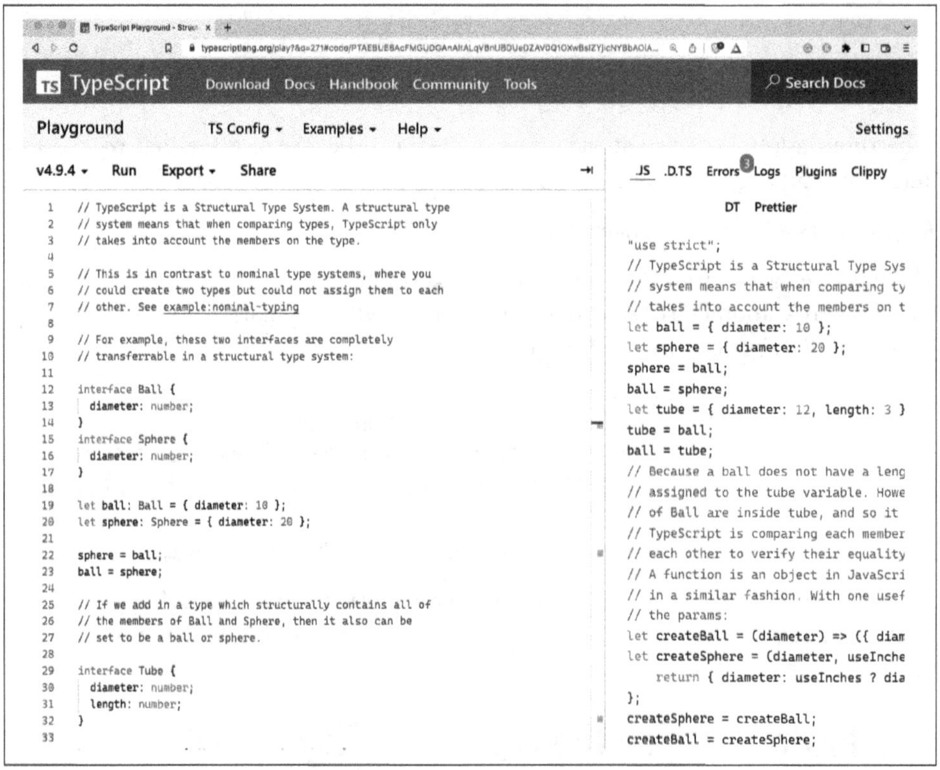

Figure 12-1. The TypeScript playground showing one of the built-in examples

For your regular development practices, the TypeScript playground is a great way to develop types in isolation, independent from your current project. As TypeScript configurations grow, they become confusing, and it becomes hard to understand which types contribute to your actual project. If you encounter weird or unexpected behavior in your types, try re-creating them in the playground, in isolation, without the rest of your project.

The playground doesn't feature a full *tsconfig.json*, but you can define the important pieces of your configuration via a user interface, as seen in Figure 12-2. Alternatively, you can set compiler flags using annotations directly in the source code:

```
// @strictPropertyInitialization: false
// @target: esnext
// @module: nodenext
// @lib: es2015,dom
```

Not as comfortable but highly ergonomic as it allows you to share compiler flags much more easily.

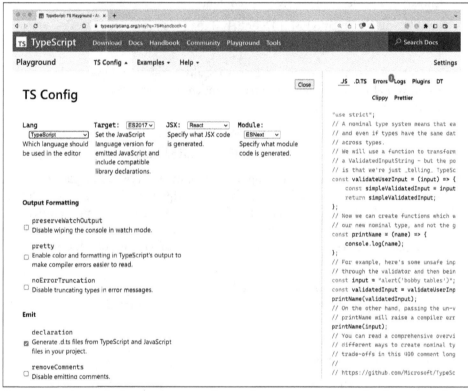

Figure 12-2. Instead of writing an actual tsconfig.json, you set compiler flags using the TSConfig panel

You also can compile TypeScript, get extracted type information, run small pieces of code to see how they behave, and export everything to various destinations, including other popular online editors and IDEs.

You can select various versions to ensure that your bug isn't dependent on version updates, and you can run various, well-documented examples to learn the basics of TypeScript while trying out actual source code.

As noted in Recipe 12.10, developing JavaScript would be nothing without using dependencies. In the TypeScript playground, it's possible to fetch type information for dependencies directly from NPM. If you import, for example, React within the TypeScript playground, the playground will try to acquire types:

1. First, it will look at the respective package on NPM and check if there are types defined or *.d.ts* files somewhere in its contents.

2. If not, it will check on NPM if Definitely Typed type information exists and will download the respective `@types` package.

This is recursive, meaning that if some types require types from other packages, type acquisition will also go through the type dependencies. For some packages, you can even define which version to load:

```
import { render } from "preact"; // types: legacy
```

Here, `types` is set to `legacy`, which loads the respective legacy version from NPM.

There's more to the ecosystem. An important tool of the TypeScript playground is *Twoslash*. Twoslash is a markup format for TypeScript files that lets you highlight code, handle multiple files, and show the files the TypeScript compiler creates. It's fantastic for blogs and websites—you basically have an inline TypeScript compiler for code examples—but it's also fantastic if you need to create complex debugging scenarios.

The compiler flag annotations are handled by Twoslash, but you can also get inline hints on current types by adding a marker in a comment directly under a variable name:

```
// @jsxFactory: h
import { render, h } from "preact";

function Heading() {
    return <h1>Hello</h1>
}

const elem = <Heading/>
//     ^?
// This line above triggers inline hints
```

You can see the result in Figure 12-3.

```
1   // @jsxFactory: h
2   import { render, h } from "preact";
3
4   function Heading() {
5       return <h1>Hello</h1>
6   }
7
8   const elem = <Heading/>
9   //      ^? const elem: h.JSX.Element
```

Figure 12-3. Twoslash in action: setting compiler flags via annotations

Twoslash is also part of the bug workbench (*https://oreil.ly/jVU3u*), which is a fork of the playground with an emphasis on creating and displaying complex reproductions of bugs. Here, you can also define multiple files to see how imports and exports work:

```
export const a = 2;

// @filename: a.ts

import { a } from "./input.js"
console.log(a);
```

Multifile support is triggered by the first @filename annotation. Everything before this line becomes a file called *input.tsx*, basically your main entry point.

Last but not least, the playground can work as your entire demo suite for workshops and trainings. Using Twoslash, you can create multiple files in a GitHub Gist repository and load the TypeScript files along with documentation as part of a Gist docset, as seen in Figure 12-4.

This is immensely powerful for immersive learning. From mere reproductions to full-fledged demo suites, the TypeScript playground is the one-stop source for TypeScript developers—whether you need to file bugs, try out something new, or work on types in isolation. It's a great resource to start with, and from there you can easily migrate to "real" IDEs and tools.

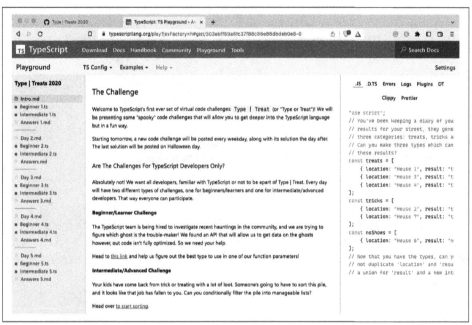

Figure 12-4. A Gist docset in the playground

12.10 Providing Multiple Library Versions

Problem

You write external types for a library and want to maintain type updates relative to library version updates.

Solution

Use reference triple-slash directives, as well as modules, namespaces, and interfaces for declaration merging.

Discussion

Programming would be tough without external libraries that take care of a lot of work for you. JavaScript's ecosystem is arguably one of the richest when it comes to third-party dependencies, mainly through NPM (*https://npmjs.org*). Also, most of them come with TypeScript support, either through built-in types or through types from Definitely Typed. According to the TypeScript team, almost 80% of NPM is typed (*https://oreil.ly/G2Ktl*). However, there is still the odd holdout: for example, libraries are not written in TypeScript, or legacy code from your own company that you still need to make compatible with today's software.

Think of a library called *"lib"*, which exposes a `Connector` class that you can use to target internal systems. This library exists in multiple versions, and features have been added constantly:

```
import { Connector } from "lib";

// This exists in version 1
const connector = new Connector();
const connection = connector.connect("127.0.0.1:4000");

connection.send("Hi!");

// This exists in version 2
connection.close();
```

It's worth noting that this library can be used by multiple projects within your organization, with varying versions. Your task is to write types so your teams get proper autocomplete and type information.

In TypeScript, you can provide multiple versions of a library's types by creating an ambient module declaration for each version of the library. An ambient module declaration is a file with a *.d.ts* extension that provides TypeScript with the types for a library not written in TypeScript.

By default, TypeScript is greedy: it includes type definitions and *globs* everything it can. If you want to limit TypeScript's file access, make sure to use the `"exclude"` and `"include"` properties in *tsconfig.json*:

```
{
  "compilerOptions": {
    // ...
    "typeRoots": [
      "@types"
    ],
    "rootDir": "./src",
    "outDir": "dist",
  },
  "include": ["./src", "./@types"]
}
```

We create a folder *next to* the folders we included in *tsconfig.json*. Here, we create a file called *lib.v1.d.ts*, where we store the basic information on how objects are created:

```
declare module "lib" {
  export interface ConnectorConstructor {
    new (): Connector;
  }
  var Connector: ConnectorConstructor;

  export interface Connector {
    connect(stream: string): Connection;
  }
```

```
    export interface Connection {
      send(msg: string): Connection;
    }
  }
```

Note that we use modules to define the name of the module and that we also use interfaces for most of our types. Both modules and interfaces are open to declaration merging, which means we can add new types in different files and TypeScript merges them together. This is crucial if we want to define multiple versions.

Also note that we use the constructor interface pattern (see Recipe 11.3) for `Connector`:

```
  export interface ConnectorConstructor {
    new (): Connector;
  }
  var Connector: ConnectorConstructor;
```

In doing so, we can change the signature of the constructor and make sure that an instantiable class is being recognized by TypeScript.

In another file called *lib.v2.d.ts*, next to *lib.v1.d.ts*, we redeclare "lib" and add more methods to `Connection`. Through declaration merging, the `close` method gets added to the `Connection` interface:

```
  /// <reference path="lib.v1.d.ts" />

  declare module "lib" {
    export interface Connection {
      close(): void;
    }
  }
```

Using triple-slash directives, we refer from *lib.v2.d.ts* to *lib.v1.d.ts*, signaling that everything from version 1 is to be included in version 2.

All those files exist in a folder called *@lib*. Using the configuration we declared earlier, TypeScript won't pick them up. We can, however, write a new file *lib.d.ts* and put it in *@types*, and from there, refer to the version we want to include:

```
  /// <reference path="../@lib/lib.v2.d.ts" />

  declare module "lib" {}
```

A simple change from "*../@lib/lib.v2.d.ts*" to "*../@lib/lib.v1.d.ts*" will change the version we target, while we still maintain all library versions independently.

If you are curious, try looking into the included library files from TypeScript. They are a treasure trove of external type definitions, and there is a lot to learn. If you use your editor to find references, for example, to `Object.keys`, you will see that this function exists in multiple locations, and based on your TypeScript configuration, the right file will be included. Figure 12-5 shows how Visual Studio Code displays various file locations for `Object.keys`. TypeScript is so flexible that you can use the same techniques for your project, even extending TypeScript's built-in types themselves (see Recipe 9.7).

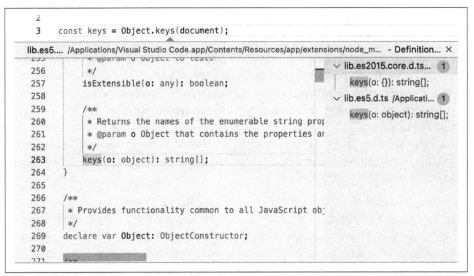

Figure 12-5. Finding references to built-in types in Visual Studio Code shows you how TypeScript manages multiple versions of ECMAScript and the DOM

In conclusion, providing multiple versions of a library's types in TypeScript can be done by creating ambient module declarations for each version of the library and referencing the appropriate declaration in your TypeScript code. Hopefully, you will be able to use package managers in your project to manage different versions of libraries and their corresponding types, making it easier to handle dependencies and avoid conflicts.

12.11 Knowing When to Stop

Problem

Writing elaborate and complicated types is exhausting!

Solution

Don't write elaborate and complicated types. TypeScript is gradual; use what makes you productive.

Discussion

I want to end this book with some general advice on how to stop at the right time. If you have read through the entire book and ended up here, you have read through more than one hundred recipes with a lot of advice about everyday TypeScript problems. Be it project setup, complicated situations where you need to find the right type, or workarounds when TypeScript runs into a situation where it's too strict for its own good, we have covered it all.

Solutions can get very complex, especially when we enter the area of conditional types and everything around them, like helper types, variadic tuple types, and string template literal types. TypeScript's type system is undoubtedly powerful, especially if you understand that every decision, every feature, has its roots in the fact that JavaScript lies underneath it all. Creating a type system that gives you strong, static types for a programming language that is so inherently dynamic is an amazing achievement. I have nothing but the deepest admiration for the bright minds in Redmond who made all of this possible.

However, undeniably, things can get very complicated at times. Types can be hard to read or create, and the fact that the type system is its own Turing-complete metaprogramming system that needs testing libraries doesn't help. And developers take pride in understanding every aspect of their craft and tools, often preferring a complex type solution over simpler types that don't give the same type safety but are ultimately easier to read and understand.

A project that goes into the nitty-gritty of the type system is called Type Challenges (*https://tsch.js.org*). It's a fantastic project of brainteasers that show what's possible with the type system. I fiddle around with some of the more challenging riddles, getting great ideas for how to explain the type system better. And while puzzles are fantastic for training a developer's mind, most of them lack a significant grasp of real-world, everyday situations.

And those are the situations where we often overlook TypeScript's wonderful capability that you don't often see in mainstream programming languages: its gradual adoption of types. Tools like any, generic type parameters, and type assertions and the fact that you can write simple JavaScript with a couple of comments make the barrier to entry so much lower. The latest effort from the TypeScript team and TC39 is to lower the barrier even more by adding type annotations to JavaScript (*https://oreil.ly/yQnIO*), a proposal currently in discussion. The goal of this proposal is not to make JavaScript type safe but to remove compile steps if we want to have simple, easy-to-understand type annotations. JavaScript engines can treat them as comments, and type-checkers can get real information on the program's semantics.

As developers, project leaders, engineers, and architects, we should use this feature. Simple types are always better types: easier to understand and much easier to consume.

The TypeScript website (*https://typescriptlang.org*) changed its claim from "JavaScript that scales" to "JavaScript with syntax for types," which should give you an idea of how to approach TypeScript in projects: write JavaScript, annotate where necessary, write simple but comprehensive types, and use TypeScript as a way to document, understand, and communicate your software.

I think TypeScript follows the Pareto principle (*https://oreil.ly/smytJ*): 80% of type safety comes from 20% of its features. This doesn't mean the rest of it is bad or unnecessary. We just spent one hundred recipes to understand situations where we effectively need TypeScript's more advanced features. It should just give you an idea of where to put effort. Don't run into advanced TypeScript trickery on every occasion. Monitor if loser types are a problem. Estimate the effort to change types in your program, and make well-informed decisions. Also know that in a refinement process (see Recipe 12.2), the reason for multiple steps is to easily be able to stop.

Index

Symbols

! (exclamation mark), 332
(pound sign; hash), 307
$ (dollar sign; CLI convention), 6
{} (empty object) type, 42-44

A

abstract classes
    describing constructors and prototypes,
        313-316
    when to use, 322-323
access modifiers, 304-309
accumulation technique, 180-183
addEventListener function, 55
AllOrNone<T, K> helper type, 231-235
ambient module declarations, 272
annotation-like type-checking, 357-361
annotations (see type annotations)
any type
    basics, 12
    disabling type-checking with, 27
    exceptions and, 84
    generic type parameters as alternative to,
        116-118
    Serialize<T> and, 164
    testing complex types, 362
    typing polymorphic components with, 301
    unknown type versus, 39-42
    uses for, 40
APIs
    creating exclusive or (XOR) models with
        optional never, 85-88
    enabling loose autocomplete for string sub-
        sets, 106-108

function overloads and, 50-52
arguments (see function arguments)
Array.prototype.includes, 259-262
arrays
    annotating with tuple types, 45-47
    defining custom hooks, 281-283
    tuple types and, 45-47
    typing a concat function for, 189-192
as components, 299
    (see also polymorphic components)
as keyword, type assertions and, 88-91
assertion signatures, modifying objects with,
    127-130
assertNever function, 70-74
autocomplete, 106-108

B

backend requests, 183-187
base class, 309-313
basic types
    annotating effectively, 35-39
    any and unknown, 39-42
    choosing the right object type, 42-44
    defining function overloads, 50-52
    interfaces versus type aliases, 48-50
    overview, 35
    this parameter types, 53-56
    tuple types, 45-47
    value and type namespaces, 59-62
    working with symbols, 56-59
Boolean constructor, filtering nullish values
    with, 263-264
bottom types, 72
builder pattern, 335-336

buttons, 276-279, 299

C

callbacks
  promisify functions and, 192-196
  typing in React's synthetic event system,
    296-298
  void as substitutable type for, 79-82
catch clauses
  error types in, 82-85
  in JavaScript, 84
class hierarchies, 313-316
classes
  choosing the right visibility modifier,
    304-309
  deciding when to use classes or namespaces,
    319-323
  describing constructors and prototypes,
    313-316
  explicitly defining method overrides,
    309-313
  overview, 303
  using generics in, 316-319
  working with strict property initialization,
    328-332
  working with types in, 332-336
  writing decorators, 336-342
  writing static classes, 324-328
CommonJS, 27-30
complex types, testing, 361-363
components (SPA framework), 139
compound types, 42
concat function, 189-192
conditional types
  combining with conditional types for typing
    a curry function, 197-199
  creating an enum from a tuple, 206-210
  filtering with never, 147-151
  function overloads versus, 370-377
  grouping elements by kind, 151-157
  inferring types in conditionals, 160-165
  managing complex function signatures,
    143-147
  overview, 143
  refining types by adding, 355-357
  removing specific object properties, 157-160
  writing a formatter function, 174-177
configurations, predefined, 33-34
const context

defining custom hooks, 283
literals and, 76
const modifier, 138-142
constants, enums and, 97-102
constructor interface pattern, 313-316
context API, type definitions for, 288-293
contracts, checking with satisfies operator,
  357-361
contravariance, 239-242
covariance, 239-242
curry function
  currying defined, 197
  typing, 197-199
  typing a flexible curry function, 200-203
  typing the simplest curry function, 203-206
custom event system, 168-170
custom hooks, defining, 281-283
custom type definitions, augmenting global
  namespace with, 267-271

D

data modeling, 63-68
declaration merging, 48-50
  extending modules, 264-266
  filtering nullish values, 263-264
  type maps and, 133
decorators, 336-342
DeepPartial<T> type, 218-220, 243-245
DeepRemap<T> helper type, 220-222
defineProperty, 253-258
definite assignment assertion, 332
DefinitelyTyped repository, 13-16
Deno, 30-33
dependencies
  Deno and, 32
  migrating a JavaScript project to TypeScript,
    11
discriminated union types, 68-70
  controlled components and, 279-281
  exhaustiveness checking with assertNever,
    70-74
  template literals as discriminants, 183-187
distributive conditional type
  for filtering with never, 147-151
  grouping elements by kind with, 153

E

ECMAScript
  decorator proposal, 337

About the Author

Stefan Baumgartner is a developer and architect based in Austria. He is the author of *TypeScript in 50 Lessons* and runs a popular TypeScript and technology blog (*https://fettblog.eu*). In his spare time, he organizes meetups and conferences, like the Rust Linz meetup and the European TypeScript conference (*https://tsconf.eu*). Stefan enjoys Italian food, Belgian beer, and British vinyl records. Stefan is also an independent consultant and trainer for Rust and TypeScript at oida.dev (*https://oida.dev*).

Colophon

The animal on the cover of *TypeScript Cookbook* is a plum-headed parakeet (*Psittacula cyanocephala*). These birds are endemic to the Indian subcontinent. They are also commonly kept as pets. Like other parrots kept as pets, plum-headed parakeets require regular interaction and socialization. Compared to other parrots, they are less aggressive and possessive and are considered to be gentle, social, and affectionate.

Plum-headed parakeets are dimorphic, which means that males and females have easily distinguishable features. Both have predominantly green bodies with a variety of different shades on their breast, abdomen, back, and wings. Males have a purplish-red colored head outlined with a black collar around the neck. Females have bluish-gray heads and yellow-tinged feathers around their necks. They are medium-sized birds that are approximately 12 inches long and weigh between 2.3 to 2.8 ounces. An average lifespan for plum-headed parakeets is between 15 to 20 years.

A typical diet for these parakeets in the wild includes fruits, seeds, fleshy flower petals, and grains. They have also been known to raid agricultural fields and orchards. In captivity, they are healthiest when fed high-quality seed and pellet mixes that are supplemented with fresh fruits and vegetables (e.g., sprouts, leafy greens, berries, and peppers).

These birds typically populate woodlands and forested areas from the foothills of the Himalayas south to Sri Lanka, including India, Pakistan, and Bangladesh. While there has been a gradual decline in numbers due to habitat loss, plum-headed parakeets are not in danger of extinction. Many of the animals on O'Reilly covers are endangered; all of them are important to the world.

The cover illustration is by Karen Montgomery, based on a black-and-white engraving from *Histoire Naturelle*. The cover fonts are Gilroy Semibold and Guardian Sans. The text font is Adobe Minion Pro; the heading font is Adobe Myriad Condensed; and the code font is Dalton Maag's Ubuntu Mono.

O'REILLY®

Learn from experts.
Become one yourself.

Books | Live online courses
Instant answers | Virtual events
Videos | Interactive learning

Get started at oreilly.com.

Printed in the USA
CPSIA information can be obtained
at www.ICGtesting.com
JSHW050320120823
46425JS00005B/6

9 781098 136659